D0327004

*How They*
    *Murdered*
*the Second "R"*

# How They
## Murdered
# The Second "R"

*By* GEORGE RIEMER

W · W · NORTON & COMPANY · INC · NEW YORK

*I dedicate this book to my teachers and friends, the Jesuits,
whose proud educational objective was once "eloquentia."*

The "Dear Ken" letter appeared originally in *College Composition and
Communication*, December 1964, pp. 248–252. The Mark Twain
excerpt is titled "Simplified Spelling" and is taken from *Mark Twain,
Letters from the Earth,* published by Harper & Row, 1962.

FIRST EDITION

Copyright © 1969 by W. W. Norton & Company, Inc. All rights
reserved. Published simultaneously in Canada by George J. McLeod
Limited, Toronto. *Library of Congress catalog card no. 66-11644.*
Printed in the United States of America.

2 3 4 5 6 7 8 9 0

# Contents

7

60047

## 3 – THE DICK & JANE "COMMUNICATION" COURSE

## 4 – THE GRADE TEACHER AS EDITOR

## 5 – THE NEW EDUCAND

# 6 – THE WRITING-ORIENTED CURRICULUM

# 7 – THE ANTI-WRITING COALITION

# Acknowledgments

ഇഇഇഇഇഇഇഇഇഇഇഇഇഇഇഇഇഇഇഇഇഇഇഇഇഇഇഇഇഇഇഇഇഇഇഇഇഇഇഇ

IN THE COURSE of writing my way through this book I had to ask many people for directions and information. Before I name those who helped me, let me thank three magazine editors whose assignments first sent me to the study of children's writings: Wade Nichols and Ray Robinson of *Good Housekeeping* and Wesley Price of the *Ladies' Home Journal.* I also want to identify Walter Ong, S. J., operating through his book *Ramus: Method, and the Decay of Dialogue,* and Marshall McLuhan, operating through *The Gutenberg Galaxy,* as my spiritual advisors.

The difference between an educator and an educationist is the same as that between a statesman and a Tammany politician. Sir James Pitman and Ben Wood are educators. I'm grateful to Dr. Wood for many things but particularly for his example as an incorrigible innovator. Sir James Pitman has encouraged me in letters from London, Nigeria, Australia, and Hong Kong. I've seen him in Montreal, Denver, Washington, and New York. Consequently, I have the feeling he's everywhere at once. This is reassuring, this feeling, because Sir James is a wise, scholarly man and a ferocious fighter for the intellectual rights of children. If i.t.a. is England's way of getting even with us for winning the Revolutionary War, as a minor critic has suggested, England in the person of Sir James has been very kind and generous to us.

I am indebted to Dr. Domenico Lombrassa, Provveditore algi Studi, Brescia, and to P. Manzi, Director of Studies for the city of Milan, for sending me writings of grade-school children in Italy, and to Taro Nezake, Tondabayashi, Osaka Prefecture, for sending the writings of young Japanese children. Barbara Fisher Raitzky translated the papers written by the Italian children. I was also helped by Sylvia Carbone and Minella Belloni Aaron.

I want to thank Maggie Bushnell for being the very first person to tell me about i.t.a. and for urging me to drive down to Bethlehem, Pennsylvania, to see it work. Harold Tanyzer of the i.t.a. Research Unit of Hofstra University is next to be thanked. Dr. Tanyzer was available for answering questions around the clock and around the calendar.

I want to thank the following persons for generously turning to my aid the resources of their offices or organizations: Dr. Richard Block of the i.t.a. Foundation; William Boutwell of *Scholastic Magazine*; Gordon Carroll of the Famous Writers; Norman Cousins of *The Saturday Review*; Paul B. Diederich of the Educational Testing Service; G. K. Hodenfield of the Education Writers' Association; Charles M. Holloway of the College Entrance Examination Board; Phil King of the National Education Association; Louie Mathis of the Department of Health, Education and Welfare; and Paul Swenson of the Newspaper Foundation. I'm sorry to report that nobody from the C.I.A. offered that organization's resources, although I could have used them.

I relied on certain persons as allies and collaborators. Their names are William B. Bean, M.D.; Ann Beere; R. V. Allen, Professor of Education, University of Arizona; Harvey Alpert, Hofstra University; Edward P. J. Corbett of Creighton University; Dr. Erwin di Cyan; Jacques Barzun; Ethel Ernst; Earl H. Greeson; Nat Hammer; Josephine Huber; Rowena McNally; Joseph Mersand; Jimmy Nolan; Dr. Charles van Riper; Lenore Sandel; Dr. Rebecca Stewart; Irene F. Volkringer; Tina Thoburn; and George Baird.

There are many, many teachers of English who love and respect their language and its literature and who pass these attitudes on to their students. I have met them at a number of conferences held by the National Council of Teachers of English and have read their essays in various NCTE publications. I am grateful to Enid M. Olson, Director of Public Relations, for keeping me informed about the NCTE. It was Mrs. Olson who first told me about the Nebraska curriculum described in this book.

*12*

Speaking of Nebraska, let me thank Paul A. Olson, Frank M. Rice, and Eldonna L. Evertts, co-directors in 1966 of the Nebraska Curriculum Development Center in Lincoln.

John Teeling, S. J., of Regis College, Denver, applied the concept of writing-oriented instruction to American Indians. We attempted to help Indians write their own myths and legends. I'm grateful to Father Teeling for the research opportunities his project made possible. Dr. Ken Macrorie of Western Michigan University has dedicated his professional life to teaching students to write. I want to thank him here formally for his insights into writing instruction at the college level.

Let me thank, finally, Georgia Griggs of W. W. Norton & Company for providing that dialogic relationship that I believe is the essential editorial function; Diane Snyder for research assistance; Joan Meade Craske for her typing help; and my secretary, Margaret M. Flanagan, for managing the office and production details required to support my work. Miss Flanagan did at least six books' worth of work so that I could deliver this single book.

G.R.R.

# 1 – NOBODY REMEMBERS A NATION FOR ITS READERS

# Prologue

ϱϱϱϱϱϱϱϱϱϱϱϱϱϱϱϱϱϱϱϱϱϱϱϱϱϱϱϱϱϱϱϱϱϱϱϱϱϱϱϱϱϱϱϱϱϱϱϱϱ

THAT THE Second "R" is dead is not news. The mailman lugs its body to us in all classes of mail: fourth, third, second, and even first.

There were complaints of dirty play. A lot of people said it was done by the colleges. Some blamed high school.

In this book I present evidence which shows how writing was killed in the first grade. It died as all beings die, its body separated from its soul—its body the symbols, its soul, human communication. It was separated from reading, then led to a deserted part of education and there done in.

A variety of devices was used to complete the crime. I have tagged and exhibited them: (1) controlled-word lists, (2) multiple-choice and fill-in sentences, and (3) a most insidious tool called "child-to-teacher dictation."

But the chief instrument was one we would suspect the least, our old familiar ABCs, the English alphabet.

Teachers, I suppose, did the actual killing. They held the weapon, they employed the devices ("methods," they call them), and the body fell on their premises. Since they never intended this death, however, I am advised to reduce my charge from murder to manslaughter.

But I do charge Reading Specialists, who dominate the primary grades, with the true crime and I charge the Department of English not only with looking the other way while the evil was being done but of conducting a graduate school of crime for showing teachers how to kill.

As with other social crimes, we are all more or less at fault. We've let ourselves be coerced by a syndicate of attitudes, fallacies, prejudices—a vast conspiracy favoring reading which has influenced our culture since the invention of type.

Writing is taken for granted as a commonplace act of nature. But it took civilization thousands of years to make the leap from speech to writing. Some societies still do not have a written language even today. It should not be a scandal if some children don't learn to write. If there weren't so much print all around us we might not be so confident that the feat is at all possible.

A child learning to write is in a passage of critical importance to his personal development and of serious importance to society.

The written sentence is the awesome sacrament of cognition. It is a human judgment preserved in symbols. The child who has freely written his first sentence should be honored as one who, through literacy, has experienced his first sacred communion with society and civilization.

A nation will be remembered in time not by its listeners, but by its speakers. A nation makes its own original mark in history not through its readers but through its writers.

By learning to write, therefore, the child acquires the instrument for making his mark in life. He will not make that mark reading. It is through writing that he submits himself as a candidate to any society beyond the limits of his voice and touch, beyond his family and outside his neighborhood.

# F for Writing

TOWARD THE END of his fourth month in first grade, your child will bring home a school-made Christmas card. Don't be misled by the message—there's nothing "merry" about it.

Burn it and call the principal.

The card indicates that your school is teaching only two R's. In the face of massive evidence that we fail in life if we can't communicate, your school is teaching reading as if reading is all that counts. History, science, and social studies are all taught through reading. The only communication practice your child will get will be through writing "True" or "False" in multiple-choice examinations.

A reading-oriented curriculum will hand your child up to higher schooling, to business or a profession badly equipped to satisfy his —and their—most demanding need: the need to compose his thoughts, define his feelings, and communicate with others in speech and writing.

HOLIDAY GREETINGS, invitations, and thank-you notes are the first results of grade-school writing instruction. The failure of this instruction is attested to by the size and growth of the greeting-card industry. According to the U.S. Department of Commerce, almost 6 billion 5 hundred million factory-written messages were bought during 1963, the last year for which there are records. Half these cards, 3 billion 7 hundred million, were Christmas cards while the remaining 2 billion 8 hundred million carried Mother's Day, Valentine's Day, sympathy, thinking-of-you, and a bewildering variety of other messages.

These cards are not bought primarily for their art work but for what they say. An industry representative told me: "The message sells the card. The *design attracts*, but the *message sells*."

One New York City department store stocks cards speaking for 1,500 different occasions, but a clerk told me 1,500 kinds of cards were not enough. "Yesterday somebody wanted a card for two college friends who had met in their freshman year, married in their junior year, had their first baby at graduation, and were living in a trailer. The card she wanted had somehow to meet this total situation. We didn't have such a card but I advised her to write to the publisher. That made her sad. She said, 'I'm not much for writing.' "

The inability of adults to express themselves in writing is far more serious than the failure to write their own greeting or announcement cards.

There is no profession, no business, no government office, no industry, no service, no science, no art in the United States in which communication is not expensively, frustratingly clogged by bad writing.

---

**Despite all the granting agencies, and subsidies for research, we have no institutes for the care and feeding of crippled sentences, spastic language, or chronically disabled and injured grammar. Our sweet language is approaching the glacial hardening of an old age deformed by the weight of ignorance from above and the upthrust of pomposity and bombast from below.—*William B. Bean., M.D.***

---

Consider space research, for example, our most expensive and spectacular scientific activity today.

The first thing Alexei Leonov, the Soviet cosmonaut, did after his astounding "walk" in space a hundred miles above the Black Sea was to sit down inside his craft and write about it.

"I wrote down everything I saw, so as not to forget something later," he said.

There is no record of any U.S. astronaut sitting inside his capsule and writing. The signed articles in *Life* magazine were ghost-written by *Life* writers who had tape-recorded oral interviews.

We must thank instruments for what we know about outer space. Our impressions have come from the camera. The human statement from U.S. space explorers reduces to *"Golly!"*

I'm not faulting the astronauts for not writing, say, like Columbus or Peter Freuchen or Scott of the Arctic and Antarctic, or Meriwether Lewis of our western states, or Dr. Hannes Lindemann of his canoe crossing of the Atlantic, or about fear as Graham Greene might have done; or, in the fine manner of A. J. Liebling, about what they ate; or for not exciting our imaginations as H. G. Wells or Jules Verne or Edgar Rice Burroughs, or that other Welles, Orson, did. I don't criticize N.A.S.A. for not sending up Antoine de Saint-Exupery or Isaac Asimov or Gerold Frank or Tom Wolfe.

I do criticize the reading-oriented education system which can pass intelligent, alert men through sixteen years of schooling in the English language and deliver them to their professions still unable to use English on paper.

Here are men able to supervise a countdown involving thousands of units; control the hundreds of switches, lights, dials, buttons, knobs, pipes, and wires needed to maneuver the craft in orbit; and then, finally, steer it back into atmosphere to a target in the ocean.

It's unbelievable that they should find it hard to arrange a simple prose statement without help. Isn't coupling a noun and verb on paper a comparatively simple docking maneuver?

# The Great Grade-School Scandal

THREE YEARS AGO, while collecting material for this book, I telephoned the New York Public Library and asked Information how many articles were listed under "writing" in the Education Index of the *Reader's Guide to Periodical Literature*. Information went off the line, then came back.

"Do you mean 'Handwriting'?"

"No, I mean writing, ordinary prose writing."

"Under 'Writing,' all that's listed is penmanship."

"Would you try looking under 'Composition'?"

Information went off.

"All I find under 'Composition' is music and art," she reported after some moments.

"But 'Writing' must be there some place."

Information became suspicious. "Is this for a contest?"

"No."

Information disappeared again. When she came back, she said, "You'll have to come down yourself. I can't find it, and I don't have any more time to look."

SHORTLY AFTER this experience, I discovered that a Reading Expert was formally attached to the U.S. Office of Education. I telephoned the office and asked to speak with the "writing expert." The gentleman who came to the telephone asked: "Do you mean handwriting?"

"No, I mean writing—prose composition."

"There is no specialist like that. Writing is part of English."

"Isn't reading a part of English, too?"

"Why, yes, so it is," he agreed after a pause. "Don't ask me how they came unstuck. I don't know."

THESE TWO telephone calls were my first clues that we have no grade-school writing curriculum. No one's trained to teach it. Everybody's so busy teaching Johnny to read there's nobody left to teach him to write.

October 21, 1965, a front page story in the *New York Times* headlined "MOST CITY PUPILS TRAIL THE NATION IN TESTS OF 2 R'S" described the most massive citywide school tests ever carried out in the history of the City of New York. The two R's tested were reading and arithmetic. There was no test of writing. The *Times* education editor wrote: "After years of underestimating the importance of early mastery of reading as a basic tool of learning, educators in the last decade have again acknowledged that the first R is indeed the key to educational success."

A more accurate statement might have been: After years of underestimating the importance of reading, educators are now *over*estimating its importance.

The *Times* took no note of the missing R. Its remark that "the first R is indeed the key to educational success" needs to be examined, for it is a spongy assumption.

Educational success is double-locked and needs *two* keys: reading is one key, writing is the other. Educational achievement throughout our school years is tested and proven not by reading but by written reports, written examinations, written term papers and theses.

Even university professors and universities must prove themselves by writing and publishing. The American Council on Education, after assessing quality in graduate education (May 1966), concluded that the strongest universities had important research libraries, while the strongest departments had important and successful writers.

Two false attitudes dominate our educational system:
1. Reading is *the* key to all later learning.
2. Writing is a special art, a talent possessed by a gifted few.

The uneven push exerted by these two notions distorts our entire educational plan. Its immediate effect is to warp reading and writing away from each other. Reading gets prime instruction time and

*23*

attention, starting in kindergarten. Spelling instruction begins in second grade, two years later. Teachers are trained to teach reading; they are not taught to write or trained to teach writing.

Now to separate reading from writing is bad, for like listening and talking, like inhaling and exhaling, they belong together; each makes the other intelligible. They are complementary forms of interpersonal communication.

Reading is an extension of listening as writing is an extension of talking. We cannot underexercise or overexercise one without loss to the other. It would be absurd to say inhaling is more important than exhaling, to specialize in inhaling while neglecting exhaling, to regard inhaling as essential for life and exhaling as a rare talent possessed by a gifted few. The teacher who promotes reading at the expense of writing hangs defeat on her children even as she launches them on their school careers.

Yet in announcements, reports, bulletins, and professional journals from foundations, research centers, and teacher-training schools and at conferences, workshops, institutes, and seminars reading is treated as a separate entity distinct from writing. Writing is usually not even discussed.

The U.S. Congress in 1964 officially recognized that reading has come unstuck from English when it amended the National Defense Education Act of 1958 "to strengthen instruction in reading, English, and other subjects."

WHEN I DID finally go to the New York Public Library to inspect the *Reader's Guide to Periodical Literature*, in the Education Index I found that most of the articles about writing were listed under "English—Composition." A few were wedged in another English subdvision called "Creative Activity."

I counted all the articles relating to reading and writing listed in the Index from July 1938 to June 1963. Although I didn't inspect the titles and didn't bother to count the thousands of articles listed under "Literature," I found an annual average of thirty columns of articles devoted to Reading as against seven columns devoted to English Composition.

A closer look at the articles on composition revealed that almost all articles referred to the upper grades, high school, and college. I could locate only four articles on primary-grade composition reported during twenty-five years.

At Columbia Teachers College I looked up the number of doctoral theses on *writing* in the 1952–57 file, the only file available to me at the time. There were no entries under "writing" or "composition." I found the theses on writing under "English teaching."

The score: 39 for reading, 4 for writing.

The four theses on writing included two on elementary-school writing, one on high school writing, and one on writing problems of Puerto Rican children.

The third edition of the *Encyclopedia of Educational Research* reports on research done in education between 1950 and 1960. Its articles on reading total eighty columns trailed by 422 additional references to books, study reports, and other articles.

Neither writing nor composition is mentioned in the *Encyclopedia*'s table of contents, but in its index I found "Written composition: teaching of, 460–61." The article is only two columns long with twenty-seven reference notes and it also discusses "oral composition." The authors say their report describes written composition in high schools. There is no reference to elementary-school composition.

More than five columns are given to the "hygiene of reading," a discussion of the color of paper. There are five columns on left-handedness and right-handedness. "Handwriting" requires thirteen columns and seventy-four reference notes.

There are fifteen columns on the school bus and its driver.

# Writing Is an Extension
## of Talk

SPEECH was never perfectly adequate for communication, or man would never have learned to whisper and would not have developed the gesture, the wink, or the grimace. Man developed writing as *an adjunct and extension of talk*. We write when it is inconvenient or impossible or impractical to talk. We write when face-to-face talk is embarrassing. We write to collect and save our argument in an organized way and to be able to present our talk at its best.

Writing tries to be better than talk. Good writing isn't just any speech babbled onto paper. It is speech under certain ideal conditions, speech to a listener who doesn't interrupt, who understands, accepts, and encourages. Whereas our talk may be impulsive, vague, and rambling, when we write we can compose what we want to say.

Just as reading offers certain advantages over listening, writing offers certain hard advantages not yielded by speech. Paper *saves* thoughts which would otherwise be lost in the air, for talk is fluid. We use the telephone today when we once would have written letters. We use magnetic tape to record and store the human voice. But we're still a long way from tape-recording or televising state and federal laws, marriage promises, or labor-management contracts. No cheaper, more versatile, and more practical medium has yet been invented to replace paper.

A machine may replace paper or handwriting somehow, but it will never be able to replace the process of organizing thoughts and feelings and communicating them to someone else. This process is reserved for a writer.

As organizations get bigger, move faster, reach out over greater distances, deal with far-off nations, engage more people, merge and interlock with other companies, they need to devise swifter, surer, more accurate means of communication.

A badly written news report doesn't get better with speed, nor will bouncing it off Tel-Star jolt its meanings into shape. We will improve writing by improving the writer, not by improving the machine he uses or by improving the reader. An improved machine will only deliver the same bad writing faster or louder or cheaper.

*No matter how sophisticated our communicating media become there will always be two bottlenecks: the man who writes the message and the man who reads it.*

---

For business purposes of all kinds, from the performance of humble routine tasks in industry and commerce to the most responsible executive and administrative work, efficiency is liable to turn, from time to time, on communication in speech and writing. In the professions the same is true, with the addition that language may be, in some professions, not only the vehicle of communication but also the very stuff of their activity. The scale and scope of modern industry and trade have not diminished but rather increased the importance of plain and exact communication. The speed at which business is done makes mistakes of meaning more troublesome, costly and dangerous than ever. Nor have mechanical contrivances made speech and writing any less important. The telephone and dictaphone have taken some work away from the pen, but they have added it to the voice and the typewriter. Translation, interpretation, paraphrase and summary are indispensable to modern commercial and political conferences. In science, transport and technology, though much depends on quantitative measurement and symbolic notation, the element of prose statement—explanation, directive, summary and record—cannot be eliminated. Such statements must, moreover, be exact and intelligible, to an increasing degree, to match the increasingly exact performance of the machines and the men who operate them. If this increasing complexity and refinement of performance are not answered by rising standards of plain, exact and practised expression, not only will our affairs suffer but the language itself will be debased as it struggles to perform its hopeless task. This is actually what is happening. Jargon is, to some extent, the product of haste and pressure, but it comes also from so many people having to say and write more than they have the skill to express plainly without long cogitation.—*"Language," Pamphlet No. 26, Her Majesty's Stationery Office, 1954*

---

The pervasive importance of writing in our economy is such that our whole organization ball is stuck together by written communication: contracts, promises, directives, memos, sales presentations, requests for delivery, instructions for handling and using, progress reports, proposals for change, new ideas, agreements, advertising, bulletins and abstracts, annual reports.

It is writing's importance to society that makes reading important for the individual.

Dr. Peter F. Drucker, an expert in business and industrial management, tells college students not to wait for papers to be assigned but to volunteer and plead for extra writing and to persuade all teachers to read and criticize what they write. He urges them to write poetry and insists that it will teach them to use language exactly and sensitively. According to Drucker, the ability to write clearly is the one enduring profit the student can take with him from college.

---

**If you work on a machine your ability to express yourself will be of little importance. But as soon as you move one step up from the bottom, your effectiveness depends on your ability to reach others through the spoken or the written word. And the further away your job is from manual work, the larger the organization of which you are an employee, the more important will it be that you know how to convey your thoughts in writing or speaking. In the very large organization, whether it is the government, the larger business corporation, or the Army, this ability to express oneself is perhaps the most important of all the skills a man can possess.—*Peter F. Drucker, Fortune***

---

# Two Ways Writing Makes
# (Corporate) Bodies Bigger, Better,
# and Stronger

TWO WRITTEN forms determine our nation's growth: they are the *proposal* and the *report*. The proposal—or plan or presentation, as it may also be called—is any statement which directs future action. The report is a follow-up account of an event or action.

Proposals and reports constitute the growing edge of any organization. But to serve growth, they must be clearly written. They delay, divert, or prevent growth if they are unintelligible.

As one brief example, consider the financial reports of the United States Government. Such transactions are audited by the General Accounting Office. E. H. Morse, Jr., Director of the Policy Staff, describes the importance of clear communication: "We prepare hundreds of reports each year, the most important of which are submitted to the Congress.... Such reports are the primary means by which we communicate our findings, conclusions, and recommendations.... Our findings have to be transmitted to persons who are not necessarily familiar with the subject matter; therefore, it is essential that we try to communicate the results of our work in as clear a manner as possible ... so that action will be taken when necessary."

How many proposals in the forms of amendments, petitions, and bond issues fail because voters in the poll booths can't make out what they propose?

In 1965, Congress voted $1 billion for educational projects. To get money, a school administrator had only to write up a decent proposal. Some administrators, unable or unwilling to write out their own proposals, sent in ghost-written plans supplied by publishers and manufacturers. John F. Hughes, Program Operations

Director for the U.S. Office of Education, revealed the scandal in a letter to chief state school officers: "Evidence is piling up that field representatives of educational equipment and materials companies are engaged in assembly line project write-ups for, or in conjunction with, school officials. . . . Generally, the projects are easily spotted. They arrive in bundles, there is standard phraseology, there are disproportionate amounts of money devoted to equipment and materials. . . ."

The National Science Foundation defines research as "a seeking for knowledge and understanding for the direct or indirect benefit of all." Scientists argue whether research should be pure or practical. In either kind of research, however, no one denies that the results should benefit others. The benefit is normally delivered through reports.

How can anyone benefit from reports when they are shipped in and out of organizations as boxes of junk, unassembled English with parts missing, mismatched sentences like the odd gauges and calibers in a military-surplus store? On expensive paper they sometimes look efficient, but when translated into sound the language gnashes and squeals aimlessly, disengaged from meaning and failing to communicate.

---

The blemishes may include ungrammatical constructions, confused thought, ambiguity, unjustifiable interpretation, subspecialty jargon, concealed hedging, inadequate description of statistical treatment, or imperfect controls. I am appalled by the frequent publication of papers that describe most minutely what experiments were done, and how, but with no hint of why, or what they mean. Execrable writing like this is the product of shoddy thinking, of careless condescension, or of pretentiousness. I have definite and clear-cut evidence that the scientific writing in our journals exerts a corrupting influence on young scientists—on their writing, their reading, on their thinking.—*Dr. F. Peter Woodford, "Sound Thinking Through Clearer Writing,"* Science, *May 12, 1967*

---

So far as the backers of a research project are concerned, the report is what counts. The backers pay for research but what they are buying is the report. The report *is* the knowledge and understanding which is the product of research.

Economists at the Battelle Memorial Institute have announced that from 1960 through 1965 the federal government and private industry together spent $107.2 billion for research and development.

---

Research is not an end in itself. The day comes when the pleasures of the detective hunt are over and the report must be written. At that point, fit expression no longer appears as a mere frill added to one's accumulation of knowledge. What is not properly presented is simply *not present*—and its purely potential existence is quite useless.—*Jacques Barzun and Henry Graff*, The Modern Researcher

---

Every medical scientist, for example, is expected to share discoveries with his colleagues, with medical societies, and with the medial profession. How well do doctors meet these needs for clear medical writing? Not well at all, according to William B. Bean, M.D., chief editor of *Archives of Internal Medicine*. He says: "The majority of people writing for medical journals use language as a blind man uses a shillelagh, striking out wildly but often to little or no purpose.... Writers don't think or work to make reading a pleasure and a joy. [The bad writer] says that, though his work is not elegant, as long as his meaning gets over he doesn't care. Right here his argument falls apart. What he has written may be clear to him, since he believes he knows what he is talking about; but it is clear to no one else. It is a reflection of his insensitivity rather than a measure of ability to express himself."

Every year Dr. Bean attacks bad medical writing in an article titled "Tower of Babel." "I have no illusion that I get much accomplished by my crusading efforts," Dr. Bean wrote me. "Having looked over 625 manuscripts submitted to our journal this year, I am convinced that there is no recognizable improvement; if anything, perhaps a slight decline. At least half needed major surgery. Perhaps another 20 per cent were hopeless, so hopeless that it didn't seem worthwhile telling the submitter why it was rejected—it would have been so painful. Perhaps a third of those we publish have to be entirely reorganized. I doubt if fear of writing holds many people back. I wish it did."

*31*

Dr. Bean's strongest appeal for clear writing appears in the *Journal of Laboratory and Clinical Medicine* (January 1952). His article titled "The Moral Responsibility to Be Intelligible" insists that bad writing blocks interscience communication. "Clinical research is predicated upon the belief that its significant results should be communicated and used by others. The iron curtain which disbars us from sampling in adjacent fields of science is not so much the erudition of our colleagues, as the tropical jungles of verbiage and gobbledegook in which this erudition lurks, unobserved save by the initiated."

# The Three Costs of Bad Writing

eeeeeeeeeeeeeeeeeeeeeeeeeeeeeeeeeeeeeeeeeeeeeeeeee

## 1. BAD WRITING WASTES TIME, WORK, AND MONEY

There are several factors to count on when figuring the cost of a badly written report. Say it takes sixty-five minutes to solve a very confused report that only deserves five minutes of reading time. Multiply the hour wasted by the number of people who have to read the report: 100 readers, 100 hours shot. If the report requires action, add the cost of time lost through mistakes due to misreading. Add the loss of action where people are too baffled or bored to move. If the report contains information the public should know about, add the loss of publicity where the press refuses to puzzle out its meaning.

---

The daily cost of written communication throughout the Air Force runs high. Therefore we can't afford the costly errors that come from poor logic and misleading language.—*General J. P. McConnell, U.S. Air Force Chief of Staff*

---

An American Management Association survey shows that the typical businessman spends five hours a day reading reports, publications, and correspondence. Four out of five of these executives complain that the material is repetitive, unclear, poorly organized, late, or irrelevant.

---

Prof. W. F. Carstens of the Sandia Corporation says that one-fourth of the most expensive manpower in any organization is devoted to turning out written words, and when one adds the fact that a high percentage of the product of all this effort is of poor quality, it is clear something should be done about it.

Using this one-fourth figure and considering salaries alone, we get a writing cost of $275,000 a year for our own top echelon. This does not include the cost of paper, typing, duplicating, mailing, reading, or—more important—the cost for salaries of others who write and the hundreds who read.

Now if you add three-fifths of that $275,000, or $162,000, as the cost of getting the words typed and mailed, you come out with a total of $440,000 for a portion of BLM [Bureau of Land Management] writing for a single year. We can't treat costs like these as though they were insignificant. —*John O'Hayre, "Gobbledygook Has Gotta Go," U.S. Department of the Interior*

---

A writing-cost analyst, Richard Morris, estimates that 15 per cent of all business letters and memos are merely requests for clarification of a previous letter or memo.

A study of ten activities in technical divisions within the Esso Research and Engineering Company revealed that the average technical man was spending 61 per cent of his eight-hour day in some form of communication.

| MINUTES OF DAY | SPENT ON | PER CENT OF DAY |
|---|---|---|
| 75 | writing | 16 |
| 48 | reading | 10 |
| 168 | speaking, listening | 35 |
| 189 | other business | 39 |

"Communication is expensive," A. F. Kaulakis, a vice-president at Esso concluded. "In the research, engineering, and development divisions a man's prime time is the time he spends directly applying his technical talent to a technical problem. We think the speaking, listening, and reading time could be cut down if the writing were clearer."

## 2. BAD WRITING FRUSTRATES DECISION-MAKING

The function of the writer in organization is to present clear alternatives for executive decision. If writing isn't clear and orderly, the executive has to suspend action till he can decode the writer's language. How can anyone make an intelligent decision about the problem of jet noise—or even decide if it *is* a problem—if he has to slog through a statement like the one following, from a recent issue of the *Minnesota Law Review*: "If the national interest in acquiring a cross-continental SST [supersonic transport] fleet cannot be sacrificed to the interests of a more quiet society, cost balancing not unlike that underlying the general airport noise problems seems in order." (Quoted in "The Jet Noise Is Getting Awful," *New York Times Magazine*, January 14, 1968.)

---

. . . I believe that much business strength is sapped in America because of subordinates' failure to present an epitome of their work in clear, concise language so that it can move to executive direction for decisions without an exorbitant amount of refining and clarification all along the supervisory lines.—*Letter from a government field auditor to E. H. Morse, Jr., U.S. General Accounting Office, December 1958*

---

An English professor addressed a group of engineers on the topic "The Challenge to Writers in Industry." If our future truly depends on whatever he says it depends on, wouldn't it help if he were clear so that we could decide what to do? He said: "Ultimately, it seems to me, our future will depend on a conversion of traditional and leisurely thinking into dynamic and imaginative projection of ideas. . . ."

## 3. BAD WRITING CORRODES CREDIBILITY

Bad writing disturbs confidence, creates doubts and suspicion, encourages cynicism and nominalism, weakens interhuman trust. It erodes respect for language itself. Any of these conditions make communication difficult if not impossible.

---

When American scholars forsake the clarity and bounteous possibilities of English for the protective coloration of private languages unintelligible at times even to each other, they are destructive of the ends of democratic government's relationship to its citizens.—*Lawrence R. Klein, publications editor, U.S. Department of Labor*

---

### The Nominalistic Cleaner

. . . I brought my suit to a cleaner whose shop carried a neon sign advertising: "Kleenerama—One Hour Service."

After three days I came back for my suit.

"It's not ready," the counterman told me.

"It's not ready? You've had it three days."

"But it takes four days."

"What about your sign—it says 'one hour service'?"

"That's only the name of the shop."

—*John Teeling, S. J., "Talks on Dialog"*

# The Professional Block

ALL PROFESSIONS are handicapped by bad writing, but two professions, religion and law, suffer more seriously than others. Words are the specific content of these professions. Each is concerned with preserving and interpreting a verbal tradition, the one divine, the other secular.

The religious ministry is charged with communicating the meaning of love and peace, of Jesus and the Bible. How poorly preachers meet their obligation is known by all who still listen to sermons. We have few heretics of faith in our day. We have, rather, aliens. God may or may not be dead. There is no doubt His Word is dead.

Lawyers write statements which direct our lives and affect our peace, our behavior, our income. They help protect identity by defining it. They write contracts binding individual men to organizations. They write the terms by which organizations merge. They write wills. They write treaties.

How good is legal writing? Not good at all, to extend a famous complaint by Fred Rodell, Professor of Law at Yale University: "There are two things wrong with all law review writing: one is its content and the other is its style."

This opinion was securely documented in 1949 by Arthur T. Vanderbilt, Dean of the New York University Law School. Dr. Vanderbilt, after collecting data on more than 24,000 students registered at eighty-one different U.S. law schools, charged that law students could not "think straight and write and speak in clear, forceful English."

Dean Thomas M. Cooley of the University of Pittsburgh School of Law and Dean William Warren of Columbia Law School both say the lawyer who can't write is no lawyer at all. Dean Cooley says: "All of our law schools continue to graduate every year people who are being sent into the world with our representation that they are qualified to become adequate practitioners, after the accumulation of the requisite practical experience, which law schools do not pretend to provide. This representation is false. The law student can go through the standard American law curriculum and emerge just as bad a writer—and thus very nearly as inept a lawyer—as he went in."

And Dr. Warren says: "We have men in our law school who, we are sure, have mastered substantial amounts of legal information. But they cannot put this learning into words on their examinations or in their term papers so that we who have supervised the very learning which they seek to express can understand what they are talking about. They cannot organize and express what it is that they know. How much less, then, can these unfortunates advise a client, or someone else who knows little or nothing of the substance of legal issues, of what it is that needs to be communicated?"

Thirteen thousand lawyers work in Washington, D.C. Among these are 315 Representatives and 66 Senators.

If Dean Warren is right and Dean Cooley is right and Dean Vanderbilt and Professor Rodell too are right, we're in serious trouble.

---

**Has literature a function in the state . . . ? It has to do with maintaining the very cleanliness of the tools, the health of the very matter of thought itself. The individual cannot think or communicate his thought, the governor or legislator cannot act effectively or frame his laws without words. When the very essence of their work, the application of word to thing, goes rotten, i.e., becomes slushy and inexact, or excessive or bloated, the whole machinery of social and individual thought and order goes to pot.—*Ezra Pound***

---

Since law schools are graduating lawyers who can't write, since a lawyer who can't write is "quite literally no lawyer at all," and since lawyers control 65 to 75 per cent of the legislative and executive branches of our federal government and 99 per cent of the judiciary branch, as well as state, city, and county governments— how does anything ever move?

*37*

In 1966, the Education Policies Commission asked teachers to promote seven values underlying the spirit of science: (1) longing to know and understand; (2) questioning of all things; (3) search for data and their meaning; (4) demand for verification; (5) respect for logic; (6) consideration of premises; (7) consideration of consequences.

Curiously, the Commission did not include report writing among its recommendations. Every one of its points describes a reader, isolated, passive, and contemplative. There is no indication that the scientist must ever communicate what he's discovered back to his supporters, the compact, interdependent communities of man.

Science, in itself, doesn't include communication. But there *is* no such real thing as "science in itself." Science exists only in the scientist. The scientist, however, is a social being dependent on society both at the start and at the conclusion of his research. His "longing to know and to understand" should be matched by a longing that *others* know and understand, too.

---

**I remember once going to a meeting of biologists and physicists at the University of Pennsylvania. The biologists wanted to learn about physics and the physicists wanted to learn about biology, but to my great horror the next morning people told me that the physicists did not understand the biologists and the biologists didn't understand the physicists. They would wait for the *New York Times* to find out what went on the day before. I should have been greatly flattered, but I wasn't; I was too concerned about the breakdown between scientists.—*William L. Laurence, speaking at the Brooklyn Polytechnic Institute as Science Editor of the* New York Times**

---

John Kenneth Galbraith, speaking before the British Association for the Advancement of Science, said that "the test of a writer is whether he remains with a difficult subject until he has thought through not only the problem but its exposition."

Following is a panorama of bad writing displayed by educationists, anthropologists, social scientists, and psychologists who failed Galbraith's test.

**Example 1** is from an educationist's report to a conference studying curriculum change. After reading it, quiz yourself: "What made the eleven most powerful men act?"

Several years ago I made an intensive study of why the eleven most powerful men in a school district power structure said they took action upon about twenty projects and issues. The leaders of competing groups held different political beliefs. Their reasons for supporting or opposing projects could be placed upon a liberalism-conservatism continuum. Thus, difference in operational beliefs was one of the elements explaining competition between groups in the power structure.

**Example 2** is from a social psychologist's report. It is called "Ingratiation," a subject Dale Carnegie wrote about in *How to Win Friends and Influence People*.

About five years ago, K. D. and I conducted an experiment in which subjects were induced to communicate a negative evaluation to a person who they thought was in the next room. We assumed, correctly as it turned out, that this task would create cognitive dissonance in the subjects—transmitting a hostile evaluation would be dissonant with the realization that the target person had done nothing to deserve it. We were able to show that if subjects were permissively coaxed rather than arbitrarily directed to read the derogatory message, their private impressions of the target person became more negative as a way of justifying their behavior. Shortly after completing the experiment we began to think of interesting next steps.

**Example 3** is from an anthropologist's report describing Australian desert people.

On the basis of their encounter with a few Walbiri men who were visiting the Warramunga, Spencer and Gillen asserted that the Walbiri patrimoieties had the same names as the Warramunga patrimoieties—that is, the djabangari-djaban-angga-djabaldjari-djungarai sub-sections were called the *uluura* patrimoiety, and the djambi-djimba-djangala-djaga-mara-djuburula sub-sections the *kingillimoiety*. I could not confirm this statement.

**Example 4** is from a psychologist's report describing how people meet and become acquainted.

Initial strangership represents the zero state out of which given opportunity and motivation, various kinds of relationships among persons emerge. Given, in addition, a relatively long period of time during which such relationships can develop, we may expect them to become more or less stabilized. We shall have more to say, in the following chapter, about these relationships and how they may be conceptualized. Meanwhile, we may say simply that the central objective of the study, to which arrangements assuring initial strangership and subsequent opportunity for acquaintance were instrumental, was to improve our understanding of the development of stable interpersonal relationships.

**Example 5** is from an abstract of a report read at the American Museum of Natural History.

The brevity of latent addition, the requirement of spatial summation, the irreciprocity of conduction, the occurrence of direct inhibition and the duration of delay, which characterize synaptic transmission, and the all-none response with subsequent refractoriness of the component neurons do all insure that the simple and discrete elementary signals are so related as to conform to a logical calculus of numerable, coexisting and sequential propositions. From this fact we can deduce the formal properties of cognition and conation in any nervous system that possesses receptors and controls effectors.

# "Where Did We Go Wrong?"

OUR READING environment is so encrusted with bad writing that we take it for granted, we don't see it any more, we weary of protesting, we assume it *has* to be the way it is. We even blame ourselves for reading badly.

Why can't Americans write? Whose fault is it that we don't? The fault is in school, but where in school? At which level?

• Dr. F. Peter Woodford, who conducts special classes in science writing at Rockefeller University, blames the *graduate schools*.

When science students enter graduate school they often write with admirable directness and clarity of purpose. Two years later, these same students' writing is verbose, pompous, full of fashionable circumlocutions as well as dangling constructions, and painfully polysyllabic. What has brought about the change? Clearly, the students have copied their dreary and pretentious phrases from the scientific literature. They have been dutifully studying it, as they are urged to do, and it has warped their style to the point that they can no longer walk to the door without "utilizing a pedestrian relocation" or sip their coffee without "prior elevation of the containing vessel to facilitate imbibition."—*Science*, May 12, 1967.

• But Jacques Barzun says students are bad writers *before* they enter graduate school.

Among the highly selected graduate students in the University where I teach [Columbia] I find about one in ten who needs coaching in the elements of literacy—spelling, punctuation, sentence structure and diction.—Introduction to *Tomorrow's Illiterates*.

*41*

Columbia University Dean William C. Warren agrees with his colleague, Dr. Barzun. In three successive reports in Columbia University's *Bulletin of Information* (1955–57), he assailed the *colleges* for polluting his School of Law with writing illiterates.

In our school the student's record and rank depend entirely upon some species of written work—an examination, a report or a seminar paper. We can teach them to put their thoughts in order, we cannot teach them grammar; we cannot rectify their clumsy use of language. Twenty per cent admitted to no college course in English composition. Any encouragement one might derive from the robust percentages if those who had received training in writing is shattered when one actually encounters in mass the written work of law students. Even the most tolerant of critics will concede that whatever the arts of which the students are masters, writing is not one of them.

• Stung by criticism, the colleges periodically revise English I or Composition. At the same time, they complain that they are forced to clutter their school terms with "hospital English" courses because *high schools* fail to teach the subject properly. There is evidence to justify their complaint. Each year almost 9,000 freshmen at the University of California in Berkeley take a three-hour English test, two hours of which is given to essay writing. The university admits only the top eighth of high school graduates in the state, and yet year after year 4,000 to 5,000 students fail the composition test.

Berkeley isn't the only school to be disappointed by freshmen who can't write. Two out of three American colleges offer non-credit remedial English at a yearly cost of over $10 million.

• But is high school the source of writing failure? It seems not. Even as colleges complain they have to teach remedial high school English, high schools complain they have to teach remedial grade-school English.

**It is the position of this book that the sources of bad writing must not be sought in graduate school, college, or high school but in elementary school, where writing instruction is supposed to begin.**

Most of what is called writing instruction in the primary grades is not writing instruction at all but a variety of reading instruction. The writing instruction that is accidentally right is inadequate. It starts too late, its start is wrong, its announced goals are wrong.

It is wasteful because it doesn't work: it doesn't deliver writers.

But it is worse than wasteful. It is pernicious because it does actual damage to a child's ability to communicate.

American adults don't write because they are the victims of a system intensely determined to make them readers, not writers, and because there is no true and proper curriculum designed to develop writing.

# The Reading Bias

WHICH IS more important—reading or writing? Which should be taught first in school?

Taken as events in a child's life, looking and listening come before speech. A three-month-old infant will watch his mother's mouth while she's talking and then try to imitate her. In this general sense, "reading" comes before writing. Reading—in the broad sense of observing and acquiring, of receiving impressions—precedes expression. Even when a person discovers something wholly inside himself, at night with the lights out, his eyes closed, his senses at rest, he "reads" this thought before expressing it to someone.

But does this natural precedence in time argue priority in teaching? Not at all. The infant "reads" his mother's face to imitate her speech. We read in order to act. Every bit of information we pick up out of a book helps form our attitudes and opinions, and these in turn affect our actions. There is very little reading that we do purely for our own hermetically isolated pleasure, not telling someone about it or discussing it later. We're anxious for Johnny to read because we expect reading to change him in some way, to get him to do something or influence his feelings. School reading is for expression.

---

**Several research studies have revealed that poor language ability is one of the factors related positively to pupil dropout rates. High school dropouts or graduates who use slovenly, inexact language in speaking or writing are poor job risks.—***"The National Interest and the Teaching of English,"** 1961*

---

If you ask them, educationists will assure you that reading and writing complement each other. Both are important, they will say, nodding and bobbing. This is educational theory. But if you look at the curriculum, interview teachers and discuss their training, review research grants from foundations and the Office of Education, consult such organizations as the International Reading Association, the National Education Association, the Modern Language Association, and the National Association of Independent Schools, it becomes big-as-life plain that in practice everyone thinks reading is decidedly more important.

School principals will assure you that composition is a part of "English."

"We teach *all* the language arts," they will say archly. "Listening, speaking, reading, and writing are all language arts and we teach them all."

But once writing becomes part of "English" or is dropped into "Language Arts" it gets lost. What usually happens is that literature—another word for reading—grabs most of the teacher's time, energy, and enthusiasm while speech, linguistics, and writing get left behind.

During 1963 and 1964, Professor Roger Applebee visited almost 1,500 high school classrooms in order to analyze the teaching of English. He reported to the National Council of Teachers of English that "English" was chiefly literature: "English consists of proportionate parts of language, literature and composition—a tripod, if you will. I must report that whatever theoretical support this tripod may have, it will surely collapse in practice, since, in most instances, the legs are of quite unequal length."

In a separate report describing college English, Dr. Applebee again said that literature took the bear's share of instruction time: "On the basis of some five hundred hours of classroom observation, it would appear that only about 20 per cent of class time is given to the teaching of writing."

Every year the sky is filled with reports of new reading research; they funnel out of the Office of Education like bats from a backless cave. Education researchers asked the federal government for $117 million in 1966–67. No one knows how much of this money went to reading as against writing research, but without exact information from Washington, $9.95 for reading for every nickel spent for writing is not a bad guess. The *Reading Teacher* suggests that reading is featured in nine out of ten projects planned under the federal Elementary and Secondary Education Act of 1965. Of course, there is burning, foot-shifting urgency to all reading research—as burning and urgent as "Validity of Frequency of Blinking as a Criterion of Readability" and "The Influences of Surface and Tint of Paper on the Speed of Reading."

Communication failures among business and professional people can't be blamed on jargon, although jargon is usually blamed. Jargon merely finishes a breakdown started years earlier. The failure of adults to communicate rises directly from the separation of reading from writing in grades one, two, and three.

Reading and writing separated in childhood never come back together again. In college "Introduction to Research" courses are separated from composition courses as if the two subjects had nothing to do with each other.

The ultimate origin of communication failures is in first grade, where reading is separated from writing and where reading is aggressively promoted in the absence of any true curriculum of writing instruction. Nobody in first grade thought it would go this far or get this bad. What seemed in the infant to be only a chapped lip causing no disturbance in communication, certainly none in self-expression, has matured as a total cleft in the hard and soft palate. Self-expression is now badly inhibited. Interhuman communication, not only interscience communication, is almost lost.

The growth of our nation is being blocked by the inability of our people to describe original thinking or to present plans for new development or to report research in clear, usable English.

Bad writing can stop the firing of a rocket, steal learning from children, stall an executive's career, kill a sale, put a job out of reach. The end penalty of bad writing is either nongrowth or misgrowth. It attacks growth in different ways: it eats profits, wastes time and work, spoils belief, isolates the lonely. It attacks all growth, everybody's growth.

The researcher who fails to write a clear, usable report fails the organization that supported him. He fails himself, too, for his own growth stops if he can't describe his findings to anyone.

The writer grows not only by thinking his ideas through but in being read by others. He grows in acquiring and grows in being acquired. Just as the speaker is completed in the listener, the writer is completed in the reader. He becomes more as he helps others become.

Dr. Edward W. Strong, while chancellor at Berkeley, complained to education writers: "We have some students coming here who have had calculus and other advanced math in high school. But they can't write English."

Dr. Strong's remark suggests there may be serious damage to children who are learning the new math but not learning how to speak and write, who are learning to communicate by numbers but not words. For example, let's get back to the astronauts.

If the astronauts could write, what more could they say than what the instruments have delivered? They could write the difference between the *number* and the *word*. Words can reach where instruments have not gone and cannot go. Words can grope for the inexact and unmeasurable. Words can guess and imagine and wonder. They can describe space fear, space loneliness, and space freedom. Words warm.

Colonel Thomas Stafford of Gemini 9 was prevented from docking because his target's shroud was still attached. He said it looked "like an angry alligator"—the first English metaphor spoken in space. How it fascinates, the thought up there of an "alligator." It's not an engineer's precise description, but doesn't it tell a lot?

A *Time* essay, arguing for manned flights to the moon, says Ranger's pictures of the moon contained only 500,000 "bits" of information, whereas the human eye with a glance may take in 100 million "bits."

What good are these 100 million bits if man can't describe them? The explorers who will actually land on the moon and planets must be communicative men. Let them send back numbers to feed the instruments, but let them also write diaries and take notes in language that can feed men. If the men we send to the moon can't communicate their thoughts and feelings, then, even after they have landed, no human life will have been on the moon.

47

# The Writing-Oriented School
## vs. the Non-Com Man

THE MINIMUM graduate of our schools should not be a reader but a writer who reads for both information and pleasure.

An eloquent writer with acutely refined listening and observational powers—this should be our maximum graduate.

To produce such a graduate we will have to reverse the reading orientation of our schools and make them writing-oriented.

In setting *writing* against *reading*, I set the active, expressive side of human development against its receptive, passive side. I don't mean to deny the importance of reading, listening, and observing. I do assert that writing develops the educative facets of a person. The observer who knows he must report sees more exactly. The listener who knows he must repeat what he's heard hears better. The reader who must write reads slower, perhaps, but more accurately.

By "writer," therefore, I mean to include the speaker and the doer or activist. Let children learn to make music, not merely listen to music of the classic composers—or at least let them play music themselves and not just appreciate professionals playing it. Let them learn to paint and draw and carve, not merely to make collages of other people's artifacts. They can be taught art history and art appreciation, but let them learn to make their own art, too.

Nobody remembers a nation for its readers.

In our present reading-oriented system, children are taught social studies, science, history, economics, and other subjects through lectures and through reading. Their educational progress is spot-checked by means of fill-in, multiple-choice, and true-false tests. Writing is pigeonholed in this curriculum as a part-time art, a subject which takes up its little share of the classroom clock and then is closed and put away.

48

One immediate product of this system is the unexpressed teen-ager. An ultimate product is the apathetic, disengaged, impersonal man; he reads his exercise watching televised baseball; he substitutes panel discussions for conversation. He is a noncommitted, noncommital, noncommunicative man. He is the Non-Com Man. The Gary Cooper man.

His receptive, experiential self is sophisticated; his active self is backward and immature. He can't communicate his feelings as a husband or a father because he never learned to communicate his feelings as a child. He can catch information beamed at him over thousands of miles, but can't send words a few inches away to someone he cares for.

WHAT ARE the characteristics of a writing-oriented school?

A writing-oriented school would not only teach writing as a subject in its own right, but would teach most other subjects as well through writing.

A writing-oriented school would strive to meet life's communication needs. Life needs both factual and imaginative communication.

Life's needs for writing don't begin after graduation. For the pupil, life is school. Writing should be the student's most important means of communicating what he knows about his studies. In a writing-oriented school, children would learn to communicate factual information through reports and proposals, the two forms they will use all through school and in life after school.

A writing-oriented school will teach children to think problems through to their explanation to others. It would teach children not only to solve problems but to solve the added problem of communicating their solutions.

A student can learn to think by means of reading, too. He can argue with his books. He can connect a book's new ideas with old ones of his own. A book's ideas can qualify and modify and balance his ideas.

But the reader must wait to be served. His mind must wait to agree or disagree with a book's opinions. The writer, on the other hand, must advance opinions of his own. Writing requires the student to define his own understanding of relationships: is *this* part of *that* or *that* part of *this*? Are *this* and *that* of equal importance? Do *this* and *that* contradict each other? The writer reveals not only what facts and concepts he has acquired, but how he associates them with other ideas.

A writing-oriented school would teach students not only to express themselves but to communicate that self-expression to others. Communication is a two-way channel. Television, radio, and print are frequently impositions rather than communications. Successful communication demands an ability to understand the changes and differences that individuate one's listeners and readers.

At present, children are taught early math and early science. They are learning a form of exact communication, but their expression is limited to numbers. If they don't learn to master words, their ability to communicate will be seriously warped.

In a writing-oriented school, children would be taught to respect the differences between words and numbers and to value the ambiguities of language. This is extremely important, for the differences and variables of language are closely associated with human variables and differences. Ultimately, whether we are computer engineers or biochemists or janitors, we will have to communicate with each other as human beings.

The primary-grade teacher teaches all disciplines: history, social studies, science, language, and art. She has the opportunity to prepare children for later interprofessional communication, but she wastes this opportunity in a reading-oriented school. She will not teach communication through reading. She will teach it only through communication itself.

For imaginative communication, children in a writing-oriented school will learn to use classic forms laid in our myths, fables, fairy tales, and adventure stories. Story writing is not an educational frill. Stories give us a chance to theorize, guess, and explore human conflicts. We imagine events as they might happen. We daydream life before realizing it. Stories thus save us time and wear and tear.

*50*

If we had to creep along the measured findings of social scientists, we would scarcely move anywhere.

Stories have forms or patterns and should be written to these patterns just as music is written to certain patterns. Our story patterns were created deep in our past history. They took shape in the process of being told again and again to live, reacting audiences. Storytellers discovered that certain patterns were more effective than others: they got instant attention and held it to the end. Such were the patterns which survived.

The school's object will not be to turn out fine artists and novelists, but to teach children skills and crafts related to art. Students who emerge from school as fine artists will be paced and stimulated by an audience that is better prepared to appreciate their art since it is already familiar with its craft.

# 2— i.t.a. MAKES WRITERS

## "When There Is Wars
## There Is Unpeace"

IN 1962 *Good Housekeeping* magazine sent me to West Berlin to write an article on the thoughts of children about Christmas. I intended to ask American children there what *peace on earth* meant at the Wall.

Schools were closed when I arrived in August. I found my children at swimming pools, playgrounds, the P.X. movie, and Sunday school. Seven-year-old children proved to work out best for my story purposes. Their talk was uninhibited and imaginative. I discovered that expressive children came from expressive families. I therefore began to look for children whose parents were teachers or worked for Radio Free Europe, Amerika Haus, or the U.S. Information Service.

I chartered a bus and loaded it with the liveliest American children I could find. I had about forty six- to ten-year-olds, but most of them were seven. Guided by an Army officer who gave us a talk, we toured the Wall.

After the tour we all boarded the bus and went back to Dahlem in Berlin, where the children went to school. In a classroom much like any suburban public-school classroom in the United States, I gave out pencils and little blue booklets. Then we began talking about our visit to the Wall. I asked them questions: what was it like to spend Christmas in Berlin? How was it different from home?

They talked quite readily. They told me that the United States, Japan, England, Italy, and Denmark had sent a thousand Christmas trees and that they had been lighted and placed along the Wall. The East German police had shot some of the lights out. They told about Christmas school holidays, Christmas candy, Christmas carols.

Almost everyone's hand was up, waving for my attention. Each child wanted to tell me something. They all began talking at once. I couldn't listen to them all—while one talked, others would interrupt.

"All right. Enough. Enough," I said, waving them to stop. "I can't listen to everyone at once. Open your booklets and write just what you were going to tell me. Write what you have on your minds this second."

The older children lowered their hands, opened their booklets and studied the blank pages. A few of them began to write. Many of the seven-year-olds still had their hands up, still wanting to talk, but I ignored them and gradually they dropped their hands too. There was dismay on their faces. Foreheads wrinkled. All the fun had suddenly been let out of the room.

I walked around among them to see who needed help. They all needed help. "How do you spell wreath?" a girl asked. I told her. "How do you spell sleigh?" a boy asked. I told him.

There was a lot of erasing, head scratching, and pencil sharpening. They coughed, twitched, scraped their feet. They had to go to the toilet. They asked what time it was. Two boys began pushing and punching each other. Two girls began whispering.

One boy had a plastic box full of colored pencils, erasers, scissors, and glue. He wrote "I" and one other word, which he kept erasing. He fumbled through his box, trying one pencil after another, each time using the pencil's eraser. He was eight years old and in the bus had explained quite clearly the reasons for continued four-power control of West Berlin. I couldn't make out the word he was struggling to write. He had erased a hole in the paper.

"Time's up," I announced. They were glad to quit, in a hurry to get out.

I had forty booklets when they had all gone. The nine- and ten-year-old children wrote, a few eights, but nineteen booklets were blank. The imaginative sevens had given me nothing.

Earlier I had asked a girl of six what she would like to send East Berliners for Christmas. Her answer: "Wire cutters." I was expecting a good paper from her but she didn't write so much as her name.

Clifford, seven, had *told* me: "Peace on earth is that statue that has the silver fire in its hand and thorns all around its head and stands in America. When there is wars there is unpeace."

Thomas, seven, had *said*: "Peace on earth has a lot of meanings. One meaning is when my father is reading a book and he says, 'Let me have peace and quiet.' "

But neither Clifford nor Thomas *wrote* anything.

One of my most interesting girls, Diana, had told me earlier how the Wall could be improved by decoration: "I think the Wall should be made pretty at Christmas time. We could put bells on strings and put them on the barbed wire. The barbed wire would be gold and the Wall could be colored a bluish-green. We could scrape off the ugly glass on top and put flowers in pots there and pfennigs for the children and butterflies of all colors, blue, white, orange, gray, bluish-green, and red rose ones. On the Wall we could have pictures of Jesus and the crib and Mary and Joseph and sheep and some little bears. And we could hang candy canes on the barbed wire, and candy angels and candy flowers and candy hearts and candy butterflies."

But Diana's *paper* was blank.

Only one child younger than eight had written in his book. Jonathan, who wrote his age "12 minus 6," had printed: "YOU ARE NOW LEAVING THE AMERICAN SECTOR."

THE INABILITY of nineteen talkative, articulate children to put a word of their talk on paper was a disappointing surprise to me. But then even the eight-, nine-, and ten-year-olds found writing a grinding test.

Why was writing so hard? When did children start learning to write?

The questions faded after I finished my article. Two years later they came back while I was in Bethlehem, Pennsylvania, writing for another magazine.

# Why Is It So Hard to Get English Down on Paper?

ADULT SPEECH, to a very small child, must be a continuous winding train of sounds, just a little different from music: slicking along on glides, interrupted by gasps and wheezes, wheedled out thin as a thread or blown out loud from a wide-open mouth. How will he ever manage to get all that on paper?

Since writing is an extension of speech, the English writer ought to have a symbol for each sound he wants to communicate. *Webster's International Dictionary* and the *Old English Dictionary* both identify over a hundred distinct sounds in English speech. But a hundred-letter alphabet would be too cumbersome for us to handle. What are the most basic sounds of our speech?

Using the alphabet of the International Phonetic Association, the *Pronouncing Dictionary of American English* isolates fifty sounds as the basic sounds of American English speech: seventeen vowel sounds, five diphthongs, and twenty-eight consonants. Other authorities say there are fewer than fifty basic sounds; one says as few as forty-two.

The trouble with English is that it neither looks like it sounds nor sounds like it looks. English speech has forty to fifty basic sounds waited on by only twenty-six symbols. Every symbol takes a turn at standing about silent and idle; certain symbols run themselves ragged answering an unmanageable number of sounds; a few symbols haven't done honest work for centuries.

Godfrey Dewey in his booklet *How We Spell!* distinguishes forty-one sounds that can be spelled a total of 507 different ways.

191 ways to spell 24 consonant sounds
316 ways to spell 17 vowel sounds
46 ways to pronounce 21 consonant symbols

36 ways to pronounce 5 vowels

26 silent letters (every letter from *a* in *aegis* to *z* in *rendez-vous* at some time or other is silent)

Dr. Dewey remarks: "To point up the significance of these figures, consider a simple word like *motor*. By analogy with the examples here given, this might be speld in any one of $7 \times 22 \times 14 \times 41 \times 8 = 708,168$ different ways. One might be *mneauchteourps* (compare hy*mn* b*eau* ya*cht* gorg*eous* co*rps*)."

Why do we have only twenty-six symbols when we need almost twice as many? Because we never had an alphabet custom-made for our speech.

Before the Norman conquest in the eleventh century, Anglo-Saxon writers used a Celtic, or Old Irish, alphabet, which consisted of runic characters added to the Latin alphabet. The Norman invaders destroyed this system of writing. Keeping only a few Anglo-Saxon characters, they imposed a French alphabet. The Old French alphabet, like the Old Irish alphabet, came from Latin. In rejecting the Anglo-Saxon alphabet, the French may have hurt England more than they did at Hastings and in the Common Market combined.

English spelling was thus concocted by Anglo-Saxon story-tellers, French scribes, and Dutch printers using an Italian alphabet. Frequently the Dutch printers solved English spelling problems by using Dutch spelling rules. In order to straighten out their right-hand margins they often added extra letters to words, most frequently the "e." Today these are our "silent" letters. When you examine the freak spelling system these four European allies produced, you wonder why anyone would dream of putting an atom bomb or Polaris submarine or even a supermarket or a newsstand under their joint control. But as bad as this spelling is, it could be worse. What if the English had been conquered by Hawaiians, who have only twelve letters in their alphabet?

Since Italian is a one-sound-one-symbol language, an Italian never has to spell his name to another Italian, whereas we seem always to be spelling our names to someone. A friend named Zaepcke tells telephone operators who ask him to spell his name: "Zaepcke—*z* as in *xylophone*, *a* as in *aisle*, *e* as in *eulogy*, *p* as in *pneumonia*, *c* as in *czar*, *k* as in *knee*, and *e* as in *ecstasy*."

A New York hotel telephone operator once spelled my name: "Riemer—*r* for Rudolph, *i* before e, *e* as in eye . . ." *Eye* is particularly eccentric—the two *e*'s silent and the sound of long *i* carried by the *y*.

Take the name *Cynthia. Pseegnthisaa, Zoismpthuayois, Swuiwnthuiah*, and *Schupnthehua* are four of the 764,524 ways it can be spelled. The *s* sound at its beginning can be spelled nineteen different ways: *ps* as in *pseudo*, *z* as in *waltz*, *sw* as in *sword*, and *sch* as in *schism*, for example.

The short *i* sound can be spelled twenty-seven ways, among them *ee* (*been*), *ois* (*chamois*), *ui* (*built*), *i* (*busy*). For *n* there is *gn* (*vignette*), *pn* (*pneumonia*), *mpt* (*comptroller*), and *wn* (*known*), and for the *i* sounded as a long *e* we have *uay* as in *quay*, *is* as in *debris*, *ui* as in *mosquito*, and *eh* as in *vehicle*. Finally, for the *a*, there is *ois* (*patois*), *aa* (*bazaar*), *ua* (*guard*), and *ah* as in *ah!*

---

**A distinguished old one-legged colonel**
**Once started to edit a jolonel;**
**But soon, quite disgusted,**
**Gave up—he was busted—**
**And cried, "The expense is infolonel!"**

---

## The English Language Is
## a Hell of a Trick
## to Play on a Little Kid

ADULTS LEARN to be amused by the oddities of English spelling. But to children, English writing is the opposite of amusing, a rude and cruel fun house fixed with fakery, unwanted surprises, and waste-of-time dead ends. The unfair thing is that many children committed to this crazy house believe it is themselves who are wrong and not the house which is at fault.

> **There was a young girl in the choir**
> **Whose voice rose up hoir and hoir**
> **Till it reached such a huit**
> **It was clear out of sayt**
> **And they found it next day in the spoir**

If children want their writing to be understood, they've got to make sure their spelling is w̶r̶i̶t̶e̶ r̶i̶t̶e̶ w̶r̶i̶g̶h̶t̶ right. It means dragging through a musty Smithsonian-size warehouse of Victorian curios, classic marbles, Anglo-Saxon fossils, medieval ikons, and World's Fair junk collected under the curatorship of the Collier brothers, meanwhile memorizing the catalogue.

It isn't only children whose memories are overtaxed by English spelling; their teachers sometimes bend under the strain too. In 1965 Texas teachers were urged to bombard their state's government officials with letters demanding a pay increase.

Senators and representatives who received the letters were shocked by the cowboy grammar, chicken handwriting, catch-as-catch-can spelling. One representative tacked this list of spelling errors on his bulletin board: *apreciate, appreicate, captoil, capetal, eleminate, particlar, equatable, ensifficent, proposial, purposal.*

---

**Pall Mall can't spall!**
*—Graffito reported by* Time

---

Even computers are baffled by our spellings. In a massive study of English spelling, Dr. Paul R. Hanna programmed a computer with 203 different spelling rules and then fed the machine 17,009 of our most common words. The computer spelled 8,516 (51.13 per cent) of the words wrong! His report, published by the Office of Education ("Phoneme-Grapheme Correspondencies As Cues to Spelling Improvement") reveals that the computer spelled, 6,195 words with one error, 1,941 words with two errors, and 390 words with three or more errors.

---

"Could you accomodate me by sending a list of the words most frequently mispelled by scholars? I think it shameful that an academic person should ever make a spelling error."

I agree. It was years before I learned how to spell acommodate.

The most troublesome words are, of course, the verbs that double or do not double their final consonant when an inflectional suffix is added. Yet to spell them perfectly, all one need do is commit to memory this simple mnemonic device:

> Monosyllabic words with b
> f, m, l, and d
> m, n, r, and g
> Coming last and not in double
> Never give us any trouble
> When preceded by a or e
> Or i, o, u, if only we
> Double the consonant before
> We add an ed or ing or y
> Or er or est, and many more:
> Like q, e, o, or i,
> Even u, though I don't know why.
> Never will you need to flub
> If you double the b and add ed to club.
> Polysyllables too, unless
> The ultimate doesn't receive the stress.
> If such eventuates, you can't
> Double the final consonant
> Unless it makes your heart rejoice

To write down Webster's second choice.
Even in a fit of choler
You should write control, controller.
Never should you feel bedeviled
Over the l's of level and leveled.
To be a good speller it will suffice
To remember this simple mnemonic device.
(You'd also learn, if you really knew it,
The hundred and one exceptions to it.)

*—From David Horne's column in* Scholarly Books in America, *October 1965*

---

How does a tourist in New York react if he's jeered asking for *Green-witch* instead of *Grenitch* Village? How does a customer asking for *Hay*den's "Surprise Symphony" react to the record clerk's smirk? Have *you* ever in your life said *sub*tle? Or *dour* to rhyme with *sour*? Do you sound the *th* in thyme? Do you pronouce Thames as if it were *They*(ms)?

The words we use are so intimately attached to our self-images that to have a pronunciation rejected is embarrassingly close to personal rejection. It would be interesting psychiatric research to catalogue the tics, starts, twitches, nose rubs, ear digs, blinks, furrows, stutters, gasps, and halts we have developed as a result of the inconsistent and illogical pronunciations and spellings of English.

A child will not trust the person who has deceived him once or twice. How will he learn to trust English spellings which repeatedly trick him?

---

What man is there of you,
    whom if his son ask bread
will he give him a stone?
Or if he ask a fish,
    will he give him a serpent?
        *—Matthew 7:10*

---

# The Skwrt Gun Incident

In March of 1964 I was leaning against a window sill in Marvine School, Bethlehem, Pennsylvania, watching a first-grader mold alphabet symbols in clay. I was in Bethlehem to write about a new alphabet called i.t.a., the Initial Teaching Alphabet.

It had been described to me as "a new medium for teaching reading."

A boy walked up to me, glanced to the rear of the room toward his teacher, and then furtively gave me a piece of paper rolled like a cigarette. I unrolled the paper and read:

> get mee back mie skwrt gun Jody

It was the first time I had read a note written in i.t.a. I walked to Jody's seat. He grinned nervously and held up a souvenir badge of the New York World's Fair.

"Who's got your squirt gun?"

Jody pointed to a boy nearby who was glaring at him.

"Why don't you ask Miss Schrantz?" I suggested.

He shrugged. "We're not supposed to have squirt guns."

I went back to the window sill. It occurred to me that six-year-old Jody had done something my best seven-year-olds in West Berlin had not been able to do. He had *written* me a note, a piece of talk. He had communicated what was on his mind at that moment.

After class I asked the teacher, Miss Schrantz, whether note writing was common among first-graders.

"In i.t.a. it is," she said. "Notes don't usually start this early."

She opened her desk drawer and mussed around till she found a slim packet of little papers. She drew a curl of paper from the packet. "A visitor received this message from one of my little girls."

ie liek yꞷr blꞷ dress
ie liek ᴛhe wæ yꞷ smell.

"You think i.t.a. makes the difference?"

"Oh, definitely. They write down anything they feel like say-ing."

"In other first-grade classes you've taught, did the children write notes like this?"

"Never."

Other i.t.a. teachers confirmed what Miss Schrantz said about note writing: i.t.a. children wrote themselves reminders, wrote instructions to the janitor, wrote notes from home when they had to miss school. They wrote spontaneously, not as part of class instruction and without asking help.

mistr hænεε did yꞷ fien mie sandwiᴄh?

plεεs dœn't clεεn mie desk

this wauter is hot   [note on water fountain]

# i.t.a.

THE Initial Teaching Alphabet was first revealed to the public by James Pitman in *The Times* of London on May 29, 1959, under the name of the Augmented Roman Alphabet. Pitman, the alphabet's designer, was a Member of Parliament, a former Director of the Bank of England, a publisher, and the grandson of Isaac Pitman, designer of the world-famous shorthand system which carries his name.

Pitman described his alphabet as a training device, a "walker" designed to help the beginning learner write and read successfully, without first being discouraged and, perhaps, defeated by the ambiguities and irregularities of the traditional English alphabet. "Caxton's alphabet is our *using* alphabet," Pitman said. "My alphabet is a *learning* alphabet, a teacher's tool to be left behind and forgotten when it has achieved its teaching purpose."

To emphasize that his alphabet was intended only for limited use at the beginning of a child's school career, and to reassure other publishers he was not launching a fresh spelling-reform movement, Pitman changed the name Augmented Roman Alphabet to Initial Teaching Alphabet, abbreviated "i.t.a."

When news of Pitman's augmented alphabet was published in London, the first American to react to i.t.a. was Phillip Hilaire, a reading consultant and psychologist to U.S. Air Force Dependents' Schools in England.

In the spring of 1961 Mr. Hilaire tried to install i.t.a. in the U.S. Air Force Dependents' School. His Command Superintendent stopped him on grounds that the pupils were too transient to benefit from such a novel program. He next began rocketing letters back to his hometown school, Lehigh University in Bethlehem, Pennsylvania, telling all about the new wonder alphabet.

66

æ (face) b (bed) c (cat) d (dog) ee (key)

f (feet) g (leg) h (hat) ie (fly) j (jug) k (key)

l (letter) m (man) n (nest) œ (over) p (pen) ɹ (girl)

r (red) s (spoon) t (tree) ue (use) v (voice) w (window)

y (yes) z (zebra) ʒ (daisy) wh (when) ch (chair)

th (three) th (the) ʃh (shop) ʒ (television) ŋ (ring)

ɑ (father) au (bali) a (cap) e (egg) i (milk) o (box)

u (up) ω (book) ω (spoon) ou (out) oi (oil)

Meanwhile, Ben Wood, a prominent researcher in the field of learning measurement, read a report about i.t.a. in *Think*.

Dr. Wood, as Director of Columbia University's Educational Records Bureau, invited James Pitman to speak in New York and describe his alphabet to American publishers and educators. "I took the first plane to London I could get," Dr. Wood recalls.

"I knew right off it was what we'd been needing." Working off-stage arranging meetings and obtaining funds, Dr. Wood became one of i.t.a.'s most important promoters in the United States.

Other educators, Harold Tanyzer and Anita Metzger among them, also flew to London to see Pitman's alphabet. Dr. Tanyzer's reports convinced Theodore Dolmatch, president of Pitman Publishing, Inc., to commit his company to produce i.t.a. materials. As a result of Miss Metzger's visit, in January 1963, six children aged four and five in the Anita Metzger School of Ventnor, New Jersey, became the very first children to use the new alphabet in the United States.

During his summer leave in 1961, Mr. Hilaire flew back home, bringing with him Pitman's alphabet and the designs for an experiment planned for England in the fall. He showed these to Dr. Rebecca W. Stewart, Director of Elementary Education, a handsome, gray-eyed woman of wagon-train practicality and vision.

"There may be a time bomb in this" she said, shaking her head—Mme. Curie looking at an alphabet. "I'd want to see the English results before endorsing it here. My biggest question is, once they've learned the new symbols, can they be weaned away from them and learn to read and spell in everyday ABCs?"

Dr. Albert Mazurkiewicz, head of Lehigh University's Reading Clinic, meantime obtained $148,000 from the Fund for the Advancement of Education to give i.t.a. a full-dress show in the United States. He offered to conduct a three-year demonstration that would involve all the Bethlehem-area schools.

By this time, reports flown from England had persuaded Dr. Stewart that i.t.a. carried no concealed "time bomb." She had already decided to run a small test when Dr. Mazurkiewicz came forward with his proposal and the Ford grant to back it up. She accepted at once. The Bethlehem elementary-school principals agreed unanimously, the Education Committee agreed, the School Board agreed, and the superintendent signed his approval.

Rebecca Stewart dipped her Bethlehem schools into i.t.a. by thirds. She started in September 1963 with fifteen first-grade classes. Thirty classes continued using the traditional orthography (T.O.).

In 1964 thirty classes began using i.t.a. as against fifteen using T.O. In September 1965 all of Bethlehem's 1,800 first-grade children started with the new alphabet. Foundation support ended in 1966 but Bethlehem voted unanimously to continue i.t.a. as the normal introduction to English in the primary grades.

The alphabet was not restricted to elementary schools. In March 1963 Vera Hannenberg began using i.t.a. for adult illiterates at the Brooklyn Adult Training Center in New York. Harold Tanyzer introduced i.t.a. in eleven Long Island school districts in 1964, and in February 1967 he used i.t.a. as part of a program for 3,000 disadvantaged children in New York City. Dr. Tanyzer was first to use i.t.a. with high school dropouts.

In spring of 1964 a school teacher was convicted of a crime and sentenced to San Quentin prison. Under the direction of Dr. H. J. Hastings, Supervisor of Education at San Quentin, the new inmate taught fellow prisoners how to read with the help of i.t.a. Dr. Hastings now maintains a growing i.t.a. program which is being imitated in other prisons.

In England about 2,200 schools now use i.t.a. In this country some schools in every state except South Dakota use i.t.a., but no one knows the total. It is our most intensively and frequently tested educational innovation. J. R. Block, director of the Initial Teaching Alphabet Foundation, says: "I am aware of approximately thirty separate investigations in which control groups were used. Well over 15,000 children have been used in these studies and the cost has been close to $750,000."

But note that in all these demonstrations and tests, it is i.t.a.'s role in *reading* that educators are concerned with. Teachers are surprised by i.t.a. writings but the writing is regarded by most as a pleasant and diverting side effect, not at all as a major educational gain.

## The First Four Questions
## About i.t.a.

Four questions rise naturally in the mind when anyone considers i.t.a. for the first time.

QUESTION 1: *How can learning forty-four of anything be easier than learning twenty-six of a similar thing?*

The standard first doubt raised by i.t.a. is that it *looks* hard. i.t.a. is admittedly funny-looking, as if the ABCs had been exposed to radiation and had sprouted some exotic mutations: some letters share a common spine or are linked by a Siamese connection; there are monkey-tailed *t*'s; there is a *w* with swollen sides and another terribly bloated *w* with a bubble in its middle; there is an *n* with a baby *g* hugging its rear leg.

But of course our eyes are used to the traditional alphabet. It's important to see the Initial Teaching Alphabet with the eyes of a child just starting school and not used to any alphabet at all.

It's a mistake to think the T.O. child has only twenty-six symbol shapes to remember. Since capital letters frequently look different from small letters and cursive handwriting looks different from typewriting, the T.O. child actually has to memorize between seventy and ninety symbols. A child may be able to print his name, but not recognize it if he sees it handwritten.

Other languages also have different shapes for their capital and lower-case letters. Herbert Bayer, a leading member of Germany's Bauhaus design school in 1925, used to print the following message on all his bills and correspondence: "why two symbols for one sound, 'A' and 'a'? why twice as many letters when half the number accomplishes the same? writing-printing only with lower case saves time, saves money, makes reading easier, makes learning to write and read simpler, one symbol for one sound!" The German post office objected to this spelling deviation as "Kultur-Bolshevism." In spite of harassments—stones thrown at his·house, name-calling, and hisses in the street—Bayer doggedly continued writing in lower case until the German Post refused to handle his mail.

In i.t.a. capital letters are simply larger drawings of each symbol's shape; there is no extra capital shape to memorize.

i.t.a. has still fewer shapes to be mastered if you consider that fourteen symbols are drawn by combining already familiar shapes: æ is formed by linking *a* and *e*, ie by linking *i* and *e*, ᴄh by joining *c* and *h*, and so on for oi, ꞓꞓ, ꭍh, au, ue, ꝑh. The child who learns to make *g* and *n* can easily make ŋ, or if he learns to make ŋ first he has learned two symbols for the price in labor of learning one.

i.t.a. throws out multiple shapes and also multiple spellings. There's no featherbedding in i.t.a. Every symbol has to work. Each symbol has only one job: to serve its sound and no other.

Of the forty-four i.t.a. characters, twenty-five are taken from the traditional alphabet (*q* and *x* are not used):

a a b c d e f g
apple arm bed cat doll egg finger girl

h i j k l m n o p
hat ink jam kitten lion man nest on pig

r s t u v w y z
red soap tree up van window yellow zoo

Fourteen characters combine traditional alphabet letters:

Five characters are peculiar to i.t.a.:

**QUESTION 2:** *If a child starts with i.t.a., is he stuck with it for life? When will he learn the regular alphabet everybody else uses?*

i.t.a. isn't a career alphabet. It's an expedient, limited-time-only convenience alphabet to be used only as long as it is needed and then chucked. The first and leading i.t.a. publisher in the United States, Theodore Dolmatch, advises parents not to invest in an i.t.a. home library because children grow out of it so quickly.

The child begins to transfer to the traditional alphabet halfway through the first grade. The leaders begin switching to T.O. in January and finish by the end of the year, while stragglers complete their transfer in second grade.

Under present methods of instruction, the child's transition is guided by reading materials. Gradually, book by book, more and more T.O. spellings appear until the last book, which is almost entirely in the traditional alphabet. In the writing, capitals usually appear first among the changes. For a while the writing is mixed i.t.a. and T.O. and then gradually the i.t.a. disappears.

The "story" below, from the Rosemont School in Bethlehem, Pennsylvania, contains both i.t.a. and traditional-alphabet spellings because its anonymous six-year-old writer is transferring from i.t.a. to T.O.

ted and Bob wer having a ræs. ted had number three. Bob had number seven. I said "muſher, wich wun is goiŋ to win?" muſher did not answer, Shee wos to bisy woching. ſhen mie muſher said, "Whot did yω sæ?" ſhen I did not answer becauz I wos to bisy woching too. ſhen everybody shouted huray, huray, huray, huray. I said, "hω wind?" Ted, Ted, Ted, Ted, our boy, our boy wind! I wos happy. Ted got alots ov priezez. and ſhæ gave him one dauler bill, and when his faſher found out hee gæve him a ten dauler bill. and when everybody founnd out ſhæ gæve him sum dauler billz and cækes, and caps, and more and mor muny. so one dæ ſhæ wer So rich ſhat ſhær faſher woz a presedent.

Certain features designed into i.t.a. make the crossing to traditional spelling easy. One of these is that i.t.a., except for a few symbols, looks a lot like the traditional alphabet. Another is that many of Pitman's changes affect only the middle or bottom part of his letters. When we read a row of words, our eyes skim over their skyline (this can be seen by covering the bottom half of this sentence). In i.t.a. only seven augmentations intrude on this skyline. As a child reads faster, he begins to plane over the sentence skyline and when T.O. letters are substituted, he may not even notice the difference.

## QUESTION 3: *Will i.t.a. hurt the child's spelling later?*

Some educationists have warned that i.t.a. will hurt high school and college spelling. i.t.a. hasn't been used long enough anywhere to prove them either right or wrong. The bad spelling already noted in high schools, colleges, and graduate schools suggests, however, that there may not be much to hurt.

*73*

According to Pitman, about 20 per cent of the words we use most frequently are spelled the same in i.t.a. as they are in T.O.—for example, *majesty, ranch, pumpkin.* Another 40 per cent need only slight change to be correct, like *clobberd* and *chickend out* in the following i.t.a. story:

wun dæ ʃhær wuſ ɑ boi and his næm wuſ dennee. hee had ɑ lieun for ɑ pet. wun dæ dennee wuſ gœiŋ hœm wiʈh his pet and aull ʃhe peepl wer afræd and ɑ lædee fæntid and ʃhe pœleesman cœd hav clobberd ʃhe lieun wiʈh his billee club but he ɟhickend out.—*David, 6, first grade, Bethlehem, Pa.*

Of the words remaining, 20 per cent have changes that conform to rule—for example, the "silent e" rule. The final 20 per cent must be mastered by brute memorization: *through, trough, tough, thought, bough.*

During i.t.a.'s first year in Bethlehem, Mrs. J. Huber, the first-grade teacher at Rosemont School, took 101 of the 221 words in the second-grade speller used at her school and tested her class, seven to ten T.O. words a day. There were no tricky words, no silent letters. The children were six months into i.t.a. when the tests were given. Without special preparation in traditional spelling, the class spelled 86 per cent of the words accurately.

Bethlehem abandoned the regular spelling book issued to T.O. second-graders because i.t.a. children were able to spell almost half its words by midterm of first grade.

. . . Wee have all kiends ov souds theeſ ar some of the souds ee æuecæ ɟh ŋ ω ω z ʃh wh au ou ʃh The werds ar eezy like bœt [boot] b is one sound ω is enether and t is enether and yω pœt them tœgether and make the werd bœt. my mommy lieks ita better then the other reediŋ caus it mæd mee reed faster. first my dady dind.t like this reeding but nou he duſ.—*Catherine, 6, first grade, Bethlehem, Pa.*

In October 1966 Dr. Rebecca Stewart, Director of Elementary Education in Bethlehem, asked thirty-six of her second-grade teachers to compare children who had had i.t.a. with previous second-grade classes. Out of thirty-four who handed in their unsigned comments, twenty said the i.t.a. graduates were *better readers*, twenty-three said they were *better writers*, twenty-one said they *spelled better*, one said they were "no good at making capitals," two said their *pronunciation was better*.

Some children continue to use their i.t.a. symbols as pronunciation keys long after they've transferred to T.O. writing. One i.t.a. graduate in Bethlehem, Richard, seven, wrote: "... I have a dog from Holland. It is the national dog of Holland. It is a Keeshond. (pronounced Kaeshond) ... " The ae in "kaeshond" is the i.t.a. digraph æ pulled apart. The dictionary symbol for this long vowel is ā.

The reader will probably note some T.O. spellings in many of the i.t.a. samples included in this book; they indicate that the child is in some stage of transferring from i.t.a. to the regular alphabet. The paper below was written near the end of the first grade, and the writer's spellings show that she is well along in her i.t.a.-to-T.O. transition.

My house is a plipy plop house. becos it is so mesy it is disgcusting my mother ses for me to clean the seller. I alwæs clean it good but every day wen I come home my sister and fother and mother and I mes it up riet now it is a plopy plip house.

it is so mesy that you cudent eaven step in it I am serprised that my fother can get in it well I can't get in it it is so mesy Mrs. E. if you fiend a wæ to clean yaur seller please riet it down on a peas ov pæper. I hæt to clean the seller ue hæt to clean my bed room I hæt to clean my mothers' bed room I hæt to clean my sisters room and I hæt most ov all I hæt to clean the seller it is discusting and wen I mean discusting I mean discusting and dont cut it out wen you luk at my seller you will see that all ov the stuff is up to the sealing wuns my fother got or old couch and throo it down stærs it mæd a laud nios it was lowd that was a big thunder and lienting and it fluded our seller boy is our seller derty. I hæt it is is stꞷoped it stingks wen I mean it is stingky it stingks. our seller is haribul it was billt under grownd it is a under grownd seller if you goe by the sied ov the house you will see a under grownd windæ it is funy our house is a hundered years oldꞷ ie love it very very very much—*Barbara, 6, Long Island*

The sample below was written in the second month of second grade by Daniel, seven, a Bethlehem i.t.a. graduate. Only two definite traces of i.t.a. spelling appear in this paper: *cilled*—in i.t.a. *c* spells the same sound as *k*, and *doun* for down—*ou* is the sound *ow* in i.t.a.

## Meeting Van Gogh

One day when I woke up, I got my mother and father up because today my dad and I were going fishing. After they were awake and we ate our breakfast and got dressed we got our fishing things. I said good bye to my mother and then we left. We walked a mile and then we came to the harbor. We got our boat and went out to sea. Then all of a sudden I shouted "We foregot the net"! "We wont need that, because we have the fishing rod." Wheeeeeeeeeeeee! that was a close one. Let me start the motor okay? "Well I gues its okay." Pot pot pot pot pot pot Zoom! away we go. Wellp here we are twenty miles away from land. "do you have the warms"? Yep right in this bag. Well let's fish. Doun go the hooks. "Now," be quiet so we don't sckare the fish." Tug "I have one," help me pull it in. Wow a twenty nine incher. Now we have ten fish let's go home. "I can't get the motor to start," "Do we have the oars"? "Yes Im glad you mentuned it! Wellp here we are at last. Who's that? Why that's Van Gogh! "Hi," what are you doing"? "Oh nothing much." Boy "when we were out their a fish jumeped in our boat and we cilled it." "Well good bye." "Yay dad, he was painting a picture of our boat." "Well we should tell mother, I saw it to." "Hay mom guess who we saw"? "I don't know. "We saw Van Gogh"! You did? "Yep."

QUESTION 4: *i.t.a. has eighteen extra letters to memorize, eighteen extra letters to be able to draw, eighteen extra letters to spell—and then eighteen to forget. Why bother?*

It is true the i.t.a. symbols must be packed away as soon as the child outgrows them. The digraphs have to be unhooked: the *t* from the *h* in ᚦh, the *s* from the *h* in ʃh, the *c* from the *h* in ɕh, and all the long vowels lose their *e* (æ becomes simple *a* etc.). The reversed *z* (ꙅ) rounds out and becomes the *s* as it is in daisy (still pronounced *z* however). The ω and ꞷ both bloom into oo, one as in *hook*, the other in *hoot*.

That the i.t.a. child finds this impossibly hard has not proven true. What seems to be true is that the hardship is in the minds of principals, teachers, and parents. Children switch from i.t.a. almost unnoticed.

Yet many professional educationists still insist that i.t.a. must be "unlearned." Arther Trace Jr., of John Carroll University, for example, says in *Reading Without Dick and Jane:* "The chief dilemma which befalls i.t.a. is that if it is used extensively over a long period of time, say two years, then it naturally becomes increasingly difficult for the poor student to unlearn the wrong spellings and to learn the right spellings because he has seen the wrong spellings of the words for so long; or else, if he spends only a short time with the ITA, say three months, or six months, he will have learned so few words, that it hardly seems worthwhile making him learn to spell words two ways, especially since one of the ways is wrong. Furthermore, having spent so little time with the ITA he will not have had the opportunity of learning the wrong ITA spellings of many of the irregularly phonetic words which the ITA was supposed to help him with."

"*Un*learning" is easy criticism used glibly. What is learning in the first place? Must a child who first learns to read and write French have to *unlearn* that language to read English?

Safer, surer i.t.a. lets the child writer develop confidence while allowing him the pleasure of travel. There is no more *un*learning involved in switching from i.t.a. to traditional spellings than in a child's switch from a tricycle to a bicycle. No child has to *un*learn how to pedal a three-wheeler to be able to pedal a two-wheeler. If an adult can still fit on a three-wheeler, he can still ride it if he wants.

"Why bother?" Because the six-year-old child who can express himself by writing without copying and without depending on his teacher for spelling help is a new, different, and valuable educand. He can be given a writing-oriented curriculum that is closely fitted to his developing needs for personal expression while preparing him for life as he'll find it when he's finished school.

## How i.t.a. and Dick & Jane
## Meet the Perils
## of English Spelling

NOBODY EXPECTS a five- or six- or seven-year-old child to memorize the hundreds of spelling facts needed to be able to write intelligible English. One source of the trouble is our alphabet, whose twenty-six letters are not enough to match the forty or so sounds of our speech.

---

The complexities and inconsistencies of Modern English spelling have been produced by a variety of causes.... But the fundamental reason is that no alphabet ever adopted by the writers or the printers of English has been based on the policy of providing one character, and only one, for each of the separate sounds of the English language.—Webster's New International Dictionary, 2nd edition

---

We could try swallowing about fifteen of the sounds. Then we'd have enough sounds to come out even with our alphabet. This is absurd, of course, for it's talk that originates writing and not writing that should control talk.

The most logical solution would be to start at the bottom and overhaul English spelling, but the history of the spelling-reform movement is one of wasted talent and work. Some very good men went down under it. President Theodore Roosevelt failed. Benjamin Franklin failed. Mark Twain and George Bernard Shaw failed. If we want to succeed through reform we won't succeed by being purists and demanding total spelling reform.

The master strategy employed by most primary-grade teachers is provided by the *basal-reader* system, known to parents as the Dick & Jane or Jimmy & Sue or Tom & Betty books. The basal readers accept our alphabet as it is with all its "works and pomps." Dick

& Jane stand pat, hand over heart, glazed blue eyes level, reciting "My alphabet right or wrong." Their solution is to postpone the spelling ordeal by muzzling the sounds while teaching words purely as sights. Basal readers teach only consonants in first grade; vowels very late in the first grade or in second; vowel digraphs and diphthongs in grades two and three. The typical basal-reader assault on English starts with a battery of prereading or *"reading readiness"* books. These are followed by a series of paperbound *preprimers* leading to a *primer*, the child's first hardcover book. The primer steps to the *reader*. Typically, there are two readers for each grade from first through sixth grade. But keep clearly in mind all this paraphernalia has nothing to do with writing. It is used for reading.

Since 1950, the basal-reader system has been stiffly challenged by bands of innovators. Some of these rage against the system's rigid vocabulary controls, some against its total sight approach, some against its suburban segregated family image, some merely because it's big and it's there—on top. Among the leading antibasal demonstrators there is Charles E. Wingo and his phonic approach, Sister Mary Caroline and her "Breaking the Sound Barrier," Caleb Gattegno with his "words in color" approach, and Charles C. Fries and his linguistics approach. The innovators are not interested in writing, either. They have their minds fixed on reading revolution. The phonics and linguistics reformers thus correct one error but stumble past a more fundamental, more serious one—that reading and writing can be separated without hurt to the educand.

The basal readers have been angrily attacked by educators and ridiculed by almost everyone, including even television comedians, and yet they not only survive but appear to thrive on abuse. A survey showed basal readers are being used in 98 per cent of the first grades and 92 to 94 per cent of the second and third grades. The basal-reader industry is a $2 billion annual business. You may refuse to know Dick & Jane socially, but you must do business with them because in the framework of our current educational logic there is nothing to replace them with.

Why have the basal readers lasted? Because they are the materials of a brilliantly designed system that accommodates a popular learning belief: that reading is the all-important key to educational achievement while writing can be safely ignored as a bothersome but relatively unimportant subject.

i.t.a. is a compromise of logic and realism, for its solution is a limited-time alphabet reform for the sake of beginning learners. It balances the sound-symbol relationship by fixing temporary extensions to our traditional alphabet. The result is a consistent, logical spelling. i.t.a. uses no symbols which don't carry their own sound—no silent letters. It requires seventeen spellings for all vowel sounds. The entire i.t.a. memory pack consists of just forty-four phonic facts. At that, i.t.a. isn't perfect. Some inconsistency has been built into it to help the child be ready for his transition to the regular alphabet.

i.t.a. is not the only new alphabet currently being shown. There is the Diacritical Marking System (DMS), introduced in 1963 by a New Jersey reading specialist. There is the Single-Sound Unifon, a forty-sound alphabet created in 1957 by John R. Malone, a Chicago advertising executive and consulting economist who says his alphabet "is the only alphabet designed for both machine and human reading . . . for computers and for data-phone transmission."

World English Spelling (WES) is the outcome of long study and large experience by the Simplified Spelling Society in Great Britain and the Simpler Spelling Association in the United States. Godfrey Dewey, whose father created the Dewey Decimal System and who is himself a man of towering scholarship, proposes a forty-symbol alphabet which can be used on any standard typewriter because it uses no diacritical marking and no new letters.

I see no reason why the World English Spelling Alphabet could not successfully help children write, but I have no samples of children using it for communication. I have no samples of children communicating by means of the Unifon or the Diacritical Marking System, so I cannot discuss these alphabets either. In this book I restrict my remarks to the Initial Teaching Alphabet since I have some six thousand samples of writing by six-year-old children using it. They have been sent to me from Canada, England, Nigeria,

## WORLD ENGLISH SPELLING ALPHABET

| a (at) | aa (father) | ae (main) | au (cause) | b (back) |
|---|---|---|---|---|
| ch (cheap) | d (do) | dh (this) | e (bet) | ee (meet) |
| f (for) | g (get) | h (had) | i (it) · ie (time) | j (just) |
| k (can) | l (light) | m (met) | n (net) | ng (thing) |
| nk (think) | o (not) | oe (note) | oi (point) | oo (good) |
| ou (pound) | p (pack) | r (right) | s (see) · sh (shall) | t (to) |
| th (thin) | u (but) | ue (few) | uu (food) | v (very) |
| w (with) | wh (which) | y (yet) | z (please) | zh (pleasure) |

## THE NEW SINGLE-SOUND ALPHABET

| A (at) | Δ (ate) | Λ (all) | B (bow) | C (cell say) |
|---|---|---|---|---|
| Ɔ (chair) | D (dip) | E (hen) | Ǝ (he) | ⊣ (her) |
| F (fast) | G (goat) | H (hat) | ⊥ (bit) | ⊥ (bite) |
| ⅃ (jaw) | K (kiss) | L (low) | M (music) | N (no) |
| И (king) | O (lot) | Ω (old) | Φ (look) | ⊙ (out) |
| ⅁ (boy) | P (pipe) | R (run) | S (sure) | T (table) |
| Θ (thirst) | ⊥ (there) | U (up) | ⊔ (due) | ⊔ (you) |
| V (vest) | W (wig) | Σ (azure) | Y (yes) | Z (zebra) |

©1961 FCCA

Hong Kong, the United Nations School in New York City, and from many parts of the United States.

i.t.a. stands radically different from the basal-reader system and its various phonic-system dependents. i.t.a. is a *medium* whereas the basal-reader system is merely a *method*. i.t.a. is the alphabet itself— slightly altered, but still the alphabet; there are various methods for teaching it. The basal-reader system is one method for teaching or using our traditional medium, the Roman alphabet. Scott, Foresman does not happily advertise the fact, but it has put Dick & Jane into i.t.a. In other words, the *basal-reader method* can be used—if desired—to teach any alphabet, whether German or French or Italian, but of course it makes sense only when used with English. Why? Because it was designed to cope with the inconsistent traditional English spellings.

Both i.t.a. and the basal readers recognize that the mysteries of English reading are secured by a badly warped lock. Each attack that lock in a different way. Dick & Jane and Nat and his rat bend their keys to fit the lock's warp; i.t.a. temporarily corrects the lock itself.

## The Dick & Jane Writer
## Is Eye-Dependent

ACCORDING TO a distinguished spelling authority, Ernest Horn, more than half the words in *A Pronouncing Dictionary of American English* contain silent letters; about a sixth of the words contain double letters where only one letter is pronounced.

Because English sounds are not spelled with consistency or logic, it is necessary to memorize how words *look* to spell them right. No one writing any English word can be sure his spelling is right without having first seen and memorized the spelling.

We tell children that A is for Apple, for example. This is apparent only to the *eye*, for if I shut my eyes and say "A is for Apple," it doesn't make sense. My ear tells me *A* is for *A*pe or *A*che, not *A*pple. If *A* is for *A*pple, how does the child say *A*rt or *A*ltar?

---

**In the beginning, spelling is a matter of copying. . . . Finally, he [the child] undertakes actual spelling, which is knowing the order of letters in a word and putting them together in patterns he has learned to detect before attempting to write them.—*The Commission on the Curriculum of English***

---

Language is primarily audible, not visible, and is meant for the ear more than for the eye. The very word *language* is from *lingua*—tongue. It follows that since spellings represent the sounds of one's tongue they ought to call up voices. What sounds can a six-year-old child hear when he copies "I walk in the rain"? Who could possibly explain to him that *I* is the same as *i*? They look different. They sound different. And what does one say about the *i* in *rain*? We can tell him the *a* in w*a*lk and r*a*in and *a*nd are look-alikes, but how do we explain that they're not sound-alikes?

The child who learns English by the traditional alphabet is forced to learn it by *seeing* it. He is taught that "magic e" at the end of a word can change the word and make the vowel "say its name," as slid—slide, cod—code, fat—fate. He'll have lots of fun. English is full of magic like that. There's a magic *b* in *subtle*, a magic *n* in *hymn*, a *ps* in *corps*, a *k* and a *gh* in *knight*. Magic: *say* the word and they all disappear. *Colonel* is packed with magic: an *l* that disappears and an invisible *r*! And *E* has more magic! It can change its appearance: E, e, ℰ, ℯ. It can turn—pop! just like that—into a *j* as in *grandeur* or a *ch* as in *righteous*. Oh, he'll have lots of fun.

He will learn little rules that help him spell, such as: "When two vowels go walking, the first does all the talking." Of course, if the first vowel is the only one he can *hear*, he will have to *see* the word to know two vowels are there. He won't be able to write it and spell it until he has seen it. Again, he is dependent on seeing and reading for his writing.

Dick & Jane were invented precisely to cope with these problems. They coped by sound-proofing words.

Dick & Jane sentence "patterns" are taught as *visual patterns*. They sound terrible but they're not meant to be sounded. They're meant to be looked at. They guide their readers gently from reading readiness to preprimers through primers to readers, from foot bath through splash ponds to baby-pool English, the word stream so adjusted that each new book lets in more spellings, the best-behaved ones first. The words are vigilantly chaperoned. No weird spellings allowed. No shockers. No spoilers. Mostly regular, consistent, rule-abiding words.

### Fun with Father

"Sue," said Father,
"Here is a little toy house.
It is for you."
"Oh, Father," said Sue.
"A little toy house for me!
I like it."

—*from* Third Pre-Primer: The ABC All in a Day
(*Betts Basic Readers*)

Whether Sue and her Father help or don't help children to read is not included in the swing of this book. We are concerned with their effect on writing instruction and the writing habit. With this in mind, we ask what does strong visual instruction do to the Dick & Jane writer?

Dick & Jane writers have two bad habits: they don't hear themselves and they write visual patterns rather than communicate. Dick & Jane sentences stencil their minds with silhouette models of what writing should *look* like. They copy these patterns. Consequently, though their speech may be interesting and their ideas refreshingly imaginative, when they go to paper they sound flat and dull.

In the Dick & Jane basal readers, the child's memory is tracked from *eye* to *hand* through copying. No sound is involved so the ear is bypassed.

In phonics programs the child's memory is tracked from *eye* to *ear* to *hand*. *See* the patterns: mat, cat, fat, sat. They *look* alike, don't they? They *sound* alike too. Now write the words.

The natural line for writing proceeds in the opposite direction. *Hear* these words: mat, cat, fat, sat. They sound alike. *See*—they *look* alike too. Now write.

It is only a difference of direction, one may say, but the child whose memorization proceeds from *eye* to *ear* to *hand*, or simply from eye to hand, develops differently as a writer from one whose memory is tracked from *ear* to *hand* to *eye*.

The basic difference is that he comes to think of words, sentences, paragraphs, and poetry purely as soundless visual patterns. This is a false concept of writing, for the writer is first of all a talker. He doesn't *see* words, he *feels* words. He feels his mouth and his lips getting ready to form them. He sounds them and feels and hears their resonance. Each different shape of his mouth—whether opened, rounded, or flattened, whether the lips are relaxed or tightened in a hard line, whether the tongue is hissing at the teeth or up at the roof of the mouth—each change affects his speech. The writer's task is to transfer these sounds to paper, and the teacher's task is to help him do so.

*86*

If our speech and spelling matched in a one-sound-one-symbol relationship, we wouldn't have to depend on sight for correct spelling. The memory could be tracked from mouth to hand. We could write with our eyes closed as we felt the words in our mouth. We could spell by *feel*.

A touch-typist types by feel. Ask her to locate C or G on the keyboard. She'll find them quicker with her eyes shut than with them open. But ask her to locate 7 or 4. If she's not used to typing numbers, she'll find them faster by looking for them. A typist can copy Russian or Finnish or Basque without knowing these languages.

Dancers memorize intricate movements by feel. Their dancing could hardly be free if they were dependent on footprints stenciled on the floor.

A basketball dribbler learns to feel where the ball is while his eyes are on the basket or the opponent or while looking for his teammates.

Good choral directors train their singers to know music without having to look at the page.

The famous power failure that blacked out New York City and several eastern states in 1965 also blackened Carnegie Hall during a piano performance by Vladimir Horowitz. The *New York Times* reported that he continued playing the unlighted piano without a break, without a pause in timing.

## Derailing English from
## Its Soundtrack

DE-SOUNDING words and sentences alienates the writer from his speech. He feels no investment of self or feeling so he feels no pride of ownership. He becomes a writer of hieroglyphs, since words to him are merely publicly owned designs. As a communicator, he is retarded at the picture-pointing level.

For the sake of faster reading, children are taught dead-lip, dead-throat reading, moving neither as they hustle along. The ideal reading posture, they are told, is to be as silent and inert as the book itself.

---

**What is your philosophy on the relationship of silent and oral reading? . . . Do you believe silent reading should always precede oral reading even at the very beginning?**

We are now beginning to believe that there is a closer link between speech and printed words than we once thought. In the beginning stages of reading, children naturally want to express the sounds of printed language, in whispering or in reading aloud. Teachers observing children as they whisper words to themselves—or read them aloud—can see whether the process of imaging all inflections of speech is actually going on. The vocalization of children's first response to printed symbols is encouraged for the first two or three weeks. Restrictions are imposed gradually. The long-range purpose is to contribute to excellent silent interpretation.—Some Answers to Questions About Reading (Scott, Foresman)

---

Three University of California scientists can now place mesh electrodes over the thyroid cartilage to record electrical activity of the vocal muscles during reading. The reader is equipped with earphones. When he swallows he hears a burst of static. The slightest quiver of his laryngeal muscles crashes like fallen plate glass. In less than an hour, the reader can learn to keep his throat from jiggling while he reads. Hardyck, Petrinovich, and Ellsworth, who conducted the experiments, explain (in an article in *Science*, December 16, 1966) that an individual who subvocalizes in any degree is limited to a top reading speed of 150 words a minute—a maximum attainable while reading aloud.

But pointing at words, sounding them, making noises, are all part of writing because they are part of talking, and writing is an extension of speech. They help the writer feel his language, feel whether it weighs right in the mouth, whether it runs with his heart. The dead-lip, dead-throat writer is a dull writer.

Writing is individualized and personalized by sound and rhythm. The writer who doesn't hear himself writes cold. Speed reading encourages speed writing. He writes an *"eye language,"* which, like numbers, is intelligible without being heard or felt. It is made for eye skimming. Note this sample taken from a foundation report:

*"Pressing Importance* .... Although elimination of the liquidity deficiency is of pressing importance, the restoration of a permanently sound financial structure at the University of Pittsburgh requires the establishment of a stronger income base, which can be maintained, matched by a rational and continuing close supervision of expenditures."

Speed reading has to be a system of silence. It makes no attempt to bring the author's tonal and rhythmic forms to the reader's ear. But good writing was never meant just for the eye. It is meant to be *sounded*. It is directed at the ear and the heart—*literally the heart*, for written language carries the writer's heartbeat to the heart of the reader.

Dick & Jane have derailed English from its soundtrack and consequently have wrecked communication, for written communication is an expression of spoken, interhuman communication. If the school doesn't teach writing as extended speech it is failing to teach human communication itself.

You doctors and physicists who find writing a research report such agony; you lawyers who struggle to draft a simple brief or ordinance or contract; you ministers and priests who dread writing sermons as much as your congregations dread hearing them; you engineers who wish you didn't have to put your ideas down into words (if only you could use diagrams), you business administrators who can't make executive decisions because you can't translate the critical alternatives in the reports and proposals on your desks— all of you, don't blame your colleges or high schools for not teaching you to communicate better. *This* is where you went wrong: *here* in the first three years of your school life with Nat and his rat pack, Jimmy & Sue and their like.

In phonics programs children do learn sounds, but learn them through lists of regularly spelled words: gin, sin, din. Inconsistent spellings are phased into the program in its later stages. The phonics program is a *sound*-and-*pattern* drill program. It is designed to teach reading, not writing.

---

**Phonics: The study and application of elementary phonetics as a method of teaching beginners to read or enunciate.—Webster's New International Dictionary, 2nd edition**

---

Phonics may actually be effective in reading instruction. But what does it do to the writer?

Fat-Nat-sat-on-the-cat words may be fun and may help teach children to play with words. Word-play in turn will help them use language with agility. But what else? Clearly, they don't let the child *communicate himself.* He has nothing to say in this kind of language. He doesn't talk like that. The rat-a-tat-tat rhythms leave their mark on the child's own expression, as can be seen when you compare fat-mat writings with i.t.a. writings.

The writings below were praised as examples of "good creative writing" from seven-year-old second-graders using a "linguistics approach." The authors are not identified by name or city to make sure they cannot be embarrassed. Note their inhibited, jerky sentence rhythms and the limited use of words. When a teacher praises such writing she helps to reinforce the child's impression that this is good writing. The teacher should praise and reward the child who communicates. Here she praises a hollow and superficial use of language, as unmeant as it is unfelt.

*90*

The candy apples are good.
They are best of all.
"The apples are good,"
said Dan's father.
Dan said, "I will go
get apples for school

Dan is on the bus with Rags.
They are going to school.
Dan has his lunch in the bus.
He said, "I have a chicken wing for you."

Mother had six chops to cook.
She put them in the pan.
Dan looked into the pan.
Dan said, "Such big chops!  Good!"
Dan said, "I have a kiss for you, Mother."
But Mother is big and Dan is little.
Dan had to kiss her on the chin.

Dick & Jane writers in the middle grades are encouraged to "build" their vocabularies.  Since they began with little, regular words, "building" means collecting *longer-looking* and *rarer-looking* words.  "Look, Dick, look!" grows to become "Observe, Richard. Utilize your visual organs."

---

. . . I suspect that a great many Americans, trying to write a scientific medical paper, are harassed by the notion that there is something evil about 4-letter words.  The corollary belief is that if one can get 6, 8 or 10 syllables into a word it acquires merit thereby. . . .  "The white male we anticoagulated was hemorrhaging so we could not ambulate him" [means] "The patient given heparin began to bleed so we had to keep him in bed." . . .

What if "blood and sweat, toil and tears" were hemorrhage and perspiration, labor and lacrimation, which is the way most doctors would have said it.—*Dr. William B. Bean's "Tower of Babel" column in* Archives of Internal Medicine

---

Small, practical Anglo-Saxon words are so strongly associated with baby readers that adults who are insecure about their education avoid using them. Many adults who normally talk a direct and pungent language will use long, unusual words when they write.

Examine the man who has just graduated from pecking out his own letters to declaiming them to a secretary and you are likely to have a man hopelessly intoxicated with the rhythm of businessese. Conversely, if you come across a blunt yes or no in a letter you don't need to glance further to grasp that the author feels pretty firm in his chair.—*William H. Whyte, Jr.*, Fortune, *November 1950*

I wrote to the U.S. Army asking if I could inspect a certain writing instruction manual. Here is part of the officer's answer: ". . . Material requested cannot be provided since current regulations preclude the gratuitous or commercial issue of instructional material prepared by Army service schools to nonfederal governmental individuals or organizations. . . . ."

Does anyone ever hear talk like this in the Officers' Club bar?

Victor D'Amico of the Museum of Modern Art in New York City has been teaching art to children and adolescents for more than thirty-five years. "The hardest thing about teaching art," Mr. D'Amico told me, "is breaking a person's habit of putting a black outline around everything. People get this habit from working with color-me books and numbered drawings in the lower grades. Even with hard work, it may take a youngster years before he learns to look at life as it really is instead of seeing people and objects with black outlines."

What "black outline" was marked on us by our first three years of Dick & Jane baby words and Jimmy & Sue baby-sentence rhythms? How was our mind stenciled by true-false and fill-in tests repeated month after month, year after year?

A specter haunts our culture—it is that people will eventually be unable to say "They fell in love and married," let alone understand the language of Romeo and Juliet, but will as a matter of course say, "Their libidinal impulses being reciprocal, they activated their individual erotic drives and integrated them within the same frame of reference."—*Lionel Trilling*

# The i.t.a. Writer Is Ear Dependent

THE SPELLINGS OF i.t.a. children may look rowdy, but they let children accurately send the sounds and rhythms of their speech. Only five i.t.a. symbols, ∫h, ꭐ, ꭐ, ŋ, and ʒ, look very different from the familiar ABCs. ʒ is useful for writing such words as usual and television. ∫h (s + h) lets the child write words like *shabby*, *rush*, *fuchsia*, *conscience*, *sure*, *sugar*, and words that end in *tion*. An i.t.a. class in King's Park, Long Island, was asked to write a sentence using the symbol ch. A six-year-old boy turned in: mie muþher cheetz on þe wæt wotcherz.

---

mie muþher went to an auc∫hun and ∫hee got a rockiŋ chær and too launmœers and ∫hee is gœiŋ too anoþher auc∫hun on satidæ and I am goiŋ to join þe boiz club and I nœ it looks liek in þær þæ hav a televiʒun and pool tæblz and you can bie peesa [pizza]. þe end—*B. J., 6, first grade, Long Island*

---

When I look at ꭐ, I see a concert conductor; the little loop is his head and his arms are raised in direction. What children see is the symbols they use to make the *oo* sound in *school*, *rule*, *two*, *few*, *true*, *through*, and *soup*. If they want, they are able to write buoy, *denouement*, *route*, *coup*, *rheum*, *leeward*, and *bruise*. ꭐ and ꭐ let the i.t.a. child hear the difference between *hook* (ꭐ) and *hoot* (ꭐ), *good* (ꭐ) and *goof* (ꭐ), and he can write *woman*, *put*, and *should* without copying the words or memorizing a book of rules.

i.t.a. spellings reflect what the writer hears, his own pronunciations as well as those of others, correct or incorrect. If he hears "praed" for "parade," he will write it that way; "anniversary" may

93

be "anevasse"; couple days later may be "kubldaes laedr"; "samwijis" = sandwiches; "sircest" = circus. Puerto Rican children write "keel" for "kill." In some papers you can tell a child lisps by the way he spells words. If a teacher says "Feb-you-erry" or "li-berry," it shows in her class's writing.

---

mi bruth has a dekst he wont go to brefikst he wont go to luch and he wont go to diner he stæs at his dekst—*Harry, 6, first grade, Bethlehem, Pa.*

yester Day mi fother got a kard from me it sed hav u hapy fother's day and we had a terke to and I had siks glass ov milk. I likt the terky. mi fother got a rop hamic. mi fother got a baj that sed im the bos and now he hst to give it bak he is onle ald [allowed] to be the bos for one Day.—*Eugene, 6, first grade, Long Island*

---

When you read the i.t.a. writings of children you have to *listen* to the papers *rather than see* them. They are not always neatly and accurately spelled either by T.O. or i.t.a. standards. They are by six-year-olds as capable of errors as their adult readers. They are written from sounds. We don't all hear the same sounds in this big country and we don't all say them the same way. If a Kansan and a New Yorker both read the lines below out loud, to hear them you'd never think they were reading the same thing.

> Howe now owns a cow.
> The cow's known as "Mao."
> Mao wears a brown bow.
> It is a cow bow.

If you really prefer familiar spellings to communicative writing you can always have Dick & Jane:

> Books are pretty.
> Books are red.
> Books are little.
> Books are yellow.

*94*

I like books.
I have books.
Books are big.

But if you're willing to accept *meanings* instead of familiar spellings and if you can put up with some slight visual shocks and *hear* the child writing, you may become caught by a new, minor literature. There are some timeless sentences a child of six can say, sentences he'll never be able to write again in his whole life because they are authentically the products of his six-year-old self. i.t.a. children, if the alphabet is used right with them, can develop such a strength of sound and beat that their writing both sings and drums.

The family conversation is the first model of language use for the growing child. Through the rhythms and sounds of his parents' talk he learns to sense emotional patterns. These sounds and rhythms are the foundations of his own speech and music. For good or bad, for comfort or discomfort, they are the *home* patterns he will return to through the years of his growth. They influence his taste in music. They underlie his adult expression.

---

ie went too the parc an ie ran throo the sprinclr. an wen ie went down the slied ie got so scærd ie jumpt ovr the sied my fist hit my jau an ie went bac up the slied and ie got sokan wet.—*No name, 6, first grade, Bethlehem, Pa.*

I hav trublz becuz mie muthr telz mee too cleen the selr and it iz cleen.—*B. J., 6, first grade, Long Island*

wun dæ a littl girl næmd marsha went too the market. with 100$ with the 100$ shee got nien packejis ov cookees. shee put the cookees in her wagon but when shee got hœm her muther had a fit. the end—*Patricia, 6, first grade, Cleveland*

---

i.t.a. writers are full of noises. They produce in writing both sounds they hear and those they make up. They imitate machines, animals, gun fights. They imitate the world.

## it cæm from outr spæs
*[written in a shaky hand]*

ar yœ redy astnot "yes" 10 9 8 7 6 5 4 3 2 1 0 egniʃhon
blast off 4 millyon miels a wæ from erʃh. "capton weev
lost ʃhe roket! ʃhærs sum ciend ov interfeerens. capton
lœk at ʃhis. every thiŋ is koŋt out. crnll [colonel] lœk.
breepær [prepare] to craʃh! baŋ! lets get out. wæt lœk at
ʃhat ʃhadœ ror! lœk out o-o-o-o-o-o help! ror! chomp!
chomp! chomp! ʃhe liets ar back on evry thiŋ is ok. lœk
anuʃher roket is comiŋ to erʃh. worn aull ʃhe peepl. bee
alert bee alert clœz aull yœr windœs and dors. uniedenefied
roket aprœchiŋ erʃh. it had a hed liek a dienesor a body
liek a lizerd and legs liek a creecher. get a ræ gun ʃhœt it.
ie can't help! ie can't. men ræ guns and hery! hery!
hery! hery! hery! ʃhe ræ dusn't hert it. lets get out ov
heer. lets. baŋ! it nokt ʃhe dor doun. ror! "lœk out"
ror! ror! chomp! chomp! it's gœiŋ bak to ʃhe roket it's
gœiŋ a wæ. kwick ʃhœt mislz baŋ! bœm! craʃh! ʃhe end
    —*No name, 6, first grade, Cleveland*

One day Ann and me went on a picnic and I popt out of
my seat! I saw a green snake and it was skwished. When
we went to a nue plas for our picnic.—*Sharon, 6, first grade,*
*Long Island*

I cliemd out ov mie bed. mie sister wuz ʃhær first but I
scwusht her.—*Steven, 6, first grade, Long Island*

In the paper below, note that Gordon, six, of Bethlehem, spelled
out the sound of thunder, crossed it out because he was unsatisfied
with it, and then spelled it again. Note, also, he writes "Halloween"
without an *l* because that's the way he pronounces it.

ʃhis is ʃhe storm my niet on hœuwaween. ʃhe spœks wer
spœky. ʃhe pumpkin taukt. ʃhe hœus fell doun. when ʃhe
hœus fell doun it mæd a big noiz. ʃhe noiz went b~~œ̸mb~~œ̸~~m~~-
b~~œ̸~~œ bœmbœm bœmm. and ʃhe last nois it mæd woz
crac and bœm. a wich got cilld bie lietniŋ.

They spell words they've *never seen.*

Sunday niet I herd a loud nois. It went bœm-pupœp-pupœm and dœ yœ nœ wot is woz? lietaning and thunder. But I did not heer it I woz sleeping.—*Gary, 6, first grade, Long Island*

---

The fall (bababadalgharaghtakamminarronnkonnbronntonnerronntuonnthunntrovarrhounawnskawntoohooardenenthurnuk!) of a once wallstrait old-parr. . . .—*James Joyce*, Finnegan's Wake

---

### Storm

Sundæ niet at 5. o'clock I wœk up and I herd sumth go cupam-cupam. it was perity loud. Cupam-cupam. It sounded liek garbijpæls gœwing doun a rœd and then the clock bongd 5 times. Bong, bong, bong, bong, bong. Then sumthing scard me. it was lietning. I bundld up in my cuvers then it reely scærd me and I fell steræt off ov my bed and it was a hard faull. and I was still in my cuvers. My sister was still sleeping. She slept riet therœ the storm. But I was awæk riet thrœ. The hœwel storm lasted antil 7 o'clock. It was a long storm and the ræn cæm doun in buckets and it was a teribul niet.—*Barbara, 6, first grade, Long Island*

## The Dick & Jane Installment Plan for Words

IN 98 PER CENT of our schools, we pay out the forty to fifty sounds of English speech and their spelling in installments. Different installment plans have been worked out, the most "popular" being the Basal Reader Plan. *Control* is its central characteristic: in addition to a controlled release of sounds and spellings there is the controlled repetition of a controlled vocabulary.

Why control the flow of words? The authors of *A Core Vocabulary*, put out by Educational Developmental Laboratories, Inc., believe that "any well-integrated language arts program should maintain vocabulary controls that make possible short-interval learning with enough repetition and reinforcement so that each student will be assured of a minimum level of language development as he progresses from level to level."

---

**Why do you control vocabulary? Does this influence adversely the total number of words children can read?**

**Answer: . . . One of the sub-objectives of the program is to bring the words of the Basic Readers to the vocabulary level of instantaneous perception and so the introduction of new words has been repeated and maintained in order to establish complete familiarity and at-homeness. The number of words taught depends upon the use of the words. All are chosen for many uses. Words of limited usefulness are not included.**

**One person replying to the question declared that "too often controlled vocabulary is taken to be a limiting process. Controlled vocabulary means that words are bunched for mastery and spaced for maintenance."—Some Answers to Questions About Reading**

---

It should be solemnly noted that though the word-control industry says it is working for the good of the language arts, it is working solely for the good of reading. Its most basic assumption is that reading is the one and only key to educational success and that writing can be separated from reading and given less attention, if it is given any attention at all.

The fact that the student's first encounter with words in visual form is through reading indicates that reading level should be the primary factor in deciding on the grade placement of words. The same words can then be re-introduced in the following grade for spelling and writing activities.
—A Core Vocabulary

Words are metered out in more or less the following quantities. Most sound words, such as "meow" and "moo" and movement words, such as "hippity" and "zoom," are left out.

| | NUMBER OF WORDS FOR | |
| GRADE | READING | WRITING |
| --- | --- | --- |
| Kindergarten | 58 | 0 |
| 1st | 280 | 0 |
| 2nd | 440 | 280 |
| 3rd | 750 | 440 |
| 4th | 860 | 750 |
| 5th | 930 | 860 |
| Total Words | 3318 | 2330 |

What are these precious 280 words the child is given to spell in second grade? Are they from the Constitution, perhaps? The Bible, maybe?

*A Core Vocabulary* says that words for the first- to eighth-grade list "would be accepted by each state in the Union." But for their first- to third-grade list, the compilers sifted through ten basal-reader series "with the express purpose of determining by quarter-grade the points at which the required words for grades 1–3 and their variant forms should be introduced."

There's nothing at all wrong with the little service words used by the basal reader. They're clear and vigorous. The child already knows most of them from around the house and he'll use them in talk all his life. What's wrong is the fascistic authority the controlled-word lists acquire. The lists enslave elementary education.

First, they determine the child's reading level. His reading level determines his grade level. His grade level determines what books he's given. His books determine the concepts he's to be taught. His concepts, finally, affect his personal growth and development.

Shouldn't there be a vote before we give Jimmy & Sue this much power?

---

Written self-expression which is linguistically and culturally authentic in English should be the ultimate goal of our Indian students.

The greatest goal can only be achieved by a carefully planned program, with a reduction of controls so gradual that the student is never in the position of having to *invent* language.—*"The Fourth Communication Skill: Writing," State Department of Public Instruction, Division of Indian Education, Phoenix, Ariz.*

---

# The Italians

ℓℓℓℓℓℓℓℓℓℓℓℓℓℓℓℓℓℓℓℓℓℓℓℓℓℓℓℓℓℓℓℓℓℓℓℓℓℓℓℓℓℓℓℓℓℓℓℓℓ

IN 1964 I wrote to certain elementary schools in Italy asking each for samples of written compositions. I explained I wanted to compare early writing in Italian with early writing in i.t.a. The children could write about their families, pets, holidays, or anything they felt like writing about. Dr. Domenico Lombrossa, School Supervisor of Brescia, and Dr. P. Manzi, Director of Studies of the Scuola Rinnovata "Pizzigoni" in Milan, generously sent to me two shoe boxes full of unedited compositions written by different six- and seven-year-old children.

We aren't often reminded of it, but what we call the "English alphabet" is really the modern Italian alphabet. Since Italian speech uses only about twenty-seven basic sounds, the 2,000-year-old twenty-six-letter alphabet which we also use is still beautifully adequate for Italians.

---

In my family there are five, my father, my mamma, me, my small brother and a small sister of two months.

My father is tall and thin and has only a little hair in front and in back he has a lot more.

Mamma has a lot of hair but she always says: "I am continually losing my hair."

She wears size 41 [U.S. size 8] shoes and has big feet like mine.

After mamma comes me; my father wants me to cut my hair in the style of a little boy; I have the bad habit of biting my fingernails and my mamma tells me that if I continue to bite them when I'm big I'll have ugly hands.

*101*

My little brother is a brat who answers always to mamma and hits me and calls me bad names; he has chestnut colored hair and eyes; he is a real brat but I love him just the same.

My little sister is 2 months old and is very cute, she makes a lot of little smiles for me.

Yesterday evening my aunt and uncle and grandparents came over. My grandmother played with my little sister and made her laugh.—*Alessandra, 7, Brescia*

---

What difference would a one-sound-one-symbol alphabet make to a child in elementary school? What does an Italian school child have that an American school child doesn't have? Let's start with the first day of school—registration.

An Italian child enters school able to write his own name and address. Usually by the age of five he can also write a few other words and has been busy writing them on building walls. The following observation, taken from a workbook titled *How to Help Your Child in Reading, Writing and Arithmetic,* shows how retarded the American child-writer is by comparison. "Before your child has finished first grade, he will be able to print his own name; he will use capitals at the beginning of proper names, at the beginning of a sentence, and in writing the word I, he will print simple sentences and print his own tags: 'To Mother . . . To Daddy.' "

An Italian child never has to spell his name to the teacher or to another Italian child, whereas most American children have to spell their names from the time they register for first grade till they graduate from college, and they continue to spell their names forever after.

An Italian teacher can dictate Dante's "Inferno" to six-year-old first-graders. They won't understand most of what they're writing and it would be tedious work for them, but they can transcribe with a high degree of spelling accuracy. I doubt if a university professor could successfully dictate Shakespeare to a college class and expect his students to get it down right. Anyone for *Troilus and Cressida*?

Italian school children never have to buy a speller since spelling is not a subject in their curriculum. They've never heard of the spelling bee or spell-down, and such an exercise would be a dull waste of their time. They never copy spellings from a book or from the blackboard. They may cheat but they don't cheat by copying spellings from each other.

By contrast, the American child learning English must buy a speller every year from the second through the sixth grade, and in some systems through the eighth grade. The words he learns to write in the first grade are copied, as are many of the words he learns in second grade. His dictionary work is copy work. His reference-book work will be copy work. He begins systematic spelling instruction in the second grade, and from grade two through grade six he will spend ten to twenty minutes each day of the week learning how to spell. He will continue learning to spell English for the rest of his life. American secretarial schools require fifty-minute spelling drills daily for their students, yet the students are usually high school graduates and some have had college. Compare this with the fact that even the poorest of Italian secretaries is a good speller. With each of its office typewriters sold in Italy, Olivetti gives away a little brochure explaining some rare exceptions in Italian spelling. Spelling is not in the curriculum of the Italian secretarial school.

The fact that Italian children don't have any spelling in their curriculum while American children have an enormous amount of it makes a staggering difference in their school life. We should examine this difference closely and carefully. It is not the same as if the Italian child studies Garibaldi and the American child does not, for the American child studies George Washington and the Italian child doesn't.

It would be interesting to compare our early readers with early Italian science and history books and social-study readers to see what concepts are dammed from our children by our spelling controls, but the intent of my book is to deal only with writing and the expressive side of learning. With this in mind, how do the Italian and American child differ?

The ability to spell is something very closely related to the essence of education itself, for the power to spell is a person's power to define and articulate what makes him think and feel and be different from everyone else. The ability to spell affects the ability to write simple and compound sentences of various kinds. It affects the learning and use of punctuation and capitalization. It affects various forms, such as letter writing, diaries, essays, and the like.

---

My mamma is beautiful. Her complexion is like the white roses which have a little bit of pink in the center. My mamma has black hair like coal, she has eyes, eyelashes and eyebrows all black like the pollen from poppies.—*Dea, 7, Brescia*

---

The Italian child learns these forms and structures quite naturally in his primary grades. The American child must wait for his spellings before he can learn them. While the Italian child is learning how to sharpen his observations, define his feelings, and organize his thoughts, the American child is still slaving over spelling. He can't afford the time to learn the simple logic of organization, nor does he have the verbal ability to practice arranging ideas on paper.

---

**Boys and Girls:**
Write the word. Compare. If you make a mistake, find the part of the word that is hard for you. Look at that part of the word. Think about it. Try to find some way to help yourself remember it. When you have spelled the word correctly, write it three more times to make sure you can write the word quickly from memory.—*"Spelling Words List A," Board of Education of the City of New York, 1961*

---

The school papers from Brescia and Milan show that Italian first- and second-graders as a normal practice use dialogue, punctuation, and a variety of sentence lengths and constructions produced only by our head-of-the-class sixth-graders. For example:

My favorite game is playing teacher. I really like a lot of games but my favorite is playing teacher. I play teacher very often.

I play with my little brother or with my little cousin Anna. Quite often my cousin won't play with me but then she says: "All right! I'll play with you!"

But after we play awhile she says: "I quit. I'm not playing any more!" Then I ask, "But why? Why don't you want to play any more?" She pulls my hair and then says, "I just don't feel like it!" But I must say just the same that playing teacher is the game I like best. My cousin doesn't like playing teacher but it's my favorite game.—*Luisa, 7, Brescia*

Most important, the Italian children communicate meaning and feelings. Each paper authentically reflects the rhythms and sounds of the writer's speech. It's very clear that Italian children have no trouble writing down their talk. Some papers reveal personal, honest, warm insights into Italian family life. Dick & Jane writers reduce people and pets and even themselves to cardboard displays.

**Italian** One-Sound-One-Symbol Alphabet:

My dog is forty-two days old, has long hair, but not very long, his coat is smooth, and he has a cute face and sharp teeth that if he bites me it hurts.

Once in a while when he's in the garden he eats the violets or the grass and sometimes he goes into the places where there are flowers and tramples them.

Sometimes in the garden, when I am doing something to him he runs in back of me and sometimes does pirouettes.

Sometimes when he is attached to the lamp he amuses himself trying to get free but never succeeds.

Sometimes when he's in his collar, if he wants to make peepee, he can't do it on the curb but on the street.—*Giovanni, 7, second grade, Brescia*

**i.t.a.** One-Sound-One-Symbol Alphabet:

yꙍ can't feed him [a rabbit] too much or hee will dieee and

ieee sau skulls uv a rabit on a golf kos—*Eric, 6, first grade, Long Island*

**T.O.** 40–50-Sound 26-Symbol Alphabet:
> Once I had a rabbit.
> His name was Ben, the Rabbit.
> Ben had one friend and that was me.
> He would run in the fields
> and find things to do.
> One day Ben ran away.
> I was so unhappy.
> A man brought him back
> and he never ran away again.
>                   —*Name and city withheld, 7, second grade*

> Sniffles is a white rabbit.
> Sniffles and Frank play together.
> Frank's father made a cage for Sniffles.
> In the morning Frank feeds his rabbit.
> Sniffles is very happy to see Frank at night.
> Frank put Sniffles back
> in the box and went to bed.
>                   —*Name and city withheld, 7, second grade*

**Italian** One-Sound-One-Symbol Alphabet:

Last evening my small gray rabbit has made six rabbits.

Then this morning while I was going to school my father called me and had a pail in his hand with six small rabbits inside.

He told me: "These six rabbits died of the cold."

Because of unhappiness I didn't want to go to school. If I think about it again I begin to cry.

They were nude without fur.—*Nadia, 7, second grade, Caionvico*

**T.O. ("Linguistics Approach") 40–50-Sound 26-Symbol Alphabet:**

> I have a dog named Skippy.
> She didn't do anything but sleep.
> No one could wake her.
> One day we bought a new dog.
> Skippy barked and the other dog barked.
> > —*Name and city withheld, 7, second grade*

**Italian** One-Sound-One-Symbol Alphabet:

> My uncle has three dogs, the first is named Dik, he has a brown and black coat, he hunts for birds, and is thirty years old, and is of the bloodhound breed, he has a normal nose, strong jaws, long and strong teeth. His paws have long nails of a brown color.
>
> The second dog is named Falco and hunts hares, he doesn't swim but Dik does, has a coat like a sheared lamb black nails weak jaws and teeth.
>
> The third dog is named Blek, he has a brown and black coat and is for birds and weak of jaw and teeth like falco.
>
> The dog is the friend of man but the enemy of the cat.—*Fusori, 7, second grade, Brescia*

**i.t.a.** One-Sound-One-Symbol Alphabet:

I hev a jermen sheperd and he is very lasy sumtims he dusent kum wen you kaul him. I hev a tug awau with him I just stic the bat in his mouth and he bits and then we both pul and I auws win—*John, 6, first grade, Long Island*

**T.O. ("Linguistics Approach") 40–50-Sound 26-Symbol Alphabet:**

> I had a dog and I lost my dog.
> I love him.
> He loves me.

I wish I had my dog today.
One day I found my dog,
and me and my dog live happily.
    —*Name and city withheld, 7, second grade*

## Jim Pitman's Jailbreak

ƐƐƐƐƐƐƐƐƐƐƐƐƐƐƐƐƐƐƐƐƐƐƐƐƐƐƐƐƐƐƐƐƐƐƐƐƐƐƐƐƐƐƐƐƐƐƐƐƐƐƐƐƐ

JAMES PITMAN and his i.t.a. have led our kids on a jailbreak out of the Dick & Jane controlled-word list. As soon as the i.t.a. child can connect the sounds of his speech with their related i.t.a. symbols, he's able to write *all the words he can speak*.

Jeanne Chall, in *Learning to Read*, says that the typical basal readers for the *third* grade where the child is eight years old have a total vocabulary of about 1,500 different words. But according to research by Mildred Templer at the University of Minnesota in 1957, a six-year-old child's mean basic understanding vocabulary is about 12,500 words. His speaking vocabulary ranges from 1,000 to as many as 4,000 words, depending on his maturity and his word environment at home. If a first-grader can speak 4,000 different words, in i.t.a. he can write 4,000 words. No matter how long the word, no matter what his accent or dialect is, if an i.t.a. child can say a word he can write it. As English Professor Frank Hook of Lehigh University has said, "He could even write about anti-disestablishmentarianism if he had anything to say about it."

i.t.a. is the *freedom* alphabet. i.t.a. liberates the child's own sentences, revealing the order of his mind and the state of his feelings expressed in his own language without help, put on paper without spelling inhibitions.

A certain freedom comes from i.t.a.'s rationality, which permits a child to learn by discovery without the teacher's help. The Spring Garden School in Bethlehem had a boy who would get furious if asked to repeat anything he had said. His father, a physician, explained that the boy was sensitive about a malocclusion. Speech therapists had not helped. One day at the blackboard in an i.t.a. class the boy saw he was writing "das di en" when other were writing

*109*

"that's the end." He began comparing other words. Gradually, without help or correction from the teacher, he improved his own speech himself.

---

batman faut ʃhe mad-hatter. and ʃhe mad-hatter and hiz men robbd storz ʃhat ʃhe stor-keeperz had hats on. and ʃhe mad-hatter nockt out ʃhe stor-keeperz wiʃh hix electronically pouerd hat.—*No name, 6, first grade, Bethlehem, Pa.*

this is an apsterackt [abstract] and I closed my eyes to mæck it. But I had my eyes opend to color it.—*No name, 6, first grade, Bethlehem, Pa.*

Sadrdæ mie bruther and the oreeols had a bæs baull gæm. and wee went too it and mie bruther hit won riet ovr the bak stop an it went in sumwons yord and the nekst baull hee hit hee got too frst bæs. and a smoll bou wos up. an hee hit a groundr riet out in the uther feeld and that tiem mie hed wos bleeding. i got hit bie a piep and I had too goe hœm and I got too stiches. and on sundæ morning I fell in the bath tub with wotr in it. the end.—*Thomas, 6, first grade, Bethlehem, Pa.*

---

If an i.t.a. child is garrulous, he will be garrulous on paper. Two interesting things show on the six-year-old Long Island girl's paper below. Note that she uses a fill-in device ("pleas riet it wær the aro is"), and that she's aware she's wandered from the point of her paper ("now! ! ! ! lets get bak on the subjekt").

When I go to lunch Alison and I alwæx see philip he is cyœtypie. He is my boy frend and I Love him very very very much he is so sweet to all ov the girls he is just a doll and so are you you are sweet and ciend and lovabul and adoribul for yaur æj Mrs. E I Love you very very very very very very much to you are sweet. When we go to lunch I aullwæx see allot ov chillderen and I aulwæs see you and if you don't no hœ I mean I mean you Mrs. E and When I men I Love you I wasnt fooling I really love you. I wish you wer my mother for ever and you better not die becos you are so sweet to me and œnly me and Mrs. E Pleas mæ I sit neks to yaur desk I don't mean wær the uther peopel are I dœ not wunt to go thær I wud Like to go riet neks to you so wut is it yes! or no! pleass wen you riet it pleas riet it wær the aro is now!!!! lets get bak on the subjekt. When we go to lunch I aulwæs see. . . .

"'Here is a little toy house. It is for you' . . . Oh, Father. A little toy house for me! I like it,'" is dishonest. The subject is forced. The sound and rhythm of the language is false. If a child talked like that around his friends he'd be drummed out of his neighborhood. But then, "A little toy house for me!" is not meant to be *expression*. It is merely eye-chart reading.

Since the i.t.a. child is free of a controlled vocabulary, he is also free of other artificial controls. He doesn't have to wait till he's eleven to write a letter of regret. He isn't restricted to writing "The ball is red" sentences but can write complex, compound, complex-compound, even super-complex-compound sentences if he chooses.

The six-year-old child writes candidly and innocently what he feels about home and school, teachers and friends. He reveals the maturity or immaturity of his emotional state, as the following papers, all by first-graders, show.

I gave mie mother a card and a bœcae of tissue paper flouers. she did not like it. she didn't even like the artullfishill flouers. she said to mie bruther that it's a waist of muney. do you no hou much muney it caust? siks dollors. she said he worked to hard for that. that was his own muney.—*Luke, 6, Long Island*

when ie grœ up I want tœ bee a tœ danser. ie want tœ bee a tœ danser beekaus ie liek tœ dans on mie tœs ie nœ sum tiems mie tœs will bleed and beekaus ie liek ſhe pritty costœms and ſhe pritty ſhœs ſhæ wær and ie nœ ſhat it is very hard tœ bee a tœ danser—*Antoinette, 6, Long Island*

111

wun dæ I wuſ lœnlee beecuſ I wuſ bad.  I had too gœ intoo
the truck.  I wuſ lœnlee.  I wuſ bad.—*David, 6, Bethlehem,
Pa.*

wen I am watching astroboy my Mother œlwæſ seſ Ellin
will yoo pleeſ tæk the garbig outsied so I do it and by the
tiem I get back in astroboy iſ œver so I wotch sandy becker
and then wen sandy beckr iſ on my Mother seſ Ellen pleeſ
tæck the garbig sœ I bring it out—*Ellen, 6, Long Island*

happy fæseſ and sad fæseſ peepl ar different.  sum ar
broun and sum ar whiet.—*Thomas, 6, Bethlehem, Pa.*

## Spell-Bound Communication

~~~~~~~~~~~~~~~~~~~~~~~~~~~~~~~~~~~~~~~~~~~~~~~~~

WE ARE A lazy age, fat with books, content to feed in libraries. We take the magic of writing for granted. "Spelling" for most people is associated with erasures and red or blue correction marks. But look up *spelling* in a big dictionary and let its many meanings take you back to an earlier time when putting meanings onto paper still impressed people as an exciting feat of magic: spell-bind, spell-casting, spellcraft, spell-weaving, spellmonger, spell-invoking, spell-caught, spell-raised, spell-set, spell-struck, spell-riveted, spell-stopped, spell-sprung, spell-free, spell-banned, spellproof.

The word *spell* itself means story. The *gospel* was *god spel*—good story.

To most of us spelling no longer means to put a "story" on paper. It means spell *right*.

In our schools, *handwriting and spelling have been wrenched out of their natural context in clear communication.* Handwriting is taught as a drawing drill isolated from its function in communication. At best it is graphic-art instruction, not a part of writing instruction. Spelling, too, has become *a thing* by itself, something to be reckoned with on its own terms—an end, not a means. In our preoccupation with putting down the right letters we've lost sight of the goal of spelling, which is to communicate.

---

**Examining the written work of children may be quite deceptive, due to the possibility that children will mask their deficiencies by choosing only those words they believe they can spell correctly.—*William B. Gillooly*, Phi Delta Kappan, *June 1966***

---

I don't say accurate spelling and punctuation should not be taught, only that they should be taught in their proper context.

*113*

Spelling and pronunciation have this in common: they both carry meaning, one to a reader, the other to a listener. They will carry their meanings if they follow agreed-upon rules. A misspelling and a mispronunciation defeat their purpose by breaking rules. They can fail to carry meaning in three ways: (1) by being totally unintelligible, (2) by carrying an intelligible but unintended meaning, or (3) by offending, annoying, or distracting the listener or the reader.

Except among children just beginning to write, few misspellings fall into the first bin of errors by being totally unintelligible. A few carry intelligible but unintended meanings and thus fall into the second bin of errors—a child writes "there" for "their." It's the third bin that is usually full—errors that shock or bother the reader. Usually the child's reader is his teacher or his parent. The degree of error in this third bin swings with their tolerance, a tolerance affected by intelligence, a sense of humor, a concern for image.

The child will straighten out his own bad spellings when he sees that they contaminate his meanings. But his willingness to correct himself should come from his desire to be understood and his feelings of frustration should come from his inability to communicate, not from his failures in copying. The child who doesn't care whether he shocks or disturbs or annoys other people has a problem a lot bigger than a spelling problem.

There are Left and Right Wing attitudes toward spelling. The Extreme Right would like correct spelling to start with toilet training. The spelling nut in this group would have rejected Anne Frank's *Diary*.

The Left is rather more tolerant toward spellings and enjoys misspellings as an amusing primitive art: folk spellings. They regard exact spellings as dues imposed on them by the Establishment.

Complaints from the Right usually come from men exasperated with their secretaries. Their concept of education is to get children ready for the typing pool: "Teach them to read good, spell good." They have some right to be exasperated. The National Geographic Society estimates that bad handwriting alone, without bad spelling, costs American business $70 million a year in confusion, waste, and bad will.

*114*

Tolerance toward a child's spelling should match the tolerance shown toward his beginning speech. Dr. Charles Van Riper, the famous speech pathologist, warns that impatient criticism of a normal child's speech may make him overconscious of failure and induce stuttering or other speech imperfections. He offers this guideline for tolerance toward children with speech handicaps: "We hunt for excellence but accept comprehended failure. We must learn to bear error in the interests of future success!"

There are adults who would choose to suppress an opinion rather than mispronounce it and others who would avoid meeting a person to escape the possibility of getting his name wrong, and there are also people who would rather not write than misspell a word. How did they get that way? They are the product of their earliest listeners and readers. Just as our earliest listeners taught us to talk, our earliest readers more than any others in our lifetime did most to help or hurt our writing habits.

Parents are so permissive about a baby's beginning speech that they hear *mama* and *dada* when he's merely clearing his throat. They'd never insist that their baby pronounce their first and last names fully and clearly or even mo-ther or fa-ther. But they see no parallel importance in a child's first writings and they pick and nag at his spellings.

The ability to write may help a child unlock and release great secrets from his mind, and help him unload tormentful feelings. But a fear of spelling rejection may make the child afraid to try to write, drive his ideas farther back into hiding, and leave him still burdened with his torments.

Some teachers—and parents, too—correct spelling from the same compulsion that drives them to straighten pictures. Spellings stretch out in a line. They fill space. Things in space can be tidied up and compared for uniformity. They are subject to controls and can be measured. Teachers and parents alike tend to distort the importance of spelling and then wonder why children have communication troubles.

Red marks on a child's early attempts to write can make him wary and afraid to try. He'll say what's safe rather than what's accurate or natural. If we complain about how a child's writing *looks* and fail to respond to what he *means*, we teach a false, superficial value.

---

**Children want to write when the teacher is enthusiastic about their plans for a written activity. Children's writing is more fluent and more honest when they trust the teacher to accept them as individuals and to value their work.** *—"Written Communication in the Elementary Schools," Anne Arundel County Public Schools, Annapolis, Md.*

---

Many good teachers try to help their children to write by urging them: "Don't worry about the spelling. Write it any way you think it ought to be. Just get your thought down." This is admirable practice. It frees a lot of children and many can get off some good writing.

The trouble with it is that sooner or later some teacher is going to have to say: "Now, stop. Worry about the spelling a little." Too frequently by this time the child has some spelling habits that will pester him for life.

Some grade-school teachers say that their children can write fluently without i.t.a., that by "taking a stab at spellings" children have no trouble getting their meanings across to the teacher, that therefore the i.t.a. "apparatus" is unnecessary.

The guess-speller has to have a brazen self-image. He has to be able to tough it out against readers who will judge his appearance, not his meanings. Not all children have a brazen self-image.

Whether guess-spellings work depends on the reader: the reader has to be a good guesser. The teacher, of course, *is* a good guesser, but the question then is how good is a child's communication if we have to guess what he's trying to say?

In a one-sound-one-symbol alphabet such as Italian or the Initial Teaching Alphabet, there's no need for guessing or "stabbing." Spelling is a correlate of pronunciation—it's actually an extension of pronunciation, and the child simply writes the way he pronounces.

A teacher who asks her class to write on "What I Did Last Summer" might not care if the whole class had drowned. If all she wants is a paper she can correct and grade, the child knows this.

He will write, but it's an uphill job when she's up there at the top ready to swat him down.

Too often the student's reader is about the worst he could be punished with—a teacher waiting to correct his spelling, grammar, and punctuation. Who can talk to somebody who's waiting to nit-pick his every pronunciation and tell his jokes over again to make their point better, meanwhile flicking dandruff off his shoulders, staring at his mouth and teeth, and, if he gestures, looking at his nails or the spot on his sleeve?

The i.t.a. graduate meets his first serious communication challenge when he meets his second-grade teacher. She can make or break him as a writer. He is just getting used to a new, more difficult writing medium, the traditional Roman alphabet. He's usually happy to use the ABCs because it's the alphabet grownups use. He can handle its eccentricities better than the kid who hasn't had a year of i.t.a. Nevertheless, the teacher is the factor to reckon with because writing is not just a matter of spelling but one of inter-personal communication. If the teacher is a basal-reader machine, she will stamp VOID on his paper and reject him. The reading-oriented teacher is used to Dick & Jane writing. She rates a paper according to its capitalizations and indentations rather than what it communicates. She's unnerved when a child writes words that don't appear on her controlled-word list for second grade.

---

**One visitor in a second grade classroom of ex-i.t.a. children said, "I'm concerned about the spelling list the students are developing. Some of them are not second-grade words." But what is a second-grade word? —Dr. Rebecca Stewart, *National Council of Teachers of English*, 1964**

---

Both parents and teachers can frustrate and discourage a child's communication development by a negative, listless, or phony reaction to the papers he writes.

We can't really blame the teacher; she's never been trained to edit communication and doesn't know how she's expected to relate to it. She's used to Dick & Jane writers with their eye-memorized words and their copied words. For years the only thing she has been able to do with a child's paper is get him to clean it up.

We can't entirely blame parents either. What can they say when their otherwise genius son comes up to them and hands over a blanket-sized sheet of pulp paper that says:

> Dear Father and Mother,
>   I have a red ball.
> The ball is red.
> It is my ball.

# Writing-Instruction Vandals:
## The Fill-In, the Check-Off,
## the Multiple Choice

IN 1965 several Air Force Academy cadets exposed fellow students who were operating a cheating ring in the Academy. I conducted an opinion poll for *Good Housekeeping* magazine in an attempt to find what children thought of informers. A school in New York offered to distribute questions to children in third, fourth, and fifth grades. John Teeling, S.J., head of the English Department at Regis College, volunteered to find a matching group of children in Denver. Both groups of children were aged eight to ten. Here are two of the problem questions I put to the children:

1. Your mother and father are going to a party. They tell you to be in bed by 9:00 o'clock. As soon as they go, your baby sitter telephones some boys and they come to your house. They smoke cigarettes, drink beer, and play kissing games. Your baby sitter asks you not to tell your father and mother. Will you tell?

2. Is it fair to tell on somebody? Is it nice to be a tattle-tale?

The New York school neatly mimeographed the problems and arranged them so that children could check off their answers.

Is it fair to tell on somebody?     Yes . . . . .   No . . . . .
Is it nice to be a tattletale?      Yes . . . . .   No . . . . .

I read through the New York answers quite rapidly. In fact, after counting fifty papers, I "subleased" the remaining three-hundred for some one else to count.

But Denver gave me trouble. Instead of allowing for check-offs, Teeling had simply provided a three-inch space after each

*119*

problem. Some children wrote only a few words, others filled the space and continued writing down the sides of the page. I had to read each statement and decide whether the child had said yes or no. Sometimes I couldn't decide so I had to make another category: Maybe. Some children said "sometimes." and this made a new category, too.

This was a bother and slowed down the opinion count. After reading more than a hundred of the papers, I still didn't feel I knew enough about the students to "sublease" the dredge work.

When I summed up the opinions, I discovered surprising differences between the children of Denver and New York. New York children seemed to know their minds better than Denver children and were more vigorously opposed to tattlers.

I re-examined the papers. This time, I noticed there were more erasures on the check-off papers than on the free-statement papers. New York children felt their ideas pinched by tight-fitting blanks. Frequently they tried to squeeze in the words *sometimes* and *maybe* in blank spaces big enough only for an X. The erasures came from shifting their opinion from *yes* to *no*.

If I counted each erasure or faintly added word as a *doubt*, the New York children and Denver children matched.

In addition to the baby-sitter problem, I gave the children make-believe situations describing The Boy Who Pointed His Father's Gun, The Boy Who Played with Knives, The Young Shoplifters, The Schoolground Bullies, and The Third-Grader Who Smoked.

The yes-no answers supply dramatic information merely by numbers. An average 90 per cent of the children said they would inform their parents or teachers of each situation. Yet, when finally asked, "Is it nice to tell on somebody? Is it nice to be a tattletale?" 67 per cent of these same children said it was *not* nice to "tell" on anybody and 92 per cent said it was *not* nice to be a tattletale.

But Denver's full-statement papers *explained* the numbers. Many writers confessed the secret agonies of children torn between peers and parents:

No it is not nice and they call you a chicken and they won't let you play with them . . . No because everybody will be mad at me but sometimes I just have to so they won't do it again . . . They would call me a tattle-tale and different names but I will not listen . . . They say you think your a smart-aleck, don't you smarty pants? . . . Well! Some say that they would never speak to me again . . . I'd tell the principle during recess. Then I'd stay home for awhile . . . Well it isn't nice to tell on somebody but if they can damage their body or anyone I would tell . . . It is nice to tell because it will help their body or soul and no in some cases because it might have been an accident . . . No because it is important to tell but it is not very nice to . . . It might not be any of our business . . . You may not have proof . . . Sometimes they have not done anything wrong . . . You aren't being kind . . . You may lose many friends that way . . . Somebody could hurt you . . . They may laugh at you . . . They call you a liar or a fiber . . . a pig a bum and a nut . . . nastyhead . . . snot creep rat fink . . . tattle tail stick your head in the garbage pail . . . finger mouse . . . brat fink dummy . . . looselips . . . no good for nothing . . . little Miss perfect . . .

At the bottom of the fill-in papers, there was one last set of blanks: "I am a . . . . . . boy . . . . . . girl." One boy wrote in "good."

Check-off papers yielded group information faster, I concluded. But the information was only superficially surer.

The fill-in New York papers delivered merely a yes or no fact. The Denver papers gave me factual information but gave me in addition some of the reasons behind the fact. From the fill-in papers I learned that 90 per cent of the children would tell on the baby sitter. But I learned more from Denver's complete statements:

It is wrong to do that in front of little boys or girls. It is not right to drink beer because if they drink too much they could get sick and die . . . Well I think I would tell because when I get old enough to baby sit I would do the same thing and all of these things are against the fifth commandment . . . Because you will disobey your parents and you should not kiss and drink beer until you are 18 years old and drinking should be never.

Denver children were not backed up behind frustrating yes-no outlet nozzles. The information they gave about tattling was positive and revealing. They showed me, for example, that children were often more outraged by the illegality of the sitter's behavior than they were by her moral conduct: "She is taking care of you and not her boy friends. She is getting paid to baby sit not to fool around with boys."

I don't intend to joust here with psychologists as to whether fill-in statements do or don't test comprehension, although I think they don't. My objection is that fill-in, multiple-choice tests steal the opportunity to learn through writing. The hardest thing about writing is connecting the ideas—that is, connecting groups of sentences. Making such ligatures is man's most central act: the making of judgments, the making of decisions.

---

**. . . arrangement and transition are arts which I value much, but which I do not flatter myself that I have attained. . . . I worked hard at altering the arrangement of the first three chapters of the third volume. What labor it is to make a tolerable book, and how little readers know how much trouble the ordering of the parts has cost the writer!—*Samuel Johnson***

---

Writing is a process of unwrapping nouns. Dropping them as unexamined bundles on cobblestone dotted lines is not writing.

Furthermore, the student who reads knowing he has to communicate his knowledge in writing will read in a different way from the reader who doesn't have to deliver any report.

I see a man look at his watch and I ask, "What time is it?" He has to look again. His first reading was for his own benefit. He was *reading without expecting* he would have *to report.*

Suppose he looks at his watch *because* I ask him. He'll say: "It's exactly 5 after 3." Or he'll say: "It's 5 after 3 on my watch, but I dropped it and it may be slow."

Now suppose I ask this same man: "It's 3 o'clock. True or false?" Or suppose I say: "It's 5 before 3, 3 exactly, or 5 after 3. Check one."

Can I be sure he knows and that he's not guessing?

I concede it would test his knowledge if I said, "It's . . . . . . . o'clock. Fill in the blank."

But compare that stiff stublet of information with this answer: "It's 5 after 3—you'll hear the kids coming home from school in another minute."

---

**Undoubtedly one of the chief reasons for the low state of writing in the schools is overuse and misuse of workbooks and short answer tests. . . . [The child] cannot by this process develop systematic habits of composing his thoughts and writing them down clearly and coherently.**—*"Thinking and Writing," Vermont State Department of Education, 1961*

---

Grade-school writing exercise is eight years of practice in drawing underlines and circles, writing the words "True" and "False" or "T" and "F," and the letter "X." I don't mean to say such practice is not getting children ready for high school. In high school, too, they'll get furious workouts underlining and circling and T-F-Xing. Whatever skills they can acquire ahead of time will do them good, but meanwhile the fill-ins steal writing time and writing opportunity and exercise from the child. And this is not petty theft. It is wholesale, day-after-day robbery and vandalism. According to Dr. Dora V. Smith of the National Council of Teachers of English, "For every legitimate piece of composition assigned to average students, there are 20 exercises involving the filling-in of blanks or the mere checking-off of words."

The *In* flow of knowledge in schools runs through reading. The *Out* idea-flow has to be extruded through fill-in, true-false, multiple-choice devices that release a cramped, feeble, and distorted trickle. Fill-in statements are paltry, harmful substitutes for the complete human statement. They may yield some knowledge of a group, but at a high cost: what school administrators may gain in knowledge of the group, teachers lose in knowledge of the individual.

Fill-in writings are an inadequate and injurious replacement for

*123*

complete sentence and paragraph statements because they prevent the development of those intellectual habits which underlie communication. They were designed as tests. Teachers have let them become the voice of the students.

---

I have a little number.
It is right.
I like my number.
Do you like number 28?
Yes... No...
I do like 28.
It is a nice Number.
And I like number 55, too,
and 65 and 72 and 1,000,
too, and 5,555,000,000.
Do you?
Yes... No...

—*Name withheld, 7, second grade, Lunenberg, Vt.*

---

I like Spring. Do you?
Yes... No...
And spring is here.
Aren't you glad?
Yes... No...
I like Spring.
There are birds and flowers
all over the place.
I like birds. Do you?
Yes... No...
There are all kinds of birds.
Yes... No...

—*Name withheld, 7, second grade, Lunenberg, Vt.*

---

# Eleven Reasons Why
## i.t.a. Children Write Earlier,
### Easier, Better, and More

i.t.a. WATCHERS now and then note that their subjects "seem" to write more than children using the traditional alphabet. If they favor i.t.a., they credit the improved alphabet. If they don't favor i.t.a. they credit the teacher, publicity, English public-school influence, or textbook design.

It is no accident that i.t.a. children write earlier, easier, better, and more than Dick & Jane writers. i.t.a. doesn't make magic. In itself it is as inert as the traditional alphabet. If there's any magic in the writing it's made by the teacher and by the child. But i.t.a. lets them make it, the traditional alphabet stops them.

## 1. i.t.a. WRITERS HAVE A LIGHTER, EASIER WORK LOAD

A special committee of elementary English experts reporting to the National Council of Teachers of English drew this picture of a Dick & Jane child struggling to write: "A story he has developed in his imagination may be lost while he struggles to spell a difficult word or to remember how to write a q or an x. Some children who have good ideas for writing become so fatigued with the combination of mental concentration and physical exertion that they end a story weakly rather than put forth the effort required to pull it through to its climax and a smooth conclusion. At such times, the teacher takes over the role of scribe, as the child tells the final portion of his story aloud."

A great part of the Dick & Jane writer's "mental concentration" is required for coping with illogical and inconsistent English spellings. At least part of the writer's "physical exertion" is used in eye-work: *finding* the word he wants to spell, *exactly copying* it, *checking* to see if he has it right.  During this work, his idea is pushing to get out. He may feel frustrated at not being able to go fast enough and this, too, is fatiguing.  Fear of making a mistake is also fatiguing. Finally, boredom is itself tiring and a child is easily bored from writing "I have a red balloon."

The i.t.a. writer doesn't have to search through a book or over a blackboard for any spellings.  He doesn't have to wait for his teacher because he doesn't have to ask her.  He refers to himself, to his own language, to his own sounds.  The i.t.a. writer doesn't tire from eye-copying strain.  The i.t.a. writer never loses a story while he "struggles to spell a difficult word or to remember how to write a q or an x."

i.t.a. children have to struggle with their thoughts just like any other children, but they don't have to fight the medium in order to put their thoughts into writing.

Cora, a six-year-old Bethlehem first-grader, frequently wrote statements six to ten pages long—in the large hand of the beginning writer, about 150 to 200 words each statement.  Cora wrote the following in December 1964, in her third month of i.t.a.:

yesterdæ wee did not gœ tω scωl becaus ʃhe snœ ʃhat fell cuverd aull ʃhe streets and siedwauks.  mee and mie bruʃher wer around sum evergreens.  mie bruʃher mæd sum big piels ov snœ cum doun on us from ʃhe branʧhes ov ʃhe evergreen trees.  ʃhæ wer big wuns, and mie bruʃher caulld ʃhem landslieds.  ʃhæ wer fun tω bee under ʃhe landslied when it fell on us.  when wee cæm intω ʃhe hous wee had tω ʧhænj our clœʃhiŋ.  espeʃhally mie bruʃher, becaus his pants wer very wet when wee got on our drie clœʃhiŋ wee plæd a kwieet gæm insied.

A six-year-old girl using i.t.a. in University City, Missouri, wrote an eighty-page "novel."  A six-year-old girl in Long Island using i.t.a. wrote a thirty-eight-page "play."

Schools that install the new alphabet must provide for more paper in their budget or be forced to use wrapping paper halfway through the year.  When Bethlehem first began i.t.a. with fifteen i.t.a. classes, the i.t.a. classes used more paper in three months than the thirty T.O. classes used in nine.

A **Dick & Jane** Writer, Second Grade:

I like my family very much
and they like me to.
Some times when I come home
I go to the park
acros the street
from my (hoses) (hasus) (hose) house.
—*Matthew, 7, New York City*

An **Italian** Writer, Second Grade:

On Sunday, I asked my father if we could visit my grandparents if the weather was good and he said yes.

We parted at nine, we had breakfast with the grandparents and afterward we rode our bicycles until midday. At midday I ate chicken and small fried potatoes and afterwards I recited some Easter poetry and when I was finished we opened my Easter egg. Oh! What a beautiful surprise: a key holder! Then I rode my bicycle until seven in the evening. At seven I ate tortellini and a pepper with a cooked apple.

Afterward I played with my small brother Giuseppe.
—*Rosella, 7, Brescia*

An **i.t.a.** Writer, First Grade:

giv your rabbit kæœpectæt and pellets and water and carrot and kєєp your rabbit clєєn do your best when thæ ɑr sick you can get them to stæ ɑliev.—*Ruth, 6, Long Island*

## 2. i.t.a. CHILDREN WRITE SOONER

The i.t.a. writer starts in the first grade. The Dick & Jane writer starts in second. The phonics child starts in first grade, too, but several months later than the i.t.a. writer.

The i.t.a. writer may take as little as four to ten weeks to master the forty-four sound-symbols of i.t.a., depending on how good his

127

ear is and how fast he can make connections between his sounds and the i.t.a. characters. Evidence of early writing is presented by i.t.a. children themselves. When first-graders write about autumn leaves and Halloween you know they are writing in October and November.

ie am jumpεεn in lεεvſ. jumpεεn, jumpεεn, jumpεεn in and mie braſhr jumps in tω ie get kuvrd up with lεεvs—*Ruth, 6, Bethlehem, Pa.*

---

**There is no definite time for starting story writing. It just seems to happen. After five weeks one little girl handed me a paper, with this explanation, "We went for a ride yesterday, and I wrote this story about it."**

ie went tω ſhe mωuntæn on sundæ aftr mie dinnεr. ie sau culorſ ov lεεvſ. ie went betwεεn tω mωuntænſ. it woſ fun.

**That did it! Everyone wanted to write!—*Mrs. J. Huber, first-grade teacher, Bethlehem, Pa.***

---

A "**Linguistics Approach**" Writer, Second Grade:

Mother goes to the shop.
Mother gets lots of apples.
Mother cooks the apples.
Mother lets Dan and Pam have one apple.
Dan said, "I like them."
Pam likes the apples.
Dad will pick ten apples.

*—Name and city withheld, 7*

An **Italian** Writer, Second Grade:

My cat has a white coat and dark green eyes and, it has one black paw and one white one, but he is a gourmet.

One time I was on the balcony and the cat went into the kitchen, he jumped onto a chair, and saw the chicken which we were going to have for supper.

He didn't realize it but he turned the plate over and it fell on the floor, he ate the chicken but he left the bones there, and later I went in to see what happened and I saw the cat eating and called my mother because I wanted to get her but didn't succeed.

One time my father went fishing and caught 3 fish one was bigger than the others and my father removed its head because no one liked it, and gave it to the cat thinking that he'd eat it instead he didn't.—*Claudia, 7, Brescia*

An **i.t.a.** Writer, First Grade:

wun dæ a littl boi wɑs mæking his plands. his muther cauld him she sed "ie want yoo too cliem the appl tree and get mee sum appls. poot the appls in ᴛhis basket". soe he took the basket and cliemd the tree. wen hee got too the top. hee sau a bunch ov appls. soe hee cliemd œvr too them. thæ wir neer a telefoen poel. he leend œvr and he acsudently tuᴄht the telufoen wieer and fel ded.—*Deborah, 6, Cleveland*

---

Studies show that phonetics function little or not at all during the first five months of reading instruction. Teaching of phonetics begins to function in the second five months and is of great value in the second and later grades. The implication of this investigation is that phonic instruction may be delayed until the second semester of the first grade or until the child has built a sight vocabulary of 100 to 200 words. The sounds of letters and letter groups should not be introduced until the child has learned to recognize words from configuration clues such as likenesses and differences in beginnings and endings of words. . . .—*Notes to the Teacher*, Phonics Skilltext (*Charles E. Merrill Books, Inc.*)

---

## 3. i.t.a. CHILDREN WRITE MORE BECAUSE THEIR WRITING IS WAITLESS

Dick & Jane writers have to keep asking for spelling help. They raise their hands and the teacher comes to their desks or they tell her the word they want aloud and she writes it on the blackboard. A teacher with twenty-five to thirty children in her class may have fifteen of them asking for help. She can only help one at a time.

A **Phonics** Writer, Second Grade:

> We like spelling with our teacher.
> I like this School.
> I am in junior C.
> I learn many things.
> We are takeing French.
> Its nice in a School with
> people all over the world.
> —*John, 7, New York City*

An **Italian** Writer, Second Grade:

Today I observed my rose plant. It had twelve buds and one flower which was yellow. There were three buds which were beginning to show a bit of their color, which would be red and as for the other nine roses one could see only the petals.

When they are all open I will take a bunch to my teacher, for her to put in a vase in front of the crucifix.

—*Vincenza, 7, Caionvico*

An **i.t.a.** Writer, First Grade:

deer mis c. ie shud bee back in scool bie Friedæ. dω yω hav enee mœr werk for mee tω dω? ie am gettiŋ bettr in "O, N, g" frum John—*Note sent to school in Bethlehem, Pa.*

## 4. i.t.a. CHILDREN LEARN LETTERS ACCORDING TO FREQUENCY OF USE

In the textbooks created by Dr. Harold Tanyzer and Dr. Albert Mazurkiewicz, i.t.a. symbols are taught in the order of frequency of use in English—not a, b, c, etc., but a, n, t, e, b, s, etc. Thus the child is able to write and read his first few words, such as *tan* or *ant*, as soon as he learns a few symbols. It isn't necessary to follow Tanyzer and Mazurkiewicz's a-n-t-e-b-s series. Any early vowel-consonant mix will help produce early writers.

The basal readers and phonics programs don't teach vowel sounds until late first or second grade. Try playing Scrabble without vowels—and don't allow *psst* or *hmmm*.

**A "Linguistics Approach"** Writer, Second Grade:

> Dan's mother has to go
> for apples for Dad.
> Dan can have an apple.
> Pam can have two apples.
> Dan picked the apples off the tree
> for mother for candy.
>
> —*Name and city withheld, 7*

An **Italian** Writer, Second Grade:

In my courtyard there lives a baby named Fausto. And also a small sister named Adele. Fausto calls me Lena, he calls my sister Nana, he calls Carla Lala and he calls Adele Tata. When Fausto sees me he runs into my arms saying "Lena."

Fausto is full of small curls and is a beautiful baby. One day that little rascal wanted to climb on the stairs and I said no, because he would fall. But he wanted to go anyway. When he was on the third step he fell and becan to cry. Then he saw my cousin Angelo and stopped crying. Fausto is so nice!

—*Carlina, 7, Caionvico*

An **i.t.a.** Writer, First Grade:

ie got a nue bæbby. it is a sheε, ie wuntit a heε but wot yω get yω must ceep.— *Nancy, 6, Bethlehem, Pa.*

## 5. i.t.a. CHILDREN ENCODE EARLIER

Reading is decoding, writing is encoding. i.t.a. permits the earliest possible encoding. In the Tanyzer-Mazurkiewicz materials, the i.t.a. child is taught first to distinguish each of the forty or so basic sounds of English speech. As he does, he learns to identify and write the symbol that stands for each of the sounds.

The three steps are repeated with words: the child hears or sees a word, and then writes it; or he hears it, writes it, and then sees it.

**A "Linguistics Approach"** Writer, Second Grade:

> The apples in the box are good.
> Dad picked the apples for Dan.
> Dad picked the apples from the tree.
> You can have apples for dinner.
> Apples are good for you.
> —*Name and city withheld, 7*

An **Italian** Writer, Second Grade:

I had a black cat with a white face and tail.

One day my cat jumped on a tall bench with his two legs too far apart, he fell badly and ripped open his front paw.

One day in Arnaldo place in the garden I saw a blackbird with an orange beak and he was large and had thin, almost reddish legs.

I had a puppy who I used to play with he was a hunting dog and he had a long snout and as soon as I touched my brother he barked and in order to quiet him I gave him sugar.

When I put my goldfinch on my finger he bites me.
> —*Bernardi, 7, Brescia*

An **i.t.a.** Writer, First Grade:

i wanted a hors. but mie muther sed ar yard is too smal and the horss caust to much. i liek horses but if mie muther sed noe. and i ast mie muther agen but ʃhee sed thay mes up the yard too much and i wanted a cat but mie father sed i cud not get the kiten becaus it will scrach—*Denise, 6, Long Island*

## 6. i.t.a. WRITERS PRODUCE MORE
### BECAUSE THEY'RE MORE SELF-CONFIDENT

They have more confidence because they trust their alphabet. They haven't been spell-shocked. They will fearlessly attack the spelling of any new word they feel like using. They believe in i.t.a. because it's honest. It has no false-front letters without any sound to back them up, no promiscuous symbols accommodating transient sounds.

Quick learners dope out the i.t.a. spelling code even before they've learned all forty-four sounds. They can be seen peeking ahead in their sound-symbol books to spell out sounds they want to use but which haven't yet been formally taught. Their confidence speaks for the alphabet's consistency.

---

**The greater regularity of spelling permitted by i.t.a. may give the child an earlier confidence in spelling words he has not yet been taught.**—*Jeanne Chall*, **Learning to Read—The Great Debate**

---

An i.t.a. first-grader couldn't think of the word *cinnamon*. He wrote in mixed alphabets because he was in the "transition" phase: "Thaer wus sumthing that muther cooks wit. wut is that sumthing the sumthing starts wit a es."

i.t.a. children are fully aware their alphabet is different. Many refer to traditional orthography as "the old alphabet" or "the big alphabet" and call i.t.a. "the baby alphabet." Two alphabets give them a special freedom. An i.t.a. child transferring to T.O. will often remark: "What a funny way to spell!"

While switching into the regular alphabet, i.t.a. children soon enough discover that T.O.'s logic and predictability are sometimes whimsical. But, like children who are warned of an Aunt Margaret who is nice but a little nutty, they're prepared to cope with the situation. i.t.a. gives them a reliable tool for coping. Dr. Rebecca Stewart told the National Council of Teachers of English how an i.t.a. graduate adapts himself to a T.O. school world: "What is most gratifying is the interest in spelling—it's strangely wonderful to the youngsters that English is spelled as it is. And every new spelling pattern is an amazing discovery. Structural and phonetic analysis are taught as helps in spelling correctly, not as part of the instructional reading curriculum."

It seldom occurs to the T.O. child to criticize spelling. If he doesn't understand it, he assumes *he* must be at fault, not the book, not the teacher, not the system.

*133*

A **Phonics** Writer, Second Grade:

My name is Margaret ———,
I like every one in my family.
I aspachaley like my grandmother,
she is a rtest,
once my father and my mother
and my brother and I
went to my grandmothers house
and when we got there
my grandmother (shoel) shoed us two paintings
my father (likeb)liked one so moush that he took it,
he (snaucht) snouck it down to the car
and ran (bach) back,
my grandmother (ti) did not evean know it,
in til I toled her.

—*Margaret, 7, New York City*

An **Italian** Writer, Second Grade:

Saturday I took my first communion, I waited the coming of the hour to take Jesus in the consecrated wafer of the host, finally the time came to take Jesus within the wafer, and after an hour and a half, the time to leave came and all of my aunts gave me a kiss, and I said to them: "Stop kissing me."

After a little while I heard: "And you won't give your aunt a kiss"

And I told her: "You'd better come over here, because if i come over there in the midst of all my aunts I'll get buried with kisses"

After all this ended we left for my house.

My cousin said: "Let's eat the pasta"

"Yes"

"After I ate a little bit of it I felt a headache coming, then I said to my mamma: "Mamma would you give me a small piece of bread with prociutto"

"Yes, dear"                    —*Ugo, 7, Brescia*

134

An **i.t.a.** Writer, First Grade:

wen ie went tω scool on mondey ie was blœn bad. my
munεε was blœn awæ. I have a dog. and anuther gust of
wind cæm and blω my dog awæ. My hat blω awæ. yω
can not go swimming tωday in Omona Minasoda ther
havin tornnædose and hurrackæns. ie em going tω bεε
supermæn if a græt big gust of wind cæm. I saw a girl's
dress go up. I onely wor a jacket. I saw a movie cauld the
wisard ov Oz. the hous went up up up.
—*David, 6, Bethlehem, Pa.*

## 7. i.t.a. CHILDREN WRITE WORDS THEY KNOW

i.t.a. writers use familiar words they hear at home and with their
friends. Dick & Jane words are good, practical words, but there
are too few of them. They fall far short of even the slowest child's
speaking vocabulary. i.t.a. writers use a greater variety of words,
including slang, contractions, abbreviations, colloquial expressions,
place names, big words, new words, and invented words:

| | | | |
|---|---|---|---|
| keradεε | hallωsinæʃhun | substitωt teεɥer | dienisors |
| clobberd | cafitεεrεεa | traŋkwilliezer | ukωæryum |

A **Phonics** Writer, Second Grade:

My family.
What a nice family You have today.
This is My family.
How did you get your family.
—*Andrew, 7, New York City*

An **i.t.a.** Writer, First Grade:
mie granmu cæm over on sundæ and wεε had a baull
—*No name, 6, Bethlehem, Pa.*

## 8. i.t.a. WRITERS ARE NOT DRAGGED DOWN BY WORD CONTROLS

Dick & Jane pupils get spelling allowances of two to three
hundred words a year. i.t.a. writers get all their sounds as *lump*

*capital.* Spelling is the capital equipment of written communication. The i.t.a. child is in the word-making business for himself—with no partners.

A Box of **Dick & Jane** Words:

| | | | | |
|---|---|---|---|---|
| farmer | bone | boat | the | I |
| ball | gray | toy | box | this |

A **Dick & Jane** Writer, Second Grade:

> I love my family.
> My family is nice.
> I go to the park
> with my (fa) family.
> I eat dinner with my family.
> I live with my family.
> My family takes me to school.
> —*Bobby, 7, New York City*

A Box of **Phonics** Words:

| | | | | |
|---|---|---|---|---|
| pin | pot | pig | pup | pan | pit |
| pen | pet | peg | pop | pad | pat |

A **Phonics** Writer, Second Grade:

> I like my mother, father,
> sister and my building too.
> My mother is big
> and my father is big.
> On raine days I play
> with my sister.
> She is three years old.
> And she is funny sometimes
> and she likes to think she is a boy.

136

My sister likes to ride in cars.
And I like to ride in cars to.
My father is in the country.
My family goes on Jets sometimes.
We go to England.

*—Jonathan, 7, New York City*

A Box of **i.t.a.** Words:

ferdinand     majellan     ekspeetient
vascœ     balbœa     caraibbeean
santa domiŋgœ     eksploræʃhons
san sabastian     perœ     dærien
accuesd     sentenst

*—From a first-grade history reader*

An **i.t.a.** Writer, First Grade:

I liek summer bee caus wee kan gœ in the wauter end in the summer the tœlups blœm and the dæsies blœm I dœ not liek wun thing a bout summer I dœ not liek the beez and bugs.—*Ellen, 6, Long Island*

## 9. i.t.a. WRITERS USE SENTENCES THAT RUN WITH THEIR SPOKEN INFLECTIONS AND RHYTHMS

The short, evenly cut, severely controlled Dick & Jane sentences don't express the child's normal rhythms, yet by repetition and drill they become his models for writing. Children who imitate Dick & Jane sentence patterns will always write less and worse than children who imitate their own personal speech patterns.

A **Dick & Jane** Writer, Second Grade:

I like my School.
children come from lots of countrys.
We learn lots of langigs we learn French.
a girl comes from Syria.

*137*

our work man is Mr. John I like him.
at School we do lots of things.
—*No name, 7, New York City*

Some **i.t.a.** Writers, First Grade:

ħe lieon haz a ɡroulıŋ vois. it iz pouerfœl noizy.—*Debra, 6, Long Island*

If I hed a $100 ie wœd by me a big big hous and a stæshin wagin. and then I wœd by a billt in swimiŋ pœl. and then I wœd mary a man and wεε wœd get a diviŋ bord. and then. wεε wœd get intœ Pieping Rock club it wœd be fun and I wœd by 3 horsis . . .—*Deirdre, 6, Long Island*

wun dæ wen wee went in a nævee Bote. mee and B.J. and ten men went on it wen it wus midniet wee went to bed. at 1 aclok ħe ɡœst apeerddd on the dek, œ this is harubill sed B.J. this musst Bee a scæree niet sed David. lœd the boulits he ardid. But nuthing hapand. aull wee'd heer is Boo, Boo, Boo. ħe wævs cæm hie-yer and hie-yer. but the sun riesd up and wee ɡot foold. the ɡœst wus jelee fish. the nyoises were the wind. wow that's clœs.—*David, 6, Long Island*

Won ov the things wεε need ar klos [clothes] now wudinnit it be sillie to wak arond bayr? and food if we didint hav food we wud diy.—*Eugene, 6, Long Island*

if i had $100 i wood liek to showt and holler. i wood feell beder. i wood be happy. i wood be good to. i wood gigil i wood laf. i think i kood bie a king size byooteyful. i wood be as bizy as a bee. i wood by a catalak.—*Kenneth, 6, Long Island*

## 10. i.t.a. CHILDREN CAN WRITE ABOUT ANYTHING

i.t.a. writers discuss subjects that interest them. T.O. children are lock-stepped to the subject matter of their readers or to words they can spell.

Some **i.t.a.** Subjects, First Grade:

Friedæ a nue Bæby cæm too the hous. and gess wot it woz! doo you want meε too tell you. It's a nue Bæby grand peyano it is a black tienæ. It is a beεuetifool peyano. It's in a corner. Weε had cumpineε but weε cood not stæ up becaus thæ were mie mothers and fatherz compineε. Thæ wer mie ant and mie unkl. Do you næ what it feεls liek? Weε bin plæing it 1, 012, 134 hourz.—*Alison, 6, Long Island*

My dream was that my mom and dad were marryd but now they are devorsd my mom and dad are good to me.—*Name withheld, 6, Bethlehem, Pa.*

kennedy's deþh    whot doo yoo þhiŋk ov aull þhœs peεpl þhat cill þheεs importend men liek marten looþher kiŋ and nou kennedy? whot has beεcum av þhis buetifel wurld þhat god mæd? a wurld ov cillness? doo yoo wont too stop aull þhis rakkit? trie!—*Cheryl, 6, New York City*

I went too a frends hows. ∫heε ∫hot a arrœ in my mowþh. It hert very moᴅh ∫heε could not gœ to seε þhe Mery popins Moovy.—*No name, 6, Newburgh, N.Y.*

I wonted a cat and dog but I cood not beε cos þhæ wood fiet and þhe kitons wood beε kild riet awæ and I wood not liek þhat at aull beε cos I liek kitons very much. þhe end þhe butiful werld is ars for nothŋ.—*Holly, 6, Long Island*

Mrs E. mæd the clas anser sum kuesjens and she said doo you want all ov the tois in the werld? or hav lots and lots ov ferends? and that is a nother thing she sed she sed wud you liek to have a butiful werld or to hav a new toy?
                                    —*Barbara, 6, Long Island*

If I Had $100. I wold by a $100 car and it wold be a powr stering car and I hœp it drievs εεseε and smooth —*Ruth, 6, Long Island*

wun dæ ʃhær wɑz ɑ witʧh. ʃhɛɛ tɷk ʃhe kiŋs dauter. hɛɛ
sed, "blac niet get miɛ dauter and yɷ can hav ɑ dæ of. if yɷ
dɷ not yɷ wil hev nɶ dæ of."—*Diane, 7, Bethlehem, Pa.*

Some **Italian** Subjects, Second Grade:

Today I observed five swallows in a ray of light.
The mother swallow was in front and her four baby
swallows were behind her. When the mother swallow
was directly in the light she began to sing: "Ci ci"
The babies also started to sing: "Ci ci." The biggest
swallow of the four babies was last and the smallest
one was behind the mother swallow. The mother and
her four baby swallows had feathers on their backs and
tails which were black and on their breasts they had
white feathers.

How nice were these five swallows.—*Vincenza, 7,
Caionvico*

My most beautiful Easter egg was one my grandfather gave to me, it was big, it was covered with paper
that was almost gold with an embroidery of red flowers,
and small red balls. On Sunday when I broke it I
found a terrific game inside, it was a round box and
there was a small ball which you tried to get into a hole,
and I played with it and had fun. We ate right away
and I almost got indigestion.—*Mauro, 7, Milan*

Some **Dick & Jane** Subjects, Second Grade:

My family is verey big.
My family likes me
and I like my family.
My family likes to play with me
and I like to play with my family to.
I have a family
that has a dog and he has a little dog.
I have one litte litte cat.

—*Lisa, 7, New York City*

I go to the —— School,
and there I learn about children
from all over the world,
and we take French
I am in junior C two
my teacher is Miss ——
we lean about many things.
                    —*Timothy, 7, New York City*

## 11. i.t.a. WRITERS CAN WRITE TO COMMUNICATE

Children who write to communicate will always write better and more than children who write merely as a classroom exercise. By its nature Dick & Jane writing in the primary grades is mere drill. It is not designed to help the child communicate himself to his peers or his teacher.

The illegitimate school note is exciting underground communication. It isn't part of the school curriculum. Children discover it by themselves. The child can use it to "talk" to another child without being heard and punished. It is quieter, more private, and less risky than a whisper. He writes it without help because he has to: notes are forbidden. But he doesn't *want* help, either. This is strictly his own private business. He wants to send a meaning to someone. In i.t.a. circles, the child who can't write a note is out of things. In Dick & Jane classes, notes don't usually fly till the fourth grade.

The "letters" that Dick & Jane children produce in the primary grades are really only notes, and they are copied. This is clear from the following instructions to teachers that appear in Book I of *American English* by Burrows, Stauffer, and Vazquez:

Letters are a familiar and much needed form of composition. . . . Increasing steps of difficulty in dictating and copying a letter are:

1. The teacher writes one copy of the letter as the children dictate; each child signs his name.

2. The teacher supplies duplicates of the written letter;

*141*

each child signs his name on his individual copy and illustrates the letter.

3. The teacher duplicates the body of the letter; the child
inserts the date, the salutation, the closing, his signature, and
illustrates the letter.

4. The child copies the entire letter if it is brief (not over
two or three lines of writing).

. . . Some first graders may perform this last step by mid-year,
others not until the end of the year, a few not until second
grade.

Some **i.t.a.** Communications:

> For mie teecher—
> heer
> ie am sick in bed
> sick in bed aull
> sick in bed. aull
> sick with a cold
> with out mie hed.
> sick in a bed
> with a
> hed. is a good
> as good
> as good aull
> sick in a bed.
> sodu and ies
> and evrythiŋ
> nies. that's
> wut ie'm
> taukiŋ
> about. for
> good littl grls
> and good littl
> bois that's wut
> ie'm taukiŋ
> about

> *—No name, 6, Long Island*

deer mis c. ie'm feeliŋ fien. see yω on wensdæ. thank yω
for sendiŋ mie libræree bωk hœm wiþ pattee. ie mis scωl.
sien Donna and yωr nœt woz nies—*Donna, 6, Bethlehem,
Pa.* [Donna had asked her mother how to end the note. Her
mother had said, "Sign 'Donna'—And your note was nice."]

in the Library aull þe peepl ar crieit. If yω ar not crieit
yω bee cict out. yω can't pic a bωk out. in sum bωks
þæ ar wurms hω ar smat. Bee caus þæ reed Books þæ
ar caull Books wurmz in the Library þæ ar found in sum
Books in smat Books.—*David, 6, Long Island*

Sunday it lietnind and it wœk mee up. I was sœ frietand I
ran out ov my bed and cliemd in my father's bed. The
lietniŋ lit the room liek you ternd on wun liet. þe neckst
mornŋ I œver slept. I got up at 8.30 and my moþer wœk
mee up and I wanted tω sleep for 20,000 ours.—*Ellen, 6,
Long Island*

My bruther wok up and then my bruther wœk me up and I
herd the thunder and then My uther bruther came up tω
my room and I herd him and then hee took the bæby and
thrœ her on the flaur and I had tω pick her up and woke
up my muther and shee wok up and I hold her and then
I tolled my muther and shee wok up my father and went
tω my bruther and scœlded him and I pωt my head under
the cuvers and herd it agen.—*Denise, 6, Long Island*

# $3$–THE DICK & JANE
## "COMMUNICATION" COURSE

# The Xerox Generations

~~~~~~~~~~~~~~~~~~~~~~~~~~~~~~~~~~~~~~~~~~~~~~~~~~~~~~~

## DICTATORS IN BERLIN

My Christmas interviews with American children in West Berlin about peace on earth at the Wall ran in the December 1962 issue of *Good Housekeeping*. Geoffrey, eight, of St. Louis led the children with his account of the very first Christmas. Reproduced on the next page is this account in its original version.

Geoffrey's story in his own handwriting was seen by many millions of Americans. *Good Housekeeping* used it as an illustration and it was shown and discussed on NBC's *Today* show. A Munich picture magazine, *Quick*, photographed Geoffrey and published his story in German.

But I have to say my own enthusiasm was halfhearted, since Geoffrey had only *half* written his story. Every word that was printed actually and truly belonged to him. Every word had come from his mouth and mind. Nevertheless, Geoffrey had a co-author. The greater part of his story had been ghost-written, and I was the reluctant ghost.

My concept of how the story should start and end had guided him. I guided by asking questions.

"How did Joseph know the way?"

"There was a big star in the sky."

"What did it look like?"

"It was shining."

"Shining? Like what, Geoffrey?"

"Like a diamond."

"What color was the diamond?"

"Like gold and like silver, like all different colors coming out."

"Such as?"

## 1

There was this lady named Mary.
She mareid a man named Josef.
Then there was an angle Gabreale
He said hale Mary that means
Hello Mary that came down and
told Mary she was going to be
the Mother of Jesus.
That was Realy good news Becous Jesus
would be the King of the
whol world. the people thouht He
would be a King with a Crown
on his head and He would sit on
a chair and give orders and
say you do this and you do that

Josef and Mary had to go
to Bethlehem to pay taxes

## 2.

Becaus, the guviner Herod
the bad guy orderd
it and Becaus there was
no air male. they came to a
place where there was no room
and Josef was pulling the donkey.
and this showd them a little
place called a stayble
and this was where
Jesus was born.
And there was a star in the sky
and Sheperts saw it. the angels in the sky
sang Glory to God on the Highest and
on Erath ipeace to men of good will.
they came to Jesus. and the woo
thout Jesus wold be a King with a
Crown and a chair were wong.

## 3.

Jesus was only a baby.
He was Dress in this white stuff
what do you call it many swadling
bands. Its like cluaths you rape
aroond your self. He was in a manger.
The manger was almost as big as a
cuffy table. there was staw in
the manger. we get staw
from, somethig is shipt from the stayts
to keep it from Baking. three wise men
Brot sacrefises. this means they gave
something that hurts them to give it.
My little Brother Jonathan said
they Brot Gold Frankinstin and murder
But He was only Jokeking. He didint
get baby food.

## 4

The music the angels made was like
Gold Bells, like Church not the
ordenery ones that tell you to
come to Church but a different
way, a funny way with many
many different sonds hi and lo
like a box you wind up, many
Bells. And that music came from
Heven. Mabe the angels sang
like people that sing our cwnyer
at 12:30 Mass but with voises
that or much better. Womens voises
becaus Womens voises sing cleer.
Men cant sing that good unless
they try to sond like a lady.
The Big star outside was shining
like a dimen, like gold and

## 5

like silver, like all different colers
coming out red and blue and oranj und yellow
and green. It sparceld and it looked very
Beatiful. It was like the moon.
It was a happy nite for Josef and Mary
and the Wisemen and the sheperts and
the inkeepers and Everybody.

148

"Red and blue."

"Any other?"

"Orange and yellow."

"Any more, Geoffrey?"

"Green."

Of course, when I transcribed the interviews from tape I left out my questions, and the reader sees the answers without the scaffolding that held them up. He reads: "The Big star outside was shining like a dimen, like gold and like silver, like all different colers coming out red, and blue and oranj and yellow and green."

An elementary-school teacher assured me that I had not invented anything. I had merely discovered the method used in all United States schools. It is called "dictation" by some, the "experience chart" method by most.

Geoffrey's story appears in his own handwriting because after I had typed it out, his mother read it back to him. His creative phonetic spellings were allowed to stand. The metaphors are his own, too. They reflect his alert imagination.

But it had been *my* knowledge of *form* that had guided the story, *my questions* pulling out words that pleased me, *my rhythm* deciding when a sentence needed stretching or when it was finished. These are most important, for whoever owns the story form owns the story, and whoever owns the sentence's rhythm owns the sentence. An adult's rhythm has no more business in a child's prose than Type O blood in a Type A heart.

## DICTATORS IN THE UNITED STATES

At the front of almost every primary-grade classroom in the United States the visitor will see a king-sized tablet hanging from an easel or a page from it tacked to a wall. It's filled with sentences written in a giant hand. It is called the "experience chart." Teachers say that the chart serves them in a variety of ways.

The Bureau of Educational Research in New York published *Experience Charts, A Guide to Their Use in Grades 1-3* (fourth edition, 1960). The *Guide* lists four kinds of experience charts:

1. Creative Language Charts—which have as their main purpose the recording of children's own creative language.

*149*

2. Work Charts—which have as their main purpose the organization and guidance of some of the classroom activities.

3. Narrative Charts—which have as their main purpose some kind of reporting or record keeping of shared experiences of the group.

4. Reading Skills Charts—which have as their main purpose the teaching and practice of some specific reading skill.

I have no fight with the "work" or "reading skills" charts, but the "creative language" and "narrative" charts are evidence of impotence and failure. The i.t.a. writer doesn't need anyone to record his "creative language." The Italian school child has never seen an experience chart.

---

**... Individuals have more to say than they can write themselves.... This need for extended expression often shows up strongly at about the ages of seven to nine.**

**... something special is necessary for imaginative stories. Imagination needs encouragement. Hence it is wise to offer to write down some stories children invent.... You may jot down a story on your note pad as a child tells it to the group. Read it to the class, and tell them that you will write others as you have time to do it. Let the children sign their names for a chance to dictate made-up stories to you.**

**... Sit down somewhat apart from the group so that each story-dictator can feel he is telling his story just to you. Use abbreviations and any type of writing you can do fastest.... If the child gets stuck, read to him what he has dictated. Offer friendly encouragement by question or gesture, but don't tell him what to say. If he goes on too long, tell him you must give someone else a turn to dictate. If a child decides not to finish a story, tell him you will keep it so that he may complete it later if he wishes....—Burrows, Stauffer, and Vazquez, American English, Book 1**

---

Dick & Jane children don't actually write their experiences themselves. They can't. They tell their teacher what they want to say and she does the writing. The children then copy on their own papers what the teacher has written. This method is called *dictation*, but note that it is pupil-to-teacher dictation.

There are three kinds of dictation:

1. The first is the *class-dictated statement*. Guided by the teacher who asks leading questions, the entire class "tells" the teacher what to write on the blackboard. The children then copy "their" blackboard statement.

2. The second is the *individually dictated statement*. A child and the teacher sit apart from the rest of the class, the child talking, the teacher writing down what he says. Later, the child copies what the teacher has written.

3. The third is *fragment-dictation*. The children raise their hands when they want a particular word spelled out for them, and the teacher writes each word on the board. An active class will have her squeezing words on the board and charging back and forth from one side of the room to the other trying to answer all questions.

Gradually, year by year, children are weaned away from copying. When elementary-school educationists say that writing instruction in the primary grades is directed toward independence, they mean the freedom from having to copy—that is, the child is "free" when he has memorized enough little words to assemble his own little sentence "without looking." But in a truer sense no child is free as long as he has to ask his teacher how to spell his words.

---

Young school children cannot record their own "creative thinking." . . .
One teacher, for example, took her class for a walk near the school—"looking for autumn." Among other things they observed the leaves falling from the trees on the school street. The children were given the opportunity to walk through the leaves and to handle them. The children had been especially stimulated by this experience. Since the teacher had been troubled by the lack of spontaneity and the stereotyped responses which she had been getting from the children, she seized upon this stimulating experience to encourage original expression. . . .
Because the teacher felt there would be value in preserving these responses, she made a chart. Although the children could not read it—any more than they could read some of the poems she read to them—a few could identify their contributions, and some at later rereadings did learn to read many of the words. The children were pleased to have their individual responses thus respected, and all participated in the enjoyment of recalling a pleasant experience.—*Experience Charts, A Guide to Their Use in Grades 1–3*

---

Dictation is not necessary in i.t.a. classes, nor do Italian school children dictate statements to their teachers. On the other hand, Italian teachers and i.t.a. teachers can dictate *to* their classes, which is something no first-grade or even second-grade Dick & Jane teacher can do.

Alvina Treut Burrows, Doris C. Jackson, and Dorothy O. Saunders wrote *They All Want to Write* in 1939. The book is in its third edition and is recommended by the National Council of Teachers of English. The authors say their book offers teachers "a detailed, step-by-step description of a balanced writing program." They call dictation the *step between talking and writing independently*. According to cases they describe as "average," the step may take from one to six years or even longer, depending on the child's maturity.

> *3rd grade* ... During the first half of the third grade the children continued storytelling and dictating. ... Near the end of the year, a few of the children began to write stories. ...
> *5th grade* ... the teacher, though sympathetic, was new. ... There was ... less opportunity for the teacher to be the scribe for the children's ideas. ... Although writing cost him [a fifth-grader] great effort, every few days he produced a new story for our enjoyment. At length he persuaded his father to be his scribe, and the stories laboriously written at school were supplemented by those dictated at home.—*They All Want to Write*

> The teacher continues to act as secretary both for cooperative and individual efforts. Few children at this level [second grade] will be able to write independently before the second half of the year. To help those who are unable to write independently, the teacher records for them and the children may copy.
> "*Written Communication in the Elementary School (Tentative)*," *Anne Arundel County Public Schools, Annapolis, Md., 1963*

Some teachers insist that dictation is necessary to show that talk can be transferred to paper and then "heard" by a reader. Surely a child can learn this in one or two dramatic lessons, but dictation continues into the middle grades:

> Children for whom writing is difficult may need this kind of help for *several years*, even after they learn to do some writing for themselves.—*Ruth G. Strickland in an article in* Elementary English, *February 1965*

---

**Before the end of the first year, children were dictating all kinds of stories and eventually wrote for themselves such stories of personal experiences as the following with as much help in spelling as they requested:**

> **Tip is a collie.**
> **Tip is black and white.**
> **Tip is not my dog.**
> **But we have fun.**

**—*The Commission on the English Curriculum*, Vol. 2**

---

# The Eight Wrongs of Dictation

ℓℓℓℓℓℓℓℓℓℓℓℓℓℓℓℓℓℓℓℓℓℓℓℓℓℓℓℓℓℓℓℓℓℓℓℓℓℓℓℓℓℓℓℓℓℓℓℓℓℓℓℓℓ

**Pupil-to-teacher dictation is not writing instruction. As far as writing is concerned, it is anti-instruction.**

## WRONG 1: DICTATION FAKES WRITING

Teachers will tell you, "My children can write." They are sincere. They mean it. But what they mean is that their children can hold a pencil and draw words in a straight, legible line. They can copy. In the sense that I'm talking about, their children can't write. They can't communicate.

My first objection to child-to-teacher dictation is that it is called "writing."

I concede that dictation exercises certain skills. It exercises talking before a group. It gives a child practice in correct pronunciation and clear enunciation. It exercises exact copying. It exercises handwriting.

All of these are important skills, but they do not constitute writing exercises. Taken separately they don't, taken together as dictation they still don't.

Dictation may also exercise "opening channels of imagination," as some say. It may exercise "confidence and joy in invention." It may exercise meaningful "sharing." Class dictation may exercise "cooperation with one's peers in formulating meaningful expression." Group writing may help group "morale." All these benefits are claimed for it.

I don't say they aren't important benefits. I merely insist they shouldn't be called *writing* instruction. There is no substitute for the exercise of writing. The only exercise is the act of writing itself.

In the fall of 1962 a group of second-grade teachers in Indiana attempted to teach written composition by means of a wood board and a set of words on cards. Their experiment involved the use of 60,000 small word cards and 100 wood boards, each of which was slotted with nine grooves. The children used the boards as composing trays for their ideas. First they hunted for a word they might use, and then slid it into a groove. They used blank cards when they could not find the words they wanted. The children assembled "stories" on their desks and then slid the composed sentences into their grooved boards.

The teachers considered their experiment successful. Children who used the boards "wrote" longer "stories" and more "stories" than children who did not.

This was a serious endeavor and I don't want to ridicule it because at least these teachers were not using all their time trying to teach reading. But writing is learned by writing, not by shifting preprinted cards on a slotted board.

Writing in its first movement is learning to make paper "echo" the sounds of talk, the sounds of screamed words, whispered words. It is learning to make *my* sounds, my hometown talk, my dialect, my accent, even my lisp.

To write, a child must look into himself and see what he thinks, define his feelings, and then find words for these ideas and feelings. He must use his own words, those he uses when he talks. He must find these words and their spellings in his mind, not in a book or on an experience chart. He must copy them from his mind, not from the blackboard. He must make this abstraction himself or he isn't learning to write. After finding his words, he must be able to cross over *by himself alone* into symbolization. The crossover of a thought from mind to paper is an utterly lonely passage, and no amount of tender loving handholding care will make it less so. There is no alternate route for this passage.

Proper writing instruction is learning to make bridge words, bringing mind together with mind. It is learning to make metaphors, to ferry ideas on the backs of commonly shared experiences. It is

155

learning the unique powers of each, the one severely exact, the other tolerant and accommodating. It is learning to think on paper. It is learning to express the self and to communicate that self to others.

All these skills are exercised in speech, but there are special hazards and impediments to bringing them to paper. Writing, therefore, needs its own practice time. If we give talking and copying the name of writing instruction, we rob true writing instruction of its own private hour.

## WRONG 2: TALKING IS NOT WRITING

Writing is an extension of talk, and the sound and beat of spoken language should course through it. The story writer learns from the storyteller, the news writer from the town crier.

Dictation may be of some help in developing a storytelling habit of mind, but I doubt it. Storytelling skills are better developed in other ways, and they should not be attempted under the guise of writing instruction or at the expense of the writing habit.

The writing habit of mind is not the same as the talking habit of mind. Writers have stories they'll never write because they've talked them too often. The stories got into a cocktail-party talk track and never got out. If talked onto tape and then transcribed they might still be wrenched into print, but as of now they have never been on paper. There is a common illusion among would-be writers that merely *thinking* or *telling* stories and *wanting* to write makes them actual writers. It doesn't. Only a writer who writes is a writer.

## WRONG 3: COPYING IS NOT WRITING

The copyist matches visual patterns. He makes sure *this* looks like *this*. *A* like *A*, *ape* like *ape*, *ZRL* like *ZRL*.

The copyist does not *hear* what he copies. He may not feel or understand it, either. He copies shapes, mute husks of words.

A good typist can copy Turkish or Danish quite rapidly without knowing these languages. She can copy engineering reports or legal documents while listening to music, even while listening to the news. There's an academic joke as old as *Gaudeamus igitur* that defines the lecture system as the notes of the professor becoming the notes of the student without passing through the minds of either.

Dr. Donald Mintz, Assistant Professor in the Department of Psychology at City College of New York, has taught pigeons that if they peck at buttons in a certain order they will release a kernel of corn from a nearby chute and feed themselves. The pigeons learn the sequence visually. A smart pigeon can get more to eat in Dr. Mintz's Automat than he could following a garbage truck. If Dr. Mintz labels his buttons C-O-R-N, can we say he's giving his pigeons writing instruction?

The copier shuffles words about less as pieces of sounds than pieces of scenery. The child may become quite skillful at picking up word cards and arranging them in proper sequence. This may possibly exercise logic, but unless he's being trained to hang the film attractions on movie marquees (a job, by the way, that doesn't require literacy), he's not getting ready to communicate with society.

When the Dick & Jane child has memorized enough words, he will start memorizing whole sentences. These models, while they alienate him from his own expression, stencil his memory.

Repeated reliance on copying over a long period of time reinforces the eye-dependency already acquired by the inconsistent spellings of English. The memory for English spelling is deeply tracked from eye to hand, bypassing the ear. The "good writers" in the early grades are those who have memorized the most words, sentences, and paragraph models and are most skillful at shifting them around. Meanwhile, they are foreigners to their own language.

WRONG 4: DICTATION CREATES DEPENDENCIES

Telling a child who dictates and copies that he's writing is like hooking up a plastic toy steering wheel in the family car and letting the child behind it believe he's driving.

There is a more ominous comparison with driving. According to a study sponsored by the AAA Foundation for Traffic Safety and the U.S. Public Health Service, a significant number of persons learning to drive in cars equipped with dual controls tend to rely on their instructors to brake the car for them.  Dr. William G. Anderson, Assistant Professor of Education, who conducted this research project for Columbia Teachers College, believes that a learner kept too long on dual controls won't gain the confidence necessary to drive alone.

Dictation develops a variety of dependency habits.  The child who gets used to dictation is book-dependent and teacher-dependent for his spelling, his language, his outline or pattern.  He needs her *assurance*.  He is intellectually dependent and emotionally dependent.

**Children write with confidence as they know the teacher is at hand, ready to assist with the spelling of words, formation of letters, and placement of the content on the paper.**—*Course of Study, City Schools of Los Angeles*

WRONG 5: THE TEACHER AS CENSOR

A young child's paper is usually messy-looking.  Curled shavings, chips, and splinters of symbols litter the paper on all sides of his words.  There are smudges where he has swept some up.  His paper looks like a workshop, which is what it is, I suppose.  He's been hewing words out of paper.  Some children are tidy, but generally when a paper is neat and all the letters are orderly and clear, we can suspect T.P.—Teacher Presence.

If your family talks a lot and your child has learned to talk with it, and if your child's speech is fresh and colorful and yet comes home on paper looking scoured, pale, and mild, sounding a lot like Dick & Jane, two things are happening to him in school: first, he's being extruded through the controlled-word lists; second, he's dictating to his teacher.

Last sater-day I got the chikin-pocs. the ferst wun I sau wus on mie hand. And it itct. And I wutid too skrach it but then wen I wood skrach it then wen I wood skrach anuth plæs it wood ich thær. I stæd home for a hole week.—*Alison, 6, first grade, Long Island*

158

wot hapans iʃ ʃhat mie dog mæks ɑ mes. ʃhe dog tikls on it. so wεε spaŋk her. ʃhεε dus it sum mor so wee puut ʃhe dog in ʃhe bathroom. hεε dus not doo ant meses. ʃhen wee puut her in mommy's room. ʃhen shee sleeps under ʃhe bed, , , , gud bie.—*David, 6, first grade, Long Island*

---

While a class is dictating, the teacher doesn't stand flat-footed and blank. Her face is oooohing, ahhhing, and oh-nooooing like the heroine's face in the old silents. She is a choir director, a cheerleader, a guide, a personal secretary, an editor, a censor. She has to have the sense of timing of a professional fund raiser who knows exactly when to ask for money.

Usually a teacher interferes knowingly, but often she herself isn't aware of what she's doing. Children's verse meters seldom count out properly unless they echo street games or nursery rhymes. A rounded verse cleanly ended means T.P. When young children write verses that look tidy like Housman's or raggedy like Dylan Thomas', ask the teacher who her favorite poets are. Bet on this: she will tell you her favorites are Housman or Thomas.

An ex-Dick & Jane teacher in Long Island told me that in her first year of using i.t.a. she had been afraid of the transition period. It hadn't helped her to be told that thousands of other children had already successfully crossed over from i.t.a. to T.O. She was afraid her class would be different and fail. As it turned out, the class succeeded in making the transition without trouble. She was surprised, however, that when her children began writing in T.O. they wrote Dick & Jane sentences. This was strange because her children had never seen a basal reader and their writing in i.t.a. had always been personal and free-styled.

What had happened was that in her desire to help the children pass from i.t.a. to T.O. she herself had regressed to using dictation and the experience chart. The Dick & Jane sentences had unconsciously come from her. She was much more confident in her second year of teaching i.t.a. and her children made their transition without any change in their writing style. They were as free in T.O. as they had been in i.t.a.

The account below is a class-dictated version of a fire experienced by first-graders in the Rosemont School in Bethlehem. The teacher wrote it on the blackboard in i.t.a.

### an eksietiŋ emerjensy!

when wee cæm intoo scool ᴣhis morniŋ, wee smelld sumᴣhiŋ burniŋ. ᴣhe janitor caulld ᴣhe fier department. wee sau sum fier-enjins outsied. wee sau poleesmen, ᴣhe fier-cheef, ᴣhe ambuelans, and ᴣhe hook-and-ladder, too. ᴣhen missis h. toeld us too get our raps. a bell raŋ, and ᴣhe poleesman sed, "goe hoem!" when wee cæm back too scool, ᴣhe teecher sed wee wer very good in ᴣhis eemerjensy.

Teacher Presence is obvious in this composition. You see it in the title, in the outline, in the orderly sequence of events, in the proportion given to all involved. The account is unexcited. Its pace is calmly adult, like that of a tourist guide. The approving pat at the end is an adult touch.

I don't say any of the individual children's accounts of the same fire, which follow, are better than the class paper. Rather, I mean to stress that each child's paper stands for the child who wrote it. The class-dictated paper stands for the teacher.

ᴣhær wos smoek in scool and ᴣhe fier-enjins lookt for ᴣhe smoek in aull ᴣhe plæs. ᴣhe smoek wos in missis ruᴣh's class on ᴣhe steps. ᴣhe fier-enjin sau ᴣhe smoek and hee caulld ᴣhe uᴣher man. and ᴣhe man took wauter and poot ᴣhe wauter on ᴣhe smoek. ᴣhen ᴣhe smoek went awæ and ᴣhe fiermen went hoem.—*Joseph, 6*

wun dæ in scool wee smelld sumᴣhiŋ burniŋ, and wee caulld ᴣhe fier department. and ᴣhe hook-and-ladder truck cæm and ᴣhe polees cæm and ᴣhe cheef's car cæm. and ᴣhæ toeld us too get our raps and leev ᴣhem bie our desk. ᴣhen ᴣhæ sed poot ᴣhem on and goe stræt hoem and doen't fool aroud.
—*Carol, 6*

in beþlehem, þær iʒ a scool næmd roeʒmont. and at
scool, þe scool smelld terribly. soe wee desieded too goe hoem.
and þe teeçherʒ desieded too wær ær masks. and þe fiermen
had ær masks, too. and þæ found þe anser too þe problem.
it woʒ a liet, woʒ þe anser. soe þæ poot in a nue liet, and
roed in þær fier-truck, back hoem too þe fier-stæʃhon, and
wee livd happily agæn.—*David, 6*

it stiŋks. it woʒ hot in scool. it woʒ eksietiŋ!—*Denise, 6*

Dictation allows the teacher too much power over the child's
expression. If a child asks his teacher how to spell an unusual word,
and if the teacher praises it, the same word will at once appear on
ten other papers. If the teacher is wise and experienced, all is well.
But what if she is neurotically corrective? What damage will she
do or allow the class to do against the child's expression?

Burrows, Stauffer, and Vazquez give teachers using *American
English*, Book I, this advice for handling a problem:

### Correction of Gross Error in Dictation

What should you do if a child says, "They was all alike," or
"My dog ain't no trick dog"? . . . Simply write "They were all
alike" or "My dog isn't a trick dog."

What would Burrows, Stauffer, and Vazquez advise if a child
commits a Gross *Social* Error in Dictation? What if the six-year-old
Bethlehem girl who wrote the statement below had *dictated* it?

a man iʒ tækiŋ a picçhoor of wun of þe girlʒ. þe room iʒ
væry hot. sum of þe çhildren ar swetiŋ beecauz þe lietz
ar hot. þe men ar swetiŋ too. a lot of men were þær
it wuʒ fun.

Should the teacher change "sweating" to *perspiring*? (The situation
makes me think of Stan Freberg's radio censor who forced him to
sing "Old Man River" as "Elderly Man River.")

A teacher is bound to influence, affect, and alter a child's dictated
statement. She has to think of the rest of the class. She has to
*socialize* the individual statement. She can't afford to let a child

just blurt out anything that comes to his mind. But, then, is she teaching that child, or is she using the child to teach the class?

---

wun dæ mie bæbby brien pʊt his hand in his hot creem ov weet and it birnd tʊ lærs ov scin. then ie went tʊ scʊl. ie tœld mie tee╷her. ∫hɛɛ œlmœst fænted. wen ie tœld her. ∫hɛɛ tœld mɛɛ not tʊ mæc a story about it but ie did it on tʊsdæ. on wesdæ mie daddy wus læt ov picking mɛɛ up bɛɛcaus thæ tʊk brien in tʊ the docters plæs. and they pickt up grama—*Nancy, 6, first grade, Bethlehem, Pa.*

---

It's amusing but sad too that even teachers who believe noise is a part of life and should therefore be a part of the classroom, who make a big fuss over free seating arrangements, who permit free talk and play, who revolt against a syllabus, who will not abide by a time schedule, will still nevertheless see nothing wrong in dictation.

## WRONG 6: THE TEACHER AS GHOST-WRITER

Dictation is an act of subtle literary disfranchisement. Teachers will deny it, but they steal stories. They can't help it. They can't keep their hands off.

No teacher takes down exactly what the child dictates to her. It doesn't really matter in the beginning, I suppose. The child can't read it anyway. Only some heroic compulsion could capture all the faltering hemidemisemiquaverings of a shy child's statement complete with its and-uhhs, uhs, and ammms, its changes.

The teacher is not a tape recorder. She does not have the ear of a tape recorder, nor its memory, nor its fidelity of reproduction. She is not impartial like a tape recorder. She doesn't have its patience. She can show love, too. It can be fun for a child to make her show appreciation, surprise, and excitement. That is why we have her: she is *not* a machine. She is teaching, and therefore she tends to *subtract* small grammatical blemishes, speech flaws, and socially unacceptable words. She is creative, and therefore she tends to *add*. Without being aware of it herself, she changes a word, tips a phrase ever so slightly to suit her own sense of verbal balance, and right there where she does it the child is bumped out of his own statement. She will impose *her* knowledge of grammar, *her* knowledge of what is wrong and right about a statement. *She* knows how a statement ought to begin and when it ought to end. She doesn't like to leave a statement hanging, but neither can she bear to let a good statement drag on after its point has been made. *She* decides when a story is finished.

Most invasive of all, the teacher's rhythm possesses the statement. She steals the writer's signature, his own rhythm and pulse, and therefore his heart. If the teacher controls and contributes to the language, the rhythm, the form of the statement, and if she also writes it out, who is the author? She is certainly part author.

---

**Keep dictated stories in folders for later reading and re-reading. This treasuring of children's stories offers incentive for writing in later grades when the pupils become more independent.—American English,** *Book 1*

---

The writer is an *author* if he originates his own statement and delivers it to paper. If he signs his name to something copied, he assumes *author*-ity. He possesses genuine authority if he is both father and mother of his word. In dictation, the written word is fathered by the child and mothered by the teacher.

A clever teacher can make it appear her class is producing clever "creative writings" by the way she words her questions. I found out while interviewing children in Berlin that if I asked a child: "Who *put up* the first Christmas tree?" he didn't know what to answer. But if I asked: "Who *chopped down* the first Christmas tree?" three of ten children blurted out "George Washington."

A painter may choose to work from a photograph or another painting, but to be an authentic painter he must be able to abstract his subject from its three-dimensional condition in time and transfer it to his timeless two-dimensional canvas. In the same way, the authentic writer converts his own language to visual symbols. The sound-for-sound exchange takes place in his mind. It is this act, when repeated, that establishes the writing habit. The writer makes fingers and touch conduct his expression. When the habit is deeply etched, the fingers respond to anticipated speech. Some writers feel

*163*

they must hold a pencil to help them think. A clear, broad sheet of good paper can evoke the wish to write.

In dictation, the child's sound-for-symbol exchange takes place in the teacher's body. This is unfortunate, for the child is thereby deprived of authorship. If dictation continues for too long a time, the writing habit itself is short-circuited. Three other habits take its place: talking, copying, and the willingness to be ghost-written.

---

**Boy dictates: "I shot a rhinoceros."**
**Teacher writes on the board: "I shot a rat."**
**("Rhinoceros" isn't a Core Vocabulary word.)**
**Boy: "No. I shot a longer word than that!"**

---

## WRONG 7: DICTATION IS UNFAIR

Dictation isn't fair. By intent it is selective, because if a teacher has twenty-five children in her class somebody's words have to be left out. The prolific "writer" by this method is somebody who gets more than one word published on the blackboard.

Dictation discourages a hearing of the slow, the shy, the inhibited at one extreme, and the very articulate, the bold, the uninhibited at the other. Free self-expressive writing gives every child a chance to put down what's on his mind.

---

Obviously, the teacher cannot record all the statements made by six or seven-year olds about even as simple an experience as looking out of the window.... Selection is often difficult ... there are exceptional times when it may be wiser to highlight some shy child's statement even though his observation may seem quite commonplace.... Let the children sign their names for a chance to dictate made-up stories to you....—*Notes to Teacher*, American English, *Book 1*

---

Some children must find dictation an agony. Everybody turns around and looks. There's a boy wrinkling his nose. There's one showing his teeth. A pointed tongue sticking out. Grinning. Laughing. Even just stares can keep some children from trying. What if everybody laughs? It's ironic that two of the finest qualifications a writer can have, namely, imagination and sensitivity to others, often work against the child and prevent him from learning to write.

If dictation discourages the shy, it suppresses the articulate. Some children talk so freely they could easily dominate the class and use up all the teacher's time.

---

**If he goes on too long [dictating], tell him you must give someone else a turn to dictate. . . .—*Notes to Teacher*, American English, *Book 1***

---

The talkative child has to queue up with slower children so all can have a chance. That's fair in a social sense, but is it fair education for that child? Advanced readers are no great problem. They're given advanced books. But what about advanced talkers? Their only escape in class can be writing. Six-year-old i.t.a. children have been reported writing twenty to forty pages at one sitting.

Alison, six, of Mrs. Ethel Ernst's first-grade class in Locust Valley, Long Island, wrote the following story in one sitting:

### At the Farm

wuns ᛚhær wuꞅ ɑ bɵi næmd Bill. hee wuꞅ ɑ veree beræv bɵi. sœ evereebodee cold him bræv bɵi. hee lieked tꙍ ꬲæꞅ the ꬲik-enꞅ in the cꙍp beecoꞅ it wuꞅ big. Farm bɵi Bill lieked tꙍ gœ in the sielœ. hee lieked tꙍ tæk the fꙍd tꙍ the Anamlꞅ. hee lieked tꙍ tæk the fꙍd in ɑ weelbaræ and best ov aull hee lieked tꙍ hav the bigest piꬲ fork yꙍ ever sau tꙍ tæk the fꙍd tꙍ the animalꞅ. hee had anamlꞅ that cꙍd mꙍꙍꙍꙍꙍꙍ and baaaaaa but best ov all 1 niet hee dereemd ov farm animalꞅ and ɑ casl. and this wuꞅ in eejept. ᛚhær wuꞅ ɑ beeꙍtufꙍl gœld hors that had wiet wiꬾꞅ and the hœl land had 1 farm. it cuverd the hœl land from hed tꙍ tœ. on ᛚhis beeꙍtufꙍl peeꞅ ov land thær wuꞅ ɑ casl for Bill tꙍ liv in and reemember this wuꞅ in eejupt sœ hee had ɑ diemend croun and it wuꞅ fꙍl ov diemenꞅ and silver and gœld but wun dæ ɑ mesinjer cæm tꙍ the casl hee sed "yor couꞅ ar runiꬾ ʃhort ov millk and the best ꬲicenꞅ ar runiꬾ ʃhort ov the best meet and the pigꞅ ar runiꬾ ʃhort ov thær dliʃhus hot dogꞅ and the steerꞅ ar runiꬾ ʃhort ov the gꙍd

*165*

stæks that thæ gæv us and yɷ nɷ wuts hapunıŋ? yor crɷn
ıʂ ternıŋ in tɷ ɑ winter hat and yor cɷt ıʂ ternıŋ in tɷ ɑ
winter cɷt. well Bill sed ie θiŋk the ɑmarɑcinʂ ɑr tellıŋ
mɛɛ its winter thær. well! hɛɛ livd sæf for 23 ywhrʂ but
wen hɛɛ wuʂ havıŋ ɑ birthday for 23 hɛɛ sudenlɛɛ herd sum
horʂ hɷfs cumıŋ dɷn the rɷd. hɛɛ ran tɷ the dor hɛɛ ran
bakc tɷ hiʂ fother the kiŋ hiʂ fother noded hiʂ hed and
hiʂ fother caulld the dor men the dor men held the dor and!
ɑ luvlɛɛ lædɛɛ stept in the dor. ʃhɛɛ cert sɛɛd tɷ the prins
græsfuɷlɛɛ and the prins bɷd tɷ the luvlɛɛ lædɛɛ. the
prins waukt ɷever tɷ the luvlɛɛ lædɛɛ. thæ taukt for ɑ minit
then thæ seporæted the kiŋ noded hiʂ hed and thæ all went
up stærʂ. thær wuʂ ɑ nether rɷler dɷn stærʂ hɛɛ rɷld the
pɛɛpl until it wuʂ tiem tɷ gɷ. thæ taukt for ɑ haf ov an our
the kiŋ ast the lædy if ʃhɛɛ cærd tɷ marry the yuŋ prinsɷ but!
frst yɷ hav tɷ tell mɛɛ yor næm ʃhʃhʃhʃhʃhʃhʃhʃh mie
næm ıʂ clɛɛɷptru. wɷ!!!!! the kiŋ wuʂ sɷ supriɛʂd that
hɛɛ sed ie herd ov that næm meny! meny! meny! tiemʂ!
ie θiŋk mie prins ʃhɷd mary yɷ! well! ʃhɛɛ wuʂ sɷ happy
that ʃhɛɛ ran dɷn the stærʂ and ʃhɛɛ wuʂ gɷeıŋ tɷ tell the
drievr and the dor men ʃhɛɛ tɷld them and thæ wer sɷ
happy tɷ and sɷ the neks dæ thæ wer marryd and thæ livd
happule ever after the end sɷ wen hɛɛ wɷk up hiʂ muther
wuʂ thær smielıŋ and ʃhɛɛ sed "it wuʂ just ɑ derɛɛm"

the end

## WRONG 8: COPYING AND CHEATING

It shouldn't be thought that dictation and copying are easy for a
child. Copying is tedious, exacting work. It has to be learned.

Children copy from the blackboard, from picture dictionaries,
from picture reference books. They "build" their vocabulary
through copying. They copy adult hand-me-down clichés and
phrases when they want to write like an adult. Instead of writing
their own full statements, they learn to circle or underline somebody
else's writing, or they fill in an *X* or *T* or *F*, or at most they fill in a
word. They never learn to put their own authentic sound on paper.

They never learned that a sentence construction is owned by the one who writes it or that word *arrangements* are an author's private property. Writing for them is a cold, impersonal object. It's only marked-up paper.

---

**. . . Prose consists less and less of *words* chosen for the sake of their meaning, and more and more of phrases tacked together like the sections of a prefabricated henhouse. . . .—*George Orwell***

---

Can instructors who require these prolonged copying exercises be exactly sure they are not developing an unconscious habit of plagiarizing? I believe the opposite is true—we teach children to plagiarize.

## TO SUM UP . . .

The Dick & Jane pupil starts spelling at the age of seven, called by some, ironically, "the age of reason." He can't communicate in writing because he can't spell his talk. His words are metered out to him in measured, year-by-year portions. His expression is limited to words he has visually memorized. He's dependent on his teacher and on workbook forms. He cannot write without them.

In contradiction to its promised goals of "independence," current writing instruction develops such habits of dependency that the pupil, when finally left to himself, cannot write or does not want to.

Almost everyone unfamiliar with i.t.a. worries about the child's *transition* period—will he be able to come back out of the augmented alphabet and use our normal, everyday ABCs? Some unfriendly critics protest against "unlearning" i.t.a.

But it must be a time of hair-raising terror for some Dick & Jane children, that moment in fifth or sixth grade when an examination paper demands a ten- or eleven-year-old's own words. Here is a dead-serious blank sheet of paper that will measure his achievement, determine his grade, and decide his degree of success. He was taught to depend on his teacher. He got used to copying. He got used to filling in tiny blanks with X's, check marks, or yes or no.

He must fumble over this glaring blank paper now and wonder what his own words are.

Do any educationists worry about *this* transition?

Dictation is proof of the primary-grade child's inability to write and cause of the middle-grade child's inability to write. The months and years of dictation and the copying habit, and the dependencies they form—all these prevent the child from daring to commit himself on paper. They make a writing habit of mind impossible.

Do educationists ever worry about "unlearning" *these* dependencies?

THIS IS MAN'S oldest act of ownership: dragging a pointed stick over the soil—the farmer's writing, *geo-graphy*. It was how man possessed land, how man still possesses any object—by gouging his mark on it, the sign for his name.

The child first beginning to write is close to primitive man. He plows paper and roots his thoughts in it. At first he lays in simple sounds, then words, then sentences, then acres and acres of sentences. A written paper is a plot of invisible plantings which will grow in a reader.

Thinking, which is the act of seeding, must accompany handwriting. The child who copies merely transplants what the teacher has grown.

---

**The individual shall have as much justice meted out to him as he is able to mete to himself. An American shall not be treated as an infant, and have good laws without making them. He shall make his own laws, and if they are not good ones he shall smart for it until he learns how to make good ones. Better not so cheap, better not so wisely governed, provided the people be self-governed. Monarchies are doubtless cheaper, doubtless not so corrupt, as republics; but the great end of all government is the elevation of mere individuals to the dignity of self-directive *persons*; the concentration of the realized products of *all* in *each*. Hence the self-determination of the individual is the object of all government. No doubt an infant can be carried in the arms of a nurse more gracefully and with greater economy of time, but we prefer that he should learn to walk by himself.—*William Torre Harris, from the 15th Annual Report of the Board of Directors of the St. Louis Public Schools***

---

# Disguise-Words That Mask
## Nonwriters

How ARE CHILDREN taught to write? What system have we designed to teach children the communication skills so important to them in school and later in life?

Before we peek into some of the textbooks and guides responsible for teaching communication, it might be helpful to comment on their terminology. Textbooks, curriculum guides, teachers, and educationists all talk about how children write stories, poems, plays, book reports, biographies and autobiographies, diaries, business letters, and even TV scripts. You may be misled into thinking a lot is happening. The truth is that the terms are badly abused, not because their abusers are dishonest or ignorant but because they are charged with teaching a complete variety of communication forms to children who can't spell out their speech.

In the vocabulary of elementary education, the term "write" may mean telling or narrating, copying from the blackboard or from a book, or filling blanks in a workbook. According to the Commission on the English Curriculum, it may mean handwriting: "Toward the end of third grade, some pupils have been encouraged to judge writing by means of standard scales. They may even use diagnostic materials to determine the success with which they form their letters, space them clearly, keep accurately on the line, and (where cursive writing has replaced manuscript) remain consistent in slanting them."

Note how the Commission on the English Curriculum uses the words "independence" and "independent writing" in the following statement. It is typical usage in elementary English instruction.

As the child gains in ability, he is encouraged to write independently, turning to the teacher for any help he needs with placement on paper, handwriting, or spelling words. . . .

The children were able to write more independently as they improved in handwriting and spelling skills. They began to group themselves into committees of twos and threes to write a make-believe story, to record group experiences, or to compile stories already written. . . . This method of working together became popular after the children were told that it was called "collaborating." . . .

When children in the late first or in the second grade are doing simple independent writing, they can help themselves if picture dictionaries, packets of words related to a topic, and the like, are available for ready reference. Or, the child may start to write the word, leaving space for its completion until the teacher can give him the personal help he needs. . . .

*—Freedom and Discipline in English, 1965*

---

*A Brief Glossary of Grade-School Disguise-Words*

"Write"—1) Handwrite
      2) Tell or narrate, talk
      3) Copy from the blackboard or from a book
      4) Fill in blanks in a workbook

"Free Writing"—
      1) Copying from the blackboard or chart, but not from a book
      2) Copying one's own idea told to the teacher, who has written it on the blackboard
      3) Filling in bigger-than-usual blanks in a workbook
      4) Writing with the teacher nearby to be ready to help with spelling

"Independent Writing"—See "Free Writing"

"Creative Writing"—Any writing at all; see "Story"

"Story"— 1) A sentence (copied)
      2) A sentence fragment, copied or written from memory
      3) Any account of any incident
      4) Any writing at all

"Language Arts"—Reading instruction

"English"—Reading instruction

### Helping Daddy

John wrote a story about helping his daddy.
Read the story to yourself.

## Helping Daddy

Daddy cuts the lawn and
I help rake the leaves and
then we sweep up the grass.

John used too many words in his story.
Find the words he should not have used.

How many sentences did John use?
How many sentences should he have used?

Read the story again without using the and's.


TO DO BY YOURSELF

1. Copy the story that John wrote.
   Be sure to leave out the and's.
2. Now, write one sentence telling
   how you help your daddy.
   Begin your sentence this way.

## I help Daddy

—*Wolfe and Dorsey*, English, Your Language, *Book 2*

What is independence? A child walks independently when he walks without support. A child who depends on a picture dictionary, word packets, and all those helps concealed by the phrase "and the like" is no more independent that a standing six-month-old baby.

What is communication? The Tyler, Texas, curriculum guide tells second-grade teachers how to teach "communication":

Practice communicating with others
through writing

1. Issue a written invitation to classmates to attend a real or imaginary social function; be sure to tell what the event will be and when and where it will take place.

2. Eliminate unnecessary *and*'s and use correct punctuation and capitalization in paragraphs which contain run-on sentences.

3. Write and illustrate stories, poems, and rules concerning safety in summer activities.

4. Memorize poems about summer safety.

5. Use correct English in booklets of other subject areas.

Do the guide authors know what communication means? Only the first of the five ways can be considered communication practice. Surely the authors must know that memorizing poems is not such practice. Their third point is impossible unless "write" means copy—which it does, but copying communication is not communicating. Number five does not even communicate its own meaning clearly.

The very term "writing instruction" is false. Much of what is called "writing instruction" in the Dick & Jane course is not writing instruction at all, but reading instruction.

T.O. children are taught capitals and indentation before they are able to write anything they can indent and capitalize. Only the Reading Expert finds these devices important, since they were designed to aid the reader.

---

**A writing mechanics scoring ratio (correct usage of punctuation, and indentation to the number of times correct usage required) showed the i.t.a. group was significantly inferior. . . . The i.t.a. children wrote significantly longer stories.—Edward Fry, Rutgers Reading Center**

---

Only the Reading Experts believe it's extremely important for children of six to learn that capitals start the first word of each line of poetry. Poor e e cummings! Generations of children are being taught to reject him on sight.

A little boy usually knows the difference between dad's electric razor and his own battery-powered rubber face buzzer that looks like dad's machine. A little girl knows the difference between her baby sister and her Barby doll.

If a child writes a statement, why can't we call it a statement and let it go at that? We don't fool anybody by calling it a "story" or "creative writing."

I suspect children know they're not writing stories. But it's hard to tell whether textbook authors and teachers know it. Maybe a wink and quote marks in the voice once went along with the terms, but not any more. The users appear to believe what they're saying.

Barby-doll terms ought to be scrubbed out of curriculum guides and textbooks and replaced by terms that describe communication accurately and honestly. They keep us from the rueful fact that we have no writing curriculum and forestall us from doing something about it. They hide the source of our writing trouble—the alphabet itself.

How will we ever find a child's individual self if we accept an interpretation of individuality like the one following? "Often, copying a group-composed letter, for example, individuality of expression may be encouraged. If a child has the ability to form letters without close teacher guidance, he may want to add this own 'I miss you' or 'My desk is by the door.' The problem of spelling enters in, of course, and as an intermediate step. The teacher may put several alternative phrases on the board for part of the letter, allowing each child to select the one he wishes to use." (*The Language Arts in Elementary Schools*)

## "CREATIVE" AND "PRACTICAL" WRITING

Year after year in grade school, children are dragged through dummy maneuvers training them to write party invitations, greetings, and announcements. This is called "practical" writing and is distinguished from "creative" writing, which includes "jingles, poetry, radio skits, short stories, plays, and autobiographies."

By some rose-decorated school-catalogue theory, "practical" writing is intended to prepare a person for business or social communication, while "creative" writing is supposed to develop the imagination and artistic talent that will one day produce last-worthy literature.

Neither happens. It's just talk—teachers assuring each other that they are teaching.

Some teachers think "creative" writing means "inspired" writing and therefore deny that writing can be taught at all. They say a child either has a talent for it or not, but they admit that they could not recognize the talent if a child possessed it. Other teachers believe that "creative" means "achievement" and, therefore, accept *all* writing as creative. Some, sadly, display "creative writings" to show off their own creative teaching. In any case, it's hard to find out what "creative" writing means when it refers to papers by seven- and eight-year-olds who can't yet spell and are copying the words they want to use.

I have almost four hundred small, unsigned pieces of paper from primary-grade teachers telling me what "creative" and "practical" writing are. Here are a few of them:

> Practical writing involves the writing of objective material regardless of subjective aspects of the individual writer.

> Practical writing—following the conventionally accepted forms such as letters, proper sentence structure, how to answer questions.

> Practical writing is having the writer express facts in clear, logical sequence. This is writing for information.

> Creative writing means having a child or adult or anyone express his own idea in his own way. It is what the writer feels without any hesitation or fear of being laughed at. It is having the child use his imagination to create a story, play, etc. It is trying to help the child think for himself and be proud of his thought.

*174*

Creative writing is when an individual expresses the uniqueness of his perceptions and impressions in written language.

Creative writing—created by the writer—not necessarily "coaxed out" by the teacher.

Creative writing—means one's ability to put his thought on paper in an original way.

Two false impressions are printed into our children by the way "creative" and "practical" are interpreted:

1) Children sense that teachers regard practical writing as socially and academically inferior to creative writing. Practical is blue collar, creative is white collar. It is Martha vs. Mary writing, profane vs. sacred, active vs. contemplative.

2) Practical writing tries to be clear and logical. Children learn to aim announcements and invitations at certain specific readers—parents, for example. Since creative is regarded as opposite to practical, and since it deals only with *self*-expression, creative writing is not penalized for being obscure or illogical.

If the writer wants to be read, he'd better consider his reader. Writing is meant to be communicative or it wouldn't use language. The individualist who uses language is a conformist. *All* writing is practical since language itself is practical. It has a job to do: carry human meanings and feelings.

The ultimate difficulty is that English is used both as the medium of *everyday communication* and, at certain times, at rare moments by unusual men, as a medium of *high artistic communication*. This double life of language gives the college English Department cramps.

# The Non-Com Course

IN 1965 *The Instructor*, a magazine serving grade teachers, mailed a questionnaire to 5,419 elementary-school principals in forty-eight states. The survey sought to find out how schools came by their "language arts" curriculum. There were 1,164 responses.

Of the principals surveyed, 81.5 per cent said they took their "language arts" programs from textbooks. The remaining principals said they accepted the course outline prepared for them by city, county, or state education offices and distributed in curriculum guides.

As was noted earlier, written composition in grade school is taught as one of the "language arts" along with speaking, listening, and reading.

According to *The Instructor*, then, 81.5 per cent of the principals let textbook authors and publishers create and manage their writing-instruction program. Let's look at some textbooks and education-office guides and see what they understand by communication and how they propose to teach it.

An ideal report would be based on broad research of all material published for writing instruction. Ideally, such research would be pursued by somebody not easily depressed by what he sees. My report is not ideal in either respect.

I can say I surveyed the catalogues, language books, workbooks, and teachers' guides published by eight major publishers for the three primary grades. But the data seem to me to be too dull to set down. This is not ideal either, for a research reporter has no right to decide that his findings are too dull to deliver.

Ideal or not, what I offer now is a report on one English textbook and one language workbook.

## I. THE ENGLISH TEXTBOOK

*English, Your Language* was published in 1963 by Allyn and Bacon, Inc. The authors of Book 2 (second grade) are Josephine B. Wolfe and Doris E. Dorsey. It is typical of other Dick & Jane language texts in at least three respects:

1. It is enslaved to a basal-reader series. Its title page, which carries the name of William D. Sheldon as Reading Consultant, indicates that *English, Your Language* is a satellite to the Sheldon Basic Reading Series produced by the same publishers.

2. It leans heavily on copying. "Copy" and "copying" appear in the table of contents thirty-two times, compared with forty times for "write" and "writing."

3. It teachers written composition as part of a "language arts" program. The "arts" in Book 2 include talking, listening, reading, dramatizing, using, proofreading, remembering, sharing, drawing, making things, learning new words, following directions, and copying.

*English, Your Language* is a little better than the typical English book for second grade. In spite of the fierce competition from other skills, writing is given its share of time. In the back of the book the authors list 212 "new words" they have managed to sneak past Dr. Sheldon's Cumulative Vocabulary List for Grades 1 and 2. Big deal? We may jeer but it's typical for language books to be dominated by basal-reader word controls.

The authors are able English teachers. The topics they outline are natural and reasonable and are presented in a simple, open style. An interesting "language arts" teacher could make this an exciting book—for all the "arts" except writing. The book's otherwise good character falls apart in the weak, limp writing assignments. Why is this, you wonder? Why are authors who dare to introduce words like "apostrophe" and "abbreviation" to second-graders unable to give out a decent writing assignment?

For example, on the next page an assignment from *English, Your Language* shows children how to use the verb saw: "Use *saw* when you talk about things that happened in the past."

In other exercises children practice using *isn't, aren't, seen,* and even *I.*

The boys and girls had fun telling
about the things they <u>saw</u> at Mr. Allen's lot.
They took turns when they talked.
Here are some of the things they <u>saw</u>.

1. Jack <u>saw</u> a pine tree.
2. Jane <u>saw</u> holly with red berries.
3. Bob <u>saw</u> Mr. Allen spray the tree.
4. Bill and Sue <u>saw</u> the stands
for the trees.

Use <u>saw</u> when you talk
about things that happened in the past.

**TO DO BY YOURSELF**

1. Think of five sentences about the things
you believe the children <u>saw</u>
at Mr. Allen's lot.
2. Ask your teacher to write the sentences
on the chalkboard.
3. Copy the sentences on paper.

Begin your sentences with the word *I*. How is the word *I* written?

Copy these sentences on paper:

I have a telephone at my house.
I talk to my friend Joe.

i.t.a. writers and Italian children skip usage drills like this. They can communicate things that excite and interest them. Below is an Italian boy's description of moving day. It is followed by a collage of statements describing the moving of a historic house in Bethlehem, Pennsylvania. All the Bethlehem writers were in the first grade in the Rosemont School.

Yesterday we moved, we moved to 80 Independence Street.

I am on the highest floor.

The room where I am now is big and spacious, I have five rooms.

My sister's fiancé has a car and he helped us.

We put a box spring and mattress on top of the car, and on that the refrigerator.

Our dishes we carried by hand, we carried them three at a time.

The arm chairs we put on top of the car and also the bed chair.—*Luciano, 7, second grade, San Martino*

On Wednesday afternœn our class went tœ see the D.A.R. hous on Braud Street.... Mr. O thaut that it woz such an eksieting thing, hee gæv us permiſhon tœ see it....

...A truck woſ mœving the hous. Two mor trucks were gœing tœ pœt the hous in erth. The two poleesmen were blocking the street. And two mor men wer bræking the branchez from the tree sœ the hous cœd get thrœ and around the curv....

...the men had tœ sau dœun the limz ov the trees sœ the hous cœd get by.... Wee had tœ step back. Thær woſ a lien that woſ our divieded lien....

*179*

. . . It woz jieant. It had 10 wheelz. Nœ man wuʒn't on the hous. Thæ needed one truck in front and one in back. . . .

. . . It went two avenueʒ. The teeĉher sed one avenue. . . . And ie sau the sien, "Workmen." And wee were cœld. Debbie, Susan, David woz cœld. . . .

. . . The slæt on top ov the D.A.R. woz worth mor than a 100 dollarʒ. And a pees ov the slæt fell off the rœf. . . . Wee tœk it tœ scœol. Wee ar gœing tœ egʒamin it. . . .

. . . ie nœ whot D.A.R. standz for—the Dauterz ov the American Revolœʃhon. ie got a kwestion for yœ and Mrs. H. The windœez were brœk. Hœ did it? Many peeple must hav gotten arrested.

Near the end of *English, Your Language* the authors ask the children to imitate the following "story" about animals:

## Our Story About Animals

We heard a story about animals.
We learned their names.
We learned where they lived.
We saw pictures of animal homes.

i.t.a. children write naturally and easily about their pets or any animals they want to write about. They communicate what they feel, whether fear or affection.

I hav a cat and hee gœs wield for ĉheeʒ and hee's a nut and wuns wen wee went tœ nw jerʒy my father wos tæking a bath and the cat luvd water so hee jumpt intœ the bath tubb and jumpt outœ and I had tœ drie the cat—*Ellen, 6, first grade, Long Island*

I had a bird and ſhe necst morning it woʒ ded We had turdlʒ. thæ died to. we hav a cat. It got shot but it is not ded he bringʒ tics. and wuns I had wun on me. a dog comʒ and plæʒ keepawæ. He iʒ very nis dog. He is a begl. my gramathrʒ cat died in ſhe winter. do you no I liek cats?
—*Tim, 6, first grade, Long Island*

180

I have a Siamese cat whose name is Zorro, because this summer he scratched my arm and it formed a Z, just like the famous cavalier who, with his sword, made his signature on the forehead of his enemy.

One evening, returning from Aprica, my brothers were in our friend's car and my mother was in our station wagon with our maid.

But we fortunate ones: my father, Zorro and I were alone in the large car.

Arriving in Brescia, we immediately went to get my brothers but a lady invited us to dinner.

Meanwhile Zorro, was left alone in the car, was busy jumping here and there. When my father went down and opened the car door, aiee! the cat shot out across Marte Square and after much running was gotten back and put back into the car.

But since I wasn't there, he continued to jump around like a madman.

When we arrived home both Zorro and my father were infuriated.—*Francesca, 7, second grade, Brescia*

In Book 3 of *English, Your Language*, authors Wolfe and Oakes offer the following assignment for *third*-graders:

Which word below might make you feel frightened?

bubbles     wolves     whiskers

(a) Draw a picture about the word.
(b) Then, write a sentence using the word.

i.t.a. children writing ghost stories sometimes use a shaky handwriting to signify a scary subject or a shaky voice. Some use it to indicate shivering cold. More important, the i.t.a. papers communicate a six-year-old's feeling of terror.

one niet wen I woꭍ in Bed I had ɑ scæry nietmær and it woꭍ ɑull ɑbout bat poiꭍen and it went like this my father woꭍ plæing bæsball and hɛɛ throo the bat poiꭍen on me

*181*

and wɛɛ reselld [wrestled] and I one and the goste cæm tœ but he got scærd bɛɛcaus I mæd fæses—*Ellen R., 6, first grade, Long Island*

I had a niet mær it wus las niet a gœst kæm in mie rœm and hɛɛ thrœ mɛɛ down the sdæs and then hɛɛ slept in mɛɛ bed and kathy cist the monsder.—*Ellen M., 6, first grade, Long Island*

I drɛɛmd about a gœst and I am sleepiŋ wen ŧhe gœst cæm and ŧhe gœst wus wiet and hɛɛ has black ies and a red mouŧh and ŧhe gœst has nœ hans and hær and hɛɛ disupærd jest beefaur mie ies and wen I got up I wus crieiŋ bɛɛcaus it wus a sad dreem—*Irene, 6, first grade, Long Island*

I had a dreem about a woolfman hœ kæm tœ my hous. He tor my hed, tœ legs and he cilld my famly too. an he set our hous on fier. I scrrynd and holerd and sed a! a! I sed don don don. tœ bad I died. aull the plees cæm but woolfmen got a wæy.—*Deirdre, 6, first grade, Long Island*

ie had a niet mær wen I went to ŧhe mœvɛɛs and sau "How the West Wos Won" the indɛɛins wer frendlɛɛ but in mie bad nietmær thæ wer not. ŧhæ wr winiŋ. But ŧhen thæ stopt in tiem the indɛɛis wud hav won but thæ did not. thæ kood hav wun but thæ did not. ŧhe ɟhɛɛf stopt ŧhem. so it kæm troo after aull but ieem afræd ŧhat it will hapin a gen bɛɛkos I never no. mæbɛɛ I will bɛɛ wauklŋ in mie slɛɛp hoonœs mæbe? it is too skærɛɛ—*Holly, 6, first grade, Long Island*

wun time in my nietmær I was in my fathers car. an then I opend the door and help! I was ded for shur. in an other nietmær dinasors wer eding the Brij wen wɛɛ wer on it. I fell off the Brij in too the wuter. an then I was ded for shur—*Debbie, 6, first grade, Long Island*

I wos at floruda. I fond a rok. I standid on the big flat rok and ŧhen I saw a grayt big tallking monter. he kaym. he sead ŧhat he wud kum and stuf mi toe and eet it. I wok up befor he stuft mi toe.—*Eugene, 6, first grade, Long Island*

This morning we went out with the teacher to take a walk beyond the railroad crossing. My friend Daniela always runs next to the rails and never crosses because she's afraid a train might come.

We saw some meadows but there weren't any beautiful flowers and we left right away. While we were coming back we found some "eyes-of-the-Madonna" and the flowers of the chicory tree called tarassaco and also some very little white flowers that were so small they had only ten petals.

Then we got a real scare when an airplane broke the sound barrier. Giovanna started teasing and making fun of Daniela again and said "Now I'm going to push you in a hole!" And Daniela cried.

Then we passed near Mauro's orchard where there are cherry trees, almond trees, peach trees, fig trees and pomegranate trees.—*Lidia, 7, second grade, Brescia*

WHERE IS THIS TEXT BOOK TAKING US?

The authors of *English, Your Language* are frustrated by having to teach children who cannot express themselves. They must therefore be satisfied with teaching them the hollow shells of communication. *English, Your Language* typically teaches children how to make capitals, indentations, periods, and other punctuation marks without being able to teach them to communicate ideas.

Similarly, the authors teach all the parts of a letter from date to signature but cannot teach children how to write a letter they feel like writing.

They teach a child how to write a story title but are helpless to show him how to write a story. The title is about the last thing a writer needs. Many nonwriters remain nonwriters because they have a good title but haven't found a story to go with it.

The trouble with *English, Your Language* is not with its authors but with its users—children who can't write as they talk because they are victims of their own reading instruction. *English, Your Language* is helpless to free them because it itself is ensnared by the basal readers it serves.

## II. THE WORKBOOK

*Language Workbook*, Grade 2, by Mildred A. Dawson and Bonnie Scales, was published in 1957 by Harcourt, Brace & World, Inc. When we riffle its ninety-six pages we see many that have blank, lined spaces. Some pages are almost entirely empty. This seems to be as it should be. If a workbook is going to give a child practice in communicating, it has to give him space to write.

In a preface to the teacher, the authors say their workbook is "concerned primarily with the skills and techniques of written expression" for *second*-graders. They promise to "equip children with those tools of written expression that will serve their current needs and also prepare them adequately for third-grade work."

Let's turn to the *Language Workbook* index and see how much attention is actually given to the "tools" and "skills and techniques" of written expression. The index is one page divided into two columns. The first column starts with 158 references to the use of capital letters. The last item at the bottom of the second column reads as follows:

> Written expression:
> checking. See checking written work.
> copy work:
> > heading . . .
> > letters . . .
> > rhymes . . .
> > sentences . . .
> > stories . . .
> > words . . .
> original:
> > letters [3 references]
> > sentences [22 references]
> > stories [4 references]. See also the entries
> > > Letters, Sentences, Story.

Now let's pursue some of these references. Remember, we're searching for "skills and techniques." Let's start with "Copy

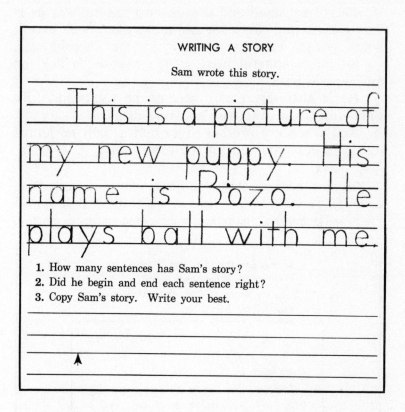

**WRITING A STORY**

Sam wrote this story.

This is a picture of
my new puppy. His
name is Bozo. He
plays ball with me.

1. How many sentences has Sam's story?
2. Did he begin and end each sentence right?
3. Copy Sam's story. Write your best.

Work . . . Stories." One reference leads us to a page titled "Writing a Story," which is shown above. Note that "writing" means *handwriting*.

Compare Sam's "story" with the Italian second-grader's paper below. Luisa did not copy nor did she ask her teacher for spelling help. She isn't more intelligent than American second-graders, though intelligent she is. She has a single enormous advantage— a one-sound-one-symbol alphabet that lets her write as she talks.

My dog is very pretty and a lot of fun.
His eyes are all green but when he was born they were yellow he has black hair like coal but underneath he has hair white like snow.

185

He is very small and is a bastard but anyway he is very playful and eats a lot and looks like a wolf except when he eats, he is even hungry for me when he eats.

But he is spiteful because he pretends to lick me and instead bites.

He is also very clever because he wants his milk only with sugar otherwise he won't drink it.

And when my brother gives him a bath he jumps and splashes water out of the tub.—*Luisa, 7, Brescia*

The first reference under "original written expression" in *Language Workbook* leads to letter writing. Let's see (below) what "skills and techniques" the authors want second-graders to practice.

---

**1.** One day the girls had a good time. They set up a lemonade stand.

Lindy wrote a letter about their good time. Read her letter.

> August 14, 19—
>
> Dear Joan,
> Last Saturday Sue and I had a good time. We made some lemonade. We sold it in our front yard. The other boys and girls came to buy. We took in fifteen cents.
>
> Your friend,
> Lindy Brown

**2.** How many capital letters do you see in the letter? Draw a line under each capital letter.

**3.** How many commas do you see? Where are they used?

**4.** Did Lindy put the right mark after each sentence?

**5.** Take a piece of paper. Write a letter about a good time you have had.

Be sure to use capital letters, periods, and commas correctly.

Ask your teacher how to spell any hard word.

### FINISHING A STORY

Here is a story that Alice wrote. She did not tell the end of her story. Think what the end ought to be.

> Our Surprise
>
> We wanted to surprise Miss Day. Another teacher called her from the room. Bob and Don brought in a pumpkin. It was filled with fruit and nuts.

Did you think how to end the story? Write the story on the next page. Add the ending you thought about. Use capital letters in the title, just as Alice did.

Here are some words that you might use in the ending. Be sure to spell them right.

came    back    liked    thanked    surprised

The second entry under "original written expression" is "Sentences." The example above, reproduced from *Language Workbook*, is titled "Finishing a Story." Let's see what "skills and techniques" this exercise teaches.

Compare the *Language Workbook*'s interpretation of "original" with the truly original statements by the i.t.a. first-graders below.

deer first græd,
iz ꝥhe test fun? ie dœn't hav ꝥhe hard meezlz. ie hav ꝥhe soft meezlz. when yꝏ hav ꝥhe meezlz yꝏ haf tꝏ stæ in bed ie will bee sik for ꝥhree dæz. mie broꝥher iꭍ scærd hee miet get ꝥhe meezlz. mie sister iꭍ scærd. ꭍhee miet get ꝥhe meezlz too. ie feel muꝯh muꝯh muꝯh better.—*Wendy, 6, Cleveland*

wons a pon a time there was a witsch. she livd in the woods.

Thanksgiving is a time to give thanks.

I am thankful for_____

_____

I am thankful for_____

_____

I am thankful for_____

_____

_____

**Work on paper:** Ask the children to finish these sentences to tell the many things they have to be thankful for. Encourage a variety of ideas. Give help with the spelling of words. If a child does not have sufficient writing skill to say what he wishes let him dictate to you and then copy his story, or write it on the page for him as he dictates.

she casht mee and maed mee intoo a witsh. shee cashis evree wun. shee has loing straglee haer and snaecs cuming owt of her haer and a blac hat and a blac girtll and bra and blac pants, blac dres, blac shoos and blac stocens and a uglee eegll and a broom. a horubl broom. the ends ar snaecs. it is horubll.—*No name, 6, Long Island*

The tenth week of school falls near the Thanksgiving holidays. First- and second-grade Dick & Jane children customarily bring home crayon drawings of turkeys and Pilgrims. A few words will be printed under the drawing, maybe "Happy Thanksgiving." Not much more. You can be pretty sure that whatever words are there have been copied or written with help from the teacher.

Reproduced above is a typical Dick & Jane workbook Thanksgiving assignment, from *American English*, Book 2. Note the instructions, and remember this is a second-grade book.

In mid-November I asked a first-grade Bethlehem i.t.a. class to write how a turkey felt the day before Thanksgiving. I talked with the teacher for twenty minutes while the children were writing, and then called for the papers. Here are a few of them. They are revealing samples of communication:

ʃhanksgiviŋ is cumiŋ. ʃhe turky i∫ sad becauz hεε gets mad and hεε gets mad becaus hεε gets ɕhoppt on hiz legs.
—*Sharon, 6*

ʃhe turky fεεlz sad. ie will fεεd ʃhe turky. and when ie am dun fεεdiŋ ʃhe turky, ie will ʃhωt him.—*William, 6*

ʃhe turky i∫ afæd ʃhat hεε will bεε killd. and hεε rεεally wurriz becaus hεε duz not wont tω bεε εεten. if hεε did get εεten, hεε wωd bεε ded, sω hεε will bεε killd.—*Gary, 6*

gωd bie huny, ie miet bεε ʃhot, but ie miet not huny. and yω miet, tω. sω if yω dω, wεε ʃhall sæ gωd bie.—*Russell, 6*

The authors of *English, Your Language*, Book 2, offer second-graders a song called "Mister Turkey" and instruct the children to listen for its rhyming words. Then, in the page reproduced on p. 190, they continue the assignment. Compare that assignment with the Bethlehem first-grader's writing below it, wherein he tosses off a rhyme without being asked.

The Valentine's Day assignment exposes the basal readers' most deplorable wrong. Dick & Jane don't give children the means to express their feelings. i.t.a. first-graders discover love, spring, and note writing all about the same time in March, and the discovery starts a cross-migration of impromptu valentines. They have no trouble expressing their feelings. Compare their notes with the *English, Your Language* assignment which follows them.

I luv yω Shæril. yω'r so cεεuet ʃhat I cud kiss yω Shæril. I ʃhωd bie yω a riŋ tωmourœ. mie storεε Sam
tonεε yω and mεε hav tω hav lædεε man tauk sωn. J

## Mister Turkey

Here are more words that rhyme.

Read them to yourself.

Your teacher will ask one of you
to read the words aloud.

thank          mother          sing
bank           another         wing

**TO DO BY YOURSELF**

1. Use your reading book to find other words
   that rhyme with thank, mother, and sing.
2. Copy the words on paper.
3. Draw a picture about the words you wrote.

ie am α turky. ie am gœiŋ too beε sittiŋ on ţhe plæt. heε
wuz α mad turky. heε cood just sæ wun wurd. ţhis iz whot
heε can sæ, "gobbl, gobbl, gobbl." ţhat's ţhe œnly thiŋ
heε nœz. hiz hed gœz bobbl and hiz neck gœs gobbl. heε
iz gœiŋ too beε on mie plæt. ie am gœiŋ too eεt him on
ţhaŋksgiviŋ.—*Lucy, 6*

do yω luv me?
No.
Yes yω do.
No  dœnt
oh yes yω do
I sed no.  stop pestriŋ me.
yω luv me
I'm gœŋ to tell . . .

*(Note confiscated at this point.  It had been traveling back and forth)*

The boys and girls wanted to make valentines for their friends.  They did not know what to write on them.  Some of them could not spell the words. . . .  Here are some valentine words that you may like to use.  Your teacher may wish to use them for your spelling lesson this week.

| love | be | mine |
|------|------|-----------|
| heart | will | valentine |

At the start of this book, I warned that the first- and second-year school-made Christmas cards were a sign of the school's failure to teach children to communicate in writing.  Part of the responsibility for this failure must be charged to textbook authors and publishers. The instructions for making Christmas cards reproduced on pp. 192 and 193, from *Language Workbook*, Grade 2, and *American English*, Book 2 (Teachers Edition), dramatically illustrate how school books can frustrate a child's free expression.

WHERE IS THIS WORKBOOK TAKING US?

In the preface to *Language Workbook*, Grade 2, the authors glibly promise to teach written expression by delivering its "tools." They fail badly.  The only tool they deliver is copying.  They cover up the poverty of their instruction by incanting the usual spew of "language arts": "However, every lesson calls for the exercise of other aspects of a well-rounded language program, such as reading to interpret directions, sentences, stories, and the like; answering

## MAKING CHRISTMAS CARDS

Here are some Christmas cards that some boys and girls made.

Make a Christmas card here. Write a greeting to your mother or father on it.

Here are some greetings you may use:

| Merry Christmas | Christmas Greetings |
|---|---|
| to Mother | to Father |

---

questions in the lessons or questions raised by the teacher; conversation and discussion concerning the lesson content; listening to directions, to poems, to stories, to dictated sentences and stories; ear-training to develop correct habits of usage; critical analysis and evaluation of models; checking and evaluation of one's own work; training in observation and in orderly thinking; study and interpretation of pictures; recognition of desirable standards of achievement."

The authors say in their preface: "At the second-grade level, children cannot be expected to take up a workbook lesson, or even an exercise, independently."

This is a bad start for it contradicts the experience of i.t.a. first-grade teachers who know that i.t.a. children can read and follow workbook directions without help.

# On Christmas morning I_____

_____

_____

_____

**Work on paper:** After the tree is finished ask the children to write what they would say as they awoke on Christmas morning and found it. To help the children, write needed words on the board for them to use as spelling reference.

Whatever the ability of the authors, the essence of the trouble is not in them but in the children they are teaching. The authors are coping with seven-year-old basal-reader cripples using a wobbly, distorted alphabet.

On the next-to-last page of *Language Workbook* the authors ask the children to display what they've learned about writing during the year, on a page titled "My Best Writing." It is reproduced on the next page.

## III. THE CURRICULUM GUIDE

The curriculum guide is a teaching plan. It may cover all subjects from kindergarten through high school, or it may concentrate on a single subject, for example, music or social studies. It defines what a course should accomplish; it breaks down the course into a series of little goals all progressing toward the master goal; and it provides a timetable for reaching the goals.

Curriculum guides may be written by state schools of education, special committees of educators, or by an expert in the field, such as a reading expert. The guides they publish may be elaborate and

---

MY BEST WRITING

It is near the end of the school year.
It is time to see how well you write. Do
you write better than you did the first
week of school? This is what Sue wrote:

## My name is Sue Lake.
## This is my best writing.
## Today is June 10.

1. Write here what Sue wrote. Use
your own name. Use the right date.

2. Look at page 47 in this book. Is
your writing today better than your
writing on that page?

3. Look on pages 3 and 4. Did you
make every letter right?

---

expensive or they may consist of a few mimeographed sheets stapled
together. New York City sells a K-2 (kindergarten to second grade)
"language arts" guide for five dollars.

In *The Instructor* report referred to earlier, 30.2 per cent of
the principals surveyed said they took their writing instruction from
a state guide; 29.8 per cent put their trust in a school-developed
guide; 28.1 per cent depended on a county or city guide.

*What do the guides say?* How do curriculum guides develop
communication in the primary grades?

In 1965 the National Council of Teachers of English (NCTE) published a list of curriculum guides. The Council recommended three guides designed for grades kindergarten to 6 (K-6). One of these, a guide from Tyler, Texas, says its general objective is to "teach children to express ideas in writing." To achieve this, the school will do two things: (1) "develop written expression" and (2) "learn the mechanics of good writing."

How will the Tyler schools "develop written expression"? Here is what their curriculum guide says:

1. Write first name at beginning of year, write full name toward end of year.
2. Copy short sentences from the board.
3. Copy experience stories.
   a. Write stories about the weather.
   b. Write the news of the day.
   c. Write original stories, jingles, and rhymes.
4. Copy stories and letters from the writing book.
5. Compose and write notes, letters, and invitations.
6. Write, draw, and read about special events and holidays.

How will the school teach the "mechanics of good writing"? We quote three of seven steps from the Tyler guide:

2. Observe the difference in the use of punctuation marks in order to read as one talks. (See the ball. What is it? Help! Help! Jane looked at Dick, but he did not see her.)
6. Learn correct pronoun usage and reference through daily conversation and reading. (Sally saw Spot. *He* was happy. Father and *I* painted boats. The ball is for Jane and *me*.)
7. Learn possessives by constantly using sentences containing words of ownership. (This is *Sally's* Tim.)

In the second grade, Tyler sets this goal for its first six weeks of school: "Learn to communicate effectively with others through writing." This is a worthy goal, but how does Tyler intend to get to it?

Here is the method suggested in Tyler's curriculum guide:

1. Use correct handwriting habits while writing the letters of the alphabet.
2. Supply the missing initial word in teacher-prepared sentence; begin it with a capital letter.
3. Write name labels for lockers and personal property.
4. Practice writing, name, street address, city, and state.
5. Write the day of the week on the board each day.
6. Write short letters to practice capitalizing the first word of the greeting.
7. Make a list of all the holidays second graders observe.
8. Write a story, capitalizing the first word of all important words in the title.
9. Observe the capitalized *I* in printed and written material.
10. Write a brief autobiography; capitalize the word *I*.
11. Practice writing headings on all papers; use the correct form.
12. Keep language papers in folders for review and comparison.

*A Developing Curriculum in English—Kindergarten through Twelve* is another guide recommended by the NCTE. It comes from Terre Haute, Indiana, home of Theodore Dreiser, and was produced by the School of Education of Indiana State University. One of the guide's first-grade objectives is "improving participation in group and individual activities." It would achieve this by writing:

1. Number 1–100
2. Alphabet A–Z
3. Names of: self, parents, brothers, and sisters

Another Indiana objective is "improving language patterns"; the curriculum guide suggests two ways of doing this:

1. Continuing practice in writing letters of the alphabet:
Writing the simple structure words "a", "an", "the",

"and", "but", "for", "of", "on", "by", and so on in big letters. Note: The simple syllable words are practiced before two or more syllable words are written.

2. Combining oral and written expression:

Scrambled sentences to be said and then written. Note: Scrambled sentences to be arranged into the simple patterns are not only amusing but most helpful in creating a foundation for understanding the "why" of English word order. Moon over the cow jumped (The cow jumped over the moon).

The Indiana guide's objective for first and second grades is similar to Tyler's objectives. Like Tyler, it advocates dictation and copying; like Dreiser's prose, it is sometimes hard to understand:

Capitalizing and punctuating:

Big letters are capitals; small letters are not capitals. Note: When children are taught to write small letters, the distinction between capitals and small in terms of capitalization is to be made.

Wyoming's *Curriculum Guide for English*, produced by the State Department of Education, says that "written language is presented as a means of preserving and sharing the kind of fun experienced in oral activities." The guide suggests the following activities "for creative thought and awareness through communication":

Grade 1 Writing:

Mostly cooperative group composition, teacher writing at group's dictation, group choosing from among several expressions often. Changes may be made after group rereads the completed composition.

Individual composition for more advanced pupils.

Reconstructing small copy of old experience chart by placing word and sentence strips in pockets in correct order opposite pictures.

Grade 2 Writing:

Cooperative group composition, teacher writing at group's

*197*

dictation, selecting best expressions, revising when completed.

Copying group composition accurately to keep and reread.

Completing an imaginative story in two or three sentences, given an appealing subject and opening, or suggested by a picture.

Planning, dictating, copying a class note, letter, or invitation.

Write two or three sentences about plans for a project, picnic, holiday, etc.

*Minimum Curriculum for Kindergarten Through Grade Five—English, Reading, and Spelling* was published in 1958 by the National Association of Independent Schools, after "careful examination of 162 curriculum outlines submitted by independent schools." A revised edition of the *Minimum Curriculum* was published in 1964. It is written by someone who loves the English language and uses it with dignified elegance. It is well worth the sixty-five cents I paid for it.

*Minimum Curriculum* plainly declares its reading bias: "Teaching a child to read is the fundamental objective in Grade 1. Phonics taught in spelling should be applied to the teaching of reading." No wonder, then, that its composition requirements in the primary grades are no more demanding than those in Wyoming or Indiana or Tyler, Texas.

Here is *Minimum Curriculum*'s objective for written composition in the first grade:

### Composition

I. Written Composition

Children should be able to write several sentences, connected in thought and punctuated properly, in which they relate personal and group experiences. To achieve this

A. The teacher may write stories which the children suggest and can copy from the board.

B. Children may write their own stories. . . .

### Punctuation

I. Periods at the ends of sentences

*198*

II. Recognition of the use of question marks at the ends of questions in reading
III. Recognition of the use of exclamation points in reading
IV. Recognition of the use of quotation marks in reading
V. Capital letters for
   A. The beginnings of sentences
   B. Proper names
   C. The word "I"

The second grade's written objectives are as follows:

Short stories and descriptions should be written in complete sentences and have logical sequence, as in
   A. Accounts of study trips, nature trips, visits to museums, etc.
   B. Simple letters
   C. Group stories written by class

More than a hundred teachers contributed ideas and lesson plans toward the contents of *Written Communication in the Elementary School*, published by the Anne Arundel County Public Schools in Annapolis, Maryland, in 1963. It is fine work, the most ambitious plan for elementary writing instruction I have seen. Its definitions of communication, creative writing, independence, originality and other concepts make sense. It offers reasonable standards for evaluating compositions. But the guide idles for three years while children are learning to spell. Till then, its gears can't catch.

The writing objectives for the first grade are as follows: "The teacher records cooperatively expressed ideas: lists of classroom duties, class plans, news, materials needed for an activity, experience stories of groups or individuals. The children copy labels for exhibits, lists of items, notes to parents, one-sentence stories under pictures, notices, messages for greeting cards. Children may write one or more independent sentences near the end of the year."

Here are the disappointing objectives for second grade: "The teacher continues to act as secretary both for cooperative and individual efforts. Few children at this level will be able to write independently before the second half of the year. To help those who are unable to write independently, the teacher records for them and the children may copy."

In every school that accepts the traditional alphabet at face value, writing can't become an honest member of the curriculum until the fourth or fifth grade.

## WHERE IS THE GUIDE TAKING US?

Curriculum guides show that grade-school writing instruction proceeds in an orderly step-by-step fashion: from short, simple sentences to long, complex sentences; from invitations to business letters; from periods to exclamation marks after imperative sentences.

The chart below is a composite of forty curriculum guides from various states, cities, and school districts.

| AGE | GRADE | KIND OF SENTENCE | TYPE OF LETTER | PUNCTUATION |
|---|---|---|---|---|
| 6 | 1 | | | Period (.) |
| 7 | 2 | Declarative Interrogative | Invitation Thank you | Question mark (?) |
| 8 | 3 | Imperative | Friendly | |
| 9 | 4 | Exclamatory | Cheer up | Exclamation mark (!) (after exclamatory sentence) |
| 10 | 5 | | Acceptance Business | |
| 11 | 6 | | Regret | ! after strong interjections ! after strong imperative sentences |

According to the chart, the child learns to write simple declarative and interrogative sentences and to use the question mark at the age of seven in the second grade. He learns the invitation and thank-you letter. At the age of eight, he learns to write an imperative and an exclamatory sentence and he learns the friendly letter. No new punctuation mark is learned at this age, but the period and question mark are practiced.

At the age of nine, the child learns to write the cheer-up letter and to use the exclamation mark after exclamatory sentences.

At the age of ten, he learns the letter of acceptance and the business letter.

At the age of eleven, he learns the letter of regret. He also learns that the exclamation mark is used after strong interjections and imperatives.

What is the principle of order in this structure? How is it expected to teach a child to write?

---

**Written composition at the second grade level has always been a major struggle for pupils and teachers alike. While children are highly articulate at this stage of development, their written expression is smothered beneath a blanket of highly intricate tasks which frequently render effective written communication impossible. To write with confidence, a child must master letter formations, spelling, sentence construction, elementary grammar, and a host of skills related to word choice, sequence, movement, and emphasis. More frequently than we would care to admit, children at this level lose their train of thought while grappling with one or more of the many frustrating mechanics of written expression.—*Donald L. Barnes in* Elementary English, *January 1964***

---

Granted that writing is hard business, how does it happen that so many different schools around the country, private and public, attack the problem of writing in virtually the same way: dictation, copying, etc.? The curriculum guides are so much alike during the first two years that we suspect a few mysterious powers have met secretly and fixed the prices of learning to write. Who are they? Who is Mr. Big?

The charts below and on the next page are from a curriculum guide designed by a committee of Vermont English teachers

## Letter Writing

| | GRADES | | | | | |
|---|---|---|---|---|---|---|
| | 1 | 2 | 3 | 4 | 5 | 6 |
| A. Writing personal letters | | | | | | |
| 1. Friendly letters | R | R | S | C | C | C |
| 2. Invitations | R | S | C | C | C | C |
| 3. Thank you letters | R | S | C | C | C | C |
| 4. Cheer-up letters | | | | S | C | C |
| 5. Letters of regret | | | | | R | S |
| 6. Letters of acceptance | | | | R | S | C |
| B. Writing business letters | | | | R | S | C |
| C. Addressing envelopes | | | S | C | C | C |

201

*Sentences*

| | 1 | 2 | 3 | 4 | 5 | 6 |
|---|---|---|---|---|---|---|
| | | | **Grades** | | | |
| A. Recognition of sentences | R | S | C | C | C | C |
| B. Writing sentences | | | | | | |
| 1. Writing a short simple sentence | RS* | S | C | C | C | C |
| 2. Varying beginnings | RS | C | C | C | C | C |
| 3. Using "and" wisely | R | R | S | C | C | C |
| 4. Avoiding run-on sentences | | | S | C | C | C |
| 5. Understanding correct use of subject and predicate | | | | R | S | C |
| C. Kinds of sentences | | | | | | |
| 1. Declarative** | R | S | C | C | C | C |
| 2. Interrogative** | R | S | C | C | C | C |
| 3. Imperative** | | | R | S | C | C | C |
| 4. Exclamatory** | | | R | S | C | C | C |

\* A minimum standard is the writing of one original sentence by the end of grade one.
\*\* These are not named as such until the middle grades.

*Punctuation*

| | 1 | 2 | 3 | 4 | 5 | 6 |
|---|---|---|---|---|---|---|
| | | | **Grades** | | | |
| A. Uses period correctly | | | | | | |
| 1. After statements | S | C | C | C | C | C |
| 2. After abbreviations and initials | R | S | C | C | C | C |
| 3. After numbers as in spelling | | R | S | C | C | C |
| B. Uses question mark correctly | R | S | C | C | C | C |
| C. Uses exclamation point correctly | | | | | | |
| 1. After exclamatory sentences | | | R | S | C | C |
| 2. After strong interjections | | | | | R | S |
| 3. After a strong imperative sentence | | | | | R | S |
| D. Uses quotation marks correctly | | | | | | |
| 1. With direct quotations | | | R | S | | |
| 2. With titles of stories or poems | | | | R | S | C |
| 3. With divided quotations | | | | | R | S |
| 4. In connected paragraphs of written conversation | | | R | R | R | S |

working for their state department of education. In presenting these charts, I want to make it clear that I am not demeaning the work of these teachers, for their guide is one of the best I have seen. I include the charts precisely because they so clearly map the course of writing instruction in the Dick & Jane system. ("R" stands for "ready" and means that a majority of students is ready to start a given phase of instruction; "S" stands for "start" and means that the subject is formally introduced and work is begun; and "C" stands for "continue" and refers to practice for mastery.)

What is the rational of these charts? How will the sequences indicated help a child learn to communicate? Why does the child start to learn how to make an exclamation mark in the fourth grade, one year after he learns to write an exclamatory sentence?

1) Is the underlying reason that directs this learning sequence related, perhaps, to a child's *growing needs*? If so, what are a child's needs for writing? How do we know them? Are they school-made or natural needs? Are they imposed on him artificially as school business or do they rise from his questioning, curious, logical nature as a thinking, feeling, social being? After a child has satisfied his need to "identify . . . his personal belongings," what other needs has he? The Commission on the English Curriculum, in *Language Arts for Today's Children* (1954), is disappointingly superficial on this point: "During the primary school years the child has an increasing number of needs for writing. He learns to write his name in order to identify the pictures he makes and his personal belongings. As other needs arise, he is taught to manage his writing equipment and to form the words he needs to use. The process develops slowly in the first year and more rapidly in the second; by the end of the third year the child is probably writing with a fair degree of skill and independence. . . ."

2) Is each writing step determined by a new stage in the child's *intellectual level*? Is he equipped with the interrogative sentence in second grade so that he can ask his way upward toward maturity using the question mark as a climber's grapple?

wind iꭺ mꭴvinꭸ ær when ᴣhe ær is still wɛɛ fɛɛl nœ wind when ær iꭺ mꭴvin wɛɛ fɛɛl ᴣhe wind—*Martin, 6, first grade, Bethlehem, Pa.*

ᴣhe magnet pics up pɑprclips and if yꭴ baꭸ ᴣhe magnet arꭴund ᴣhen yꭴ wil lꭴs ᴣhe pꭴuer—*Gary, 6, first grade, Bethlehem, Pa.*

it iꭓ not sæf too sit on a tilted ꭡær becauꭓ it will tip œver
and yoo will land on ʄhe flor ie nœ becauꭓ it happend too mee
—*Charles, 6, first grade, Bethlehem, Pa.*

3) Perhaps each writing step is determined by the child's
*emotional stages*? If this is the case, it would explain why the child
doesn't learn the letter of regret until he's almost at puberty; it
must be that he's incapable of feeling regret until then. It must be,
also, that children of six or seven are still too immature, too selfish
to wish a sick person well, and this is why cheer-up letters are not
learned until they are nine or ten. Then is it that they are still too
family-oriented at seven to know about writing friendly, social
letters?

I strted out bie tæking mie lunch and noouw I am bieing
mie lunch and this dæ I'm bringiꬻ mie lunch. I liek too
sit bie Arther in lunch. wee jest liek too blaber about wut
ar wee gœing too doo out on the plæground—*B. J., 6, first
grade, Long Island*

ie woꭓ gæiꬻ too ʄhe stor for gum. mie muʄher sed ie woꭓ
læt. ʃhee sed, "ʃhood ie keep yoor muny?" ie sed, "nœ."
ʄhen ie went too scool. ʄhe bell raꬻ. ie got in lien. ʄhe
teeꭡher sed too aull, "pass too class" wee got in our class. ʄhe
teeꭡher askt if wee had eny red cross muny. ie had siks sents
for gum. ʄhen ie gæv mie siks sents too red cross for a pin.
—*Ricky, 6, first grade, Cleveland*

My sister's name is Cinzia and she is a beautiful
baby, she has brown eyes and a nose like a little potato,
her mouth is small and pink, her cheeks are fat, white
and pink, and her back is good and strong and pudgy.
We are dressed almost always the same.
One day my sister and I (in the middle of the woods)
made a small house all out of leaves, straw, wood,
branches, and buds and we planted the ground around
it and the flowers were: roses, carnations and tulips
of the summer, and by springtime all the branches of

the flowers were full and it was so beautiful and it has been a memory of our vacation in Bolzano with the Floiren girls.

My sister is not only beautiful and good but ... she's also a bother, she keeps talking about money, money, money; saying "I have ten cents can I go and buy two candies can I momma can I?"

And my mother answers "Miss Spendthrift you're not going to buy anything!" And Cinzia is so sad.

But Cinzia is still a cute little fatty.

Three cheers for Cinzia! Yea Cinzia!

Hurrah! Hurrah! Hurrah! —*Patrizia, 8, third grade, Brescia*

As my mother had to go to the hospital to get my grandfather who had just died that night, she took me to my aunt's.

But before she left my mother gave me so many instructions that I almost lost my mind.

When I was up at my aunt's I couldn't find anything to do, after 1 or 2 hours my aunt gave me a broken box and I had to piece it together again and glue it. When I got it together, the lid was missing, but I didn't do anything about it because my aunt had to do her ironing and then go out with me.

After 20 or 30 minutes we were on the street car. We got off at Crispi Street in order to visit some lady to take a sweater to her, but the lady wasn't there and then we returned to my aunt's house.

I was very unhappy that my grandfather died and who would know how many tears my mother would cry.—*Luciano, 7, second grade, Brescia*

4) The State of New Jersey suggests, in its School Bulletin No. 7 (1951), that *effective communication* should be the rationale which determines writing instruction: "The main objective in teaching writing is to help each pupil communicate what he has to say as

effectively as possible. He should be learning to write with confidence, ease, and satisfaction."

If New Jersey is right, this explains why children first learn to make short, simple declarative statements and to ask short, simple questions. This is all their friends can handle. Their statements get longer and more involved as their friends get older and smarter. They begin as Hemingway and end as Arthur Schlesinger, Jr. ?

5) Maybe the answer is really quite simple: that the whole course is related to the child's *physical strength*. Handwriting is hard work for a six-year-old first-grader. His hand cramps up in the middle of a word. He chews his pencil, digs in to his hair, and shows other signs of tension, according to Gesell and Ilg in *The Child From Five to Ten*. Little writing is expected from him partly because he tires so quickly, according to the National Council of Teachers of English. Writing is named as a subject in first grade but it's there only in name, and the seven-year-old is limited to short, simple sentences because his hand muscles are too weak to push a pencil through a compound sentence. This could also explain why he learns to make a period in first grade, before he learns to write a declarative sentence in second grade. Periods are easy—just dots. He learns to use imperative sentences at age eleven, when he's big enough to back up his orders.

IT WOULD BE very good if *some* kind of thinking were evident in the writing-instruction course. It would make especially good sense if a child's ability to express himself in writing corresponded somehow with his intellectual and emotional growth and development. Writing would then be an excellent way of self-realization. It would help his teacher observe his growth and so be able to guide it.

But the bald, warted truth about the grade-school writing course is that it has *no* rationale directed toward writing. Its sequence is *not* determined by the child's personal needs, *not* limited by his physical strength, *not* related to his emotional or intellectual development, *not* paced by the requirements of communication. Its sequence is determined by the illogical and inconsistent spellings of the English language and by our antiquated, inadequate

"Italian" alphabet. Every child, regardless of family, color, or religion, is disadvantaged as he starts English. Instead of being structured to produce speakers and writers, the writing course is structured to produce readers.

Children ask questions from the time they can talk. They get excited and say so. They give orders. In other words, they speak declarative, interrogative, exclamatory, and imperative sentences before they come to kindergarten.

Beyond its pompous name, what's so hard about a "declarative" statement that a child has to wait till he's seven years old to write one?

Long before school, little girls make up conversation with their dolls, little boys make talk for anyone from Tonto to Tarzan. Some i.t.a. children turn in samples of dialogue as early as eight weeks after starting first grade. Quotation marks start appearing in papers after Christmas, even though they are often used inexactly.

Dick & Jane children don't start using quotation marks until they're eight or nine and don't start writing dialogue until they're a year older.

---

**Grade III**
**Quotation marks—learning to use quotation marks in dialog. (Note: At this time the meaning of direct quotations and indirect quotations should be introduced. The best material for this study is a story book. Students then can visualize from the written page the spoken sentences.)—***"A Developing Curriculum in English,"* **School of Education, Indiana State University**

---

Periods, commas, hyphens, and all the other jots and tittles of a printer's tray help the writer relate the pace of his language, the catches and pauses of speech. They may show stress and exertion. They may indicate mental states—distraction, for example, or thoughts within thoughts. They are useful devices to show balance, difference, series, or other forms of intellectual organization.

Teachers report that punctuation appears in i.t.a. writings naturally and correctly. Periods and question marks are sometimes discussed in the classroom, but often such marks appear spontaneously. How they are learned is not clearly known.

mœst ov japan haz hilż. ȼhapan iż serounded bie wauter.
"dœ yœ nœ wær thæ get thær fœd, ie nœ wær thæ get thær
fœd, from the pacific oshun?" thæ diev for seeweed, and
digd for clamż. sumtiemż thæ fish with nes. thæ get fœd
from farmerż neer bie. thæ ɛɛt with chop stis. this iż hou
thæ riet man 𝄆 . this is hou thæ riet wauter 𝄐 . thæ plæ
cardż.—*No name, 6, first grade, Long Island*

Some i.t.a. writers find our traditional signals inadequate. They
will write six or seven exclamation marks in a row, each one smaller
than the one before, to indicate fading surprise or feeling. I have
seen this on papers from different parts of the country, and it seems
to be a spontaneous invention. Some i.t.a. writers insert exclamation
marks within a sentence directly behind a word they want to stress:

shɛɛ sed ʈhat I!!!!! wuz ʈhe wun whœ pœʃhd her

**A New Kind of Sentence**

"Oh, look at the acrobat!"
"See all the arms on the octopus!"

**The two sentences above show that the children were surprised and excited.
These sentences are called *exclamations*. An *exclamation* is a new kind of
sentence.—English, Your Language, *Grade 3***

i.t.a. first-graders may use exclamation marks as early as Christmas. One Bethlehem six-year-old asked, "How do you make an
*exciting* mark?" and then wrote the paper below.

ie sɛɛ ie sɛɛ!! ie sɛɛ α christmas trɛɛ. iżnt it bɛɛuetifœl and
grand? yes!! œ! yes!! it iż α ʈhiŋ of god. ʈhat mæks it verɛɛ
grand. yes. but love Jesus too. rɛɛmember its hiż birʈhdæ!
— *Debra, 6, first grade, Bethlehem, Pa.*

œ dɛɛr! œ dɛɛr! whær ɑr mie sisdorz tœ givmɛɛ toiz and
toiz and toiz bɛɛcauz ie wunt tœ plæ with them and ie luv
ʈhem. sed mie bruthr.—*Sandra, 6, first grade, Cleveland*

According to Vermont's curriculum guide, children get ready
to write the word *brought* in third grade and start to use it in fourth

grade, when they are nine years old. Six-year-old i.t.a. writers who use *brought* in their speech use it in their writing as a normal practice.

B.J.   ie braut a triesorsris tw skwol.
        mie cusin gæv it tw mee.

In *Language Workbook*, Grade 2, the word *brought* is exercised in seven different lessons. One of these lessons is reproduced here.

---

### USING BROUGHT

Miss Lee's children brought some of their Christmas gifts to school. They told the class about them.

Jay said, "I brought the plane I made."
Betty said, "I brought my Indian doll."

Write a sentence. Tell about something you brought to school.

_____

_____

_____

---

On the next page is another chart from the Vermont curriculum guide. As before, "R" means ready to start, "S" means start, and "C" means continue and repeat. But if most of the children are ready to start writing diaries and reports in the first grade, as the chart indicates, why do they wait until the fourth grade to start? And if they are ready to write "newspaper notices and announcements" in the first grade, why wait until the fifth grade to start? Can Dick & Jane children really write plays, essays, and ballads—not to mention reviews and autobiographies—in the fifth and sixth grades, as the chart specifies? Aren't these terms inflated and false?

*A Greater Variety of Writing Tasks*

| Both types (1. Creative, 2. Practical) | GRADES | | | | | |
|---|---|---|---|---|---|---|
| | 1 | 2 | 3 | 4 | 5 | 6 |
| A. Writing reports | R | R | R | S | C | C |
| B. Writing reviews | | | | R | S | C |
| C. Playwriting | | | | R | S | C |
| D. Writing creative verse | | R | S | C | C | C |
| E. Writing autobiographies | | | | R | S | C |
| F. Writing essays | | | | | R | S |
| G. Writing dialogues | | | | R | S | C |
| H. Writing notices and newspaper announcements | R | R | R | R | S | C |
| I. Writing diaries | R | R | R | S | C | C |
| J. Writing ballads | | | | | R | S |
| K. Writing anecdotes | | | | | R | S |

Now compare Vermont's expectations with the i.t.a. paper and the Italian paper below:

I woz plæiŋ outsied. mie muƚhr caulld mɛɛ. ʃhɛɛ sed gœ and ɕhænj yœr clœƚh'z. it iʂ tiem for pɛɛanœ lessunz'. kwick ie ran tœ mie rœm and "sed"! Oh wot can ie dœ mie muƚhr "sed" ie hav tœ gœ ʃhoppiŋ. yœ stæ heer. ie herd α nok at ƚhe dœr. ie went tœ ƚhe dœr. ƚhær woz mie pɛɛanœ teɕhr. ʃhɛɛ "sed" sit doun. ie "sed" did yœ sɛɛ mie nue doll? sit doun ʃhɛɛ "sed"! sɛɛ ƚhe pikɕhœr. it iz mɛɛ. ʃhɛɛ "sed" plɛɛʂ sit doun. ʃhɛɛ sed wot iz ƚhe mattr? well ie dident dœ mie lessun. yœ wot? I œnlɛɛ gæv yœ wun pæj. well on sundæ ie went tœ ɕherɕh. on mundæ ie went to skœl. and ƚhen balæ. and on tuezdæ ie woz sick until ƚhrzdæ mœrniŋ. and on ƚhrʂdæ ie had skœl tœ. and aftr skœll it woz ɕherɕh. and heer wɛɛ ɑr α gen on friedæ.

210

well ꭍhaŋk yꚙ for ꭍhat stœreε. but if yꚙ dꚙ ꭍhat a gen yꚙ'll bεε in trubl.—*No name, 6, first grade, Long Island*

## Prologue

I have a fake dog made of velvet.

He guards me every night.

He is a dog of green velvet, and has black and brown eyes but the rest of him is green except for the ears which are on the one side green but on the other side white.

I always play with him, and in the evenings when it's really cold I take him to bed with me.

The other day I gave him something to eat but he wasn't hungry.

And after a few moments he became sick in his stomach.

Once I took him to dinner but he vomited immediately.

The next day I took him to my aunt's house to watch television which we never got a chance to do! Do you know what happened! I'll explain it to you right away.

Well, I was at my aunt's house and I had turned on the television set and that dog became blind in the middle of the best program.

Is it possible to find such a stupid dog!

Is it possible that one can become blind right in the middle of the best part of a police film! It just may be so!

He lived through it but I'm not so sure the film survived him.

## Dialogue

Claudio: "Mamma may I go to my aunt's house with Gustavo?

Mamma: "Yes.

Claudio: "Let's go.

Gustavo: "Bau!

Claudio: "Bye Bye.

Aunt: "Hi Claudio!

Claudio: "Hi Aunt! I came to watch television, do you mind?

Aunt: "No, no.

Claudio: "It's best to turn on the set.

Aunt: "Right away.

Claudio: "Do you like this Gustavo?

Gustavo: "Bau!

Claudio: "And you Aunt?

Aunt: "Yes very much, and Gustavo?

Claudio: "He has already said yes.

Aunt: "That pleases me. Claudio look at Gustavo's eyes.

Claudio: "What is it?

Aunt: "They're white what could it be?

Claudio: "Let's take him to the doctor.

Aunt: "Yes.

Doctor: "Do you have a television?

Aunt: "Yes.

Doctor: "Did you have it on?

Aunt: "Yes.

Doctor: "Was he watching?

Aunt: "Yes

Doctor: "Perhaps . . .

Claudio: "What's wrong with him?

Doctor: "He is already blind.

Claudio: "What!!

Doctor: "Don't get excited. Maybe we can do something.

Claudio: "Good! How long will it before he is cured?

Doctor: "Three days.

Claudio: "So many!

Doctor: "Yes.

Claudio: "Well, all right then.

*212*

Aunt: "Let's go home.
Claudio: "Who's going to pay?
Aunt: "You!
Claudio: "I don't have money.
Aunt: "But it's your dog.
Claudio: "But the money.
Aunt: "I don't have any money with me.
Claudio: "But, the doctor will accept credit won't you
    doctor?
Doctor: "Sure.
Aunt: "Very well.
Claudio: "Doctor is Gustavo ready?
Doctor: "Yes
Gustavo: "Bau.
Aunt: "Doctor but his eyes are white.
Doctor: "He's the kind of dog that when there's light
    his eyes become white.
Aunt: "How much do we owe you?
Doctor: "Three thousand lira [about five dollars].
Aunt: "Here it is.
Doctor: "Thanks.
[*I leave with my Aunt*]
Aunt: "Are you happy now that you made me spend
    three thousand lira, huh.
Claudio: "But my dog isn't an outcast—he belongs
    in the family, doesn't he?
Aunt: "Okay but three thousand lira to hear that he
    isn't even sick is a lot.
Claudio: "Well yes bye bye.
Aunt: "Bye.

# Summary of Charges, Part I

ELEMENTARY WRITING instruction ultimately fails because of the reading-oriented training of elementary-school teachers, particularly those destined to introduce the child to his first experience with literacy and communication, the teachers from kindergarten to grade five.

This teacher has no true curriculum of writing instruction to guide her. The curriculum she now works with was designed by reading specialists for reading instruction. This curriculum expects her to lead children through a false and foolish program against the current of treacherous spellings and still teach them how to communicate. That the teacher is sometimes able to achieve anything at all is a credit to *her*, not to her formal education.

The grade teacher's standards for writing competence are uncertain, doubtful, inadequate, or wrong, since they bear no relationship to the logical goals of writing instruction. Her standards equate writing with "self-expression." But writing is a relationship between the writer and reader, i.e., it is interhuman communication.

The grade teacher's correction norms in current writing instruction are false norms because they don't relate to life's writing needs. They treat spelling and handwriting as independent skills isolated from their function in communication, and look at errors as wrongs in themselves rather than as blocks to communication.

The grade teacher's methods, devised to work with our illogical alphabet on its own terms, develop harmful dependencies in the child and interfere with the formation of a writing habit of mind. The worst of these methods is pupil-to-teacher dictation, which is not writing instruction in any way but is anti-instruction.

This, then, is how American children learn to write: by copying and memorizing. They begin copying in first grade and they continue copying in second grade, third grade, fourth grade, and even beyond. They copy from books or from the blackboard or from cards they've made earlier by copying. It is all visual exercise. They draw the mere black shapes of words, joining silent lines with soundless circles.

But a child who learns to write by eye memorizations of whole-word spellings is not learning to write his talk. The opposite is true: he is being alienated from his own sounds and rhythms. All the steps intended to teach him to write—dictation-copying, work-book copying, filling in blanks, and vocabulary building—continue his alienation and make him a stranger to his own voice.

Since reading instruction is visual instruction, reading is taught first in school. It is wrenched from writing and the two are never brought back together. Reading is given prime administrative time and attention while writing, lagging behind, is neglected. Writing is exploited as a means to teach reading instead of being taught for the sake of its own proper values.

Writing instruction in the grades doesn't serve life's writing needs. "Creative" and "practical" writing as interpreted in grade-school programs are a waste of time for the teacher, the pupil, and society.

Writing is the student's most *practical* means of communicating what he knows about other school subjects, yet writing is treated as a part-time *art*. Fill-in, multiple-choice, and true-false devices are used in almost all subjects as proof of competence and mastery; but more, they are used as the means for normal instruction and as a substitute for writing. These completion devices steal a valuable exercise from the pupil: decision-making or the making of judgments on paper. The theft deprives him of intellectual and social growth.

Any writing-instruction system in the early grades that accepts our alphabet at face value cannot possibly serve life's writing needs. Writing instruction that accepts Dick & Jane reading instruction as its companion is either misdirected or fraudulent.

The Dick & Jane basal-reader system means the basal rot of communication instruction. The controlled vocabularies at the heart of this system were developed to help the beginning reader cope with the inconsistent spellings of English, but they harm the beginning *writer* since they repress him and frustrate his interest in communicating.

The Dick & Jane basal-reader system not only stifles the child but stifles the child's teacher. It trains her to work with copied writings and puts her attention on the externals of communication—periods, capitalizations, and indentations—instead of on the content of communication. When some child does accidentally reveal some little trace of self in his writing the teacher is likely to miss it and pick on his spelling.

Children cope with superficial assessment of their writing by learning to write superficially and falsely. They learn to avoid saying what's on their minds and, instead, scheme to give the school what it appears to want.

---

Students in the better schools have learned the knack of answering the kind of questions now asked on the College Board Examination in English: they know the fundamentals of grammar and vocabulary, and they do not seem to make frequently the kind of crude errors in their writing that we met quite often 10 years ago. Nevertheless, we feel that this improvement lies only on the surface as demonstrated on these tests, but in fact they are less competent to write an effective composition than were the students of 10 years ago. There is a grave weakness in their powers of analysis and organization; even the brightest students sometimes show that they lack basic training in the ways of beginning, developing, and concluding an argument or exposition. This is a much more troublesome weakness than any small errors in usage, for it shows a lack of mental discipline in the basic principles of human thought.—*A joint statement of Louis L. Martz, Chairman, and Frederick W. Hilles, Former Chairman, of the Department of English at Yale in* Attitudes Toward English Teaching, *1958*

---

# 4—THE GRADE TEACHER AS EDITOR

# The Teacher's Non-Com Course

eeeeeeeeeeeeeeeeeeeeeeeeeeeeeeeeeeeeeeeeeeeeeeeeeeeee

NOW THERE she is, then, a million other things to do, the Grade Teacher as Editor.

Directing not just one subject, but history, geography, music, drawing, spelling, handwriting, reading, science, social studies, and "creative writing"; leading different groups over separate hurdles to separate goals, all the while keeping her class under control.

*What are the standards and goals by which she directs and edits the communicative expression of twenty-eight to thirty-one children every year?*

When she marks papers, which will get the better grade—spelling or thoughts? Neatness or feeling?

How well is she qualified for her job as editor? (Has anybody asked?)

---

**One-fourth of all elementary teachers are not college graduates.
— 69,500 elementary teachers did not meet even the minimum standards established as legal for teaching by various states. (Official figures reported in 1959 by state departments of education.)
As many as 200,000 teachers completed no more than two years of college.**—*"The National Interest and the Teaching of English," National Council of Teachers of English, 1961*

---

My book is not addressed to the problem of writing instruction in high school or college. The meaning of this book is that writing failures are made in the primary grades where the first attitudes toward writing are formed. It is waste work to keep plastering and painting over upper-level English damage if its continuing cause is that lower-level English is out of joint. High school and college English courses, however excellent and well-thought-out they may be, are built on top of faults. They are doomed to trouble and it shouldn't surprise anyone that they get it.

My only reason for looking at college English even superficially is to see what the elementary-school teacher is taught about writing. According to state-certification rules, virtually all students preparing to teach in the primary grades must take freshman English. Since so many teachers show the same broken ideas of English, it's reasonable to examine the stamp that has impressed them all. That stamp is their college English course.

In an earlier chapter we saw that reading was split from writing at the start of grade school. We saw readers aggressively nurtured and pampered while writers got a hollow, figurehead curriculum of instruction. The split is not mended in college. It gets worse.

## HER TRAINING

Late in September 1960 the National Council of Teachers of English sent a special questionnaire to the chairmen of departments of education in 2,000 colleges. Within forty-five days it had 569 answers from schools that prepared elementary-school teachers. The answers revealed serious failures in the preparation of teachers in English:

* More than 94 per cent of the colleges failed to require work in the English language.
* Almost half of the colleges failed to require a course on teaching the English language.
* In more than three-fifths of the colleges students were not required to complete work in grammar and usage.
* Only 19.7 per cent of the programs specified study in composition beyond the freshman level.

## HER INFLUENCES, I: KLEIN'S HEAD-MAN THEORY

Lawrence R. Klein, publications editor in the U.S. Department of Labor, spent a year—August 1962 to August 1963—studying government writing in the social sciences. At the start of his work a "distinguished business journalist" wrote him: "I'd make one point, and one point only, about your project. Writing can be improved whenever and wherever superiors in an organization are interested in good writing; if praise and promotion are meted out to persons who express themselves well, if this is a standard throughout the organization, then persons all along the line will try to express themselves well."

"I scoffed at first," Mr. Klein says in the report of his study published in 1964. "But before long I learned that his point was a good one, and I offer the theory of the Head Man. In any department of Government *writing will be just about as good as the head of the agency wants it to be and insists that it be*."

Klein's Head-Man Theory can be directly applied to our school system. Where a teacher is convinced that writing is important, you will find her class writing. Where a principal really wants good writing you will find teachers who teach writing. Where a school superintendent insists on good writing and finds ways of publicly rewarding it, you will have the schools in his district or state delivering it. I would guess, from the curriculum guides produced by Vermont, Anne Arundel County (Maryland), and San Diego County, that the grade schools there produce decent writing.

Unfortunately, any Head Man influence on grade teachers is quite impossible when those who direct her training misunderstand or ignore or belittle the importance of writing.

I believe Klein's theory explains why English scientists, educators, and politicians are better writers than American scientists, educators, and politicians. British students who graduate from a writing-oriented tutorial system know the value of good writing. Wherever they go, they will naturally require good writing from assistants who work for them. If they become school headmasters, their schools will produce writers.

Colleges used to require a writing sample along with the application for admission. Such a sample might forewarn applicants that the college valued writing. At the same time, this college requirement would put pressure on high schools and grade schools to demand more writing themselves in order to prepare their students for college acceptance.

From 1900 to 1926 the College Entrance Examination Board used nothing but essay examinations. Then, between 1926 and 1941, it began mixing in objective tests. In 1965, out of the 545 colleges that were members of the College Entrance Examination Board, only seventy-two required a candidate to submit a writing sample. In 1967 the Board had 782 members and it voted to abolish the writing sample entirely. What the colleges communicate to high schools is that writing examinations are too much trouble to administrate, that the information received from them is difficult to assess, that multiple-choice information is more exact.

The future grade teacher in college doesn't have to be a Rhodes candidate to see that her Head Man has made reading the king subject in English. Any catalogue will show her that literature courses boss the English section. At the same time, she is *never made to feel that writing is important.*

## HER INFLUENCES, II: THE JARGON JUNGLE

From freshman year to graduation, the future grade teacher is swaddled and rolled in the glutenous word-batter of educationist jargon. The stuff gets in her hair, in her shoes, under her nails— she can't escape it. It comes in her mail, it's on bulletin boards, in the school paper, in her textbooks. Wherever she turns there's more of it. She gets used to it and comes to take it as inevitable.

What must the future teacher think of writing when the leaders in her profession cannot communicate what they mean by communication? For example, note this excerpt from "The Fourth Communication Skill: Writing," published by the Arizona Department of Education: "The greatest weakness with many teachers is *too much* and *too early* concern with creative writing with students which provides no consistent progress toward good writing and serves only to undermine progress achieved in better controlled parts of a good audio-lingual program of second language teaching."

*Communication in the Elementary Schools* was published by the Wisconsin Council of Teachers of English (1964). Its table of contents includes such titles as "Intensional Orientation," "Two-Dimensional Orientation," and "Phatic Communication." Here are two typical passages:

> The use of language to accurately express thoughts with recognition to its important place in accurate thinking is not to be minimized. A student impressed with this awareness but not yet habituated in its practice may become tense in talking and almost afraid to express himself because he might not do it accurately. At this point we take into account a fourth principle of general semantics, that called phatic communication. . . .

> As our world shrinks we live more closely together with the result of more interactions between people. Interactions between people multiply as numbers are added. Between two people there are two interactions; person A reacts to person B and person B reacts to person A (A ↔ B). Between three people there are six interactions; A reacts to B and C, B reacts to A and C, and C reacts to A and B (A ↔ C ↔ B). Between four people there are twelve interactions for each of the four persons react to each of the other three and four times three are twelve. . . .

I bought *Communication in the Elementary Schools*, for $1.50, to find out what "phatic communication" means. It means talk.

How can any curriculum guide be accepted as an authority on writing when its own writing is terrible? Note this directive to grade teachers:

> Writing compound sentences. Note: A discussion of the meaning of conjunctions as structure words is very important in the light of joining simple sentences to make a compound sentence. As a matter of fact, too much time cannot be spent on "meaning" that is apparent only when conjunctions are used in sentences.

> Writing complex sentences. Note: The concept of adjunct sentence in place of dependent clause may be introduced as a means of clarification.—"*A Developing Curriculum in English*," *School of Education, Indiana State University*.

How will she learn that writing should communicate when her textbook authors haven't?

## Differentiation of Specific Emotions

The evident excitement (violent mass activity and crying) exhibited by neonates when they are aroused by intense, noxious, and prolonged stimuli is analogous in intensity of feeling tones to the emotional states of older children.— *"Psychology of Emotion," an article in* Educational Research.

And note this sample of "intense, noxious, and prolonged" jargon:

## Communication

The key in reading is "communication," communication of ideas, feelings, understandings and information. We now realize that effective communication takes place through either oral or written media to the extent that the individual can bring personal meaning to *these* ideas in *this* context. Personal meaning is developed through contact. This experience must be direct and personal until such time as enough background has been accumulated in each type of situation that it may be synthesized by the individual. Only then can it provide a basis for bringing personal meaning to the reading vicariously. Individuals may be able to attach similar verbalizations to various situations but this may only reflect others' statements and carry virtually no real meaning.
—*"Reading As Contact,"* Educational Leadership, *February 1967.*

## HER COMPOSITION COURSE

The elementary-school teacher spends upward of 40 to 50 per cent of her time teaching English and language arts, yet she spends *less than 8 per cent* of her total time in college learning English and how to teach it.

What is the 8 per cent like? What kind of "creative writing" is she up to in college? Does she learn the Thank-You Novel in freshman year, the Cheer-Up Novel in sophomore year, the Business Novel in junior year, the Novel of Regret in senior year? And what "practical writing" does she learn? The Letter Accepting a Fulbright? The Job Application Letter? The Friendly Letter to the draft board?

The English Composition class may be a class in logic or psycholinguistics. It may discuss the media of Marshall McLuhan or Ong's *Ramus, Method and the Decay of Dialogue: From the Art of Discourse to the Art of Reason*. It may, week after week, analyze *The New Yorker* or Tom Wolfe (dead or alive). It may be a flat, dull class droning with snores or a cold needle shock to the mind.

One thing you can bet on: it will be a class *about* writers and *about* writing—somebody *else's* writing, not the students'.

What the future grade teacher learns in college is that "English" is *reading*. *Composition* is an isolated, derided, embarrassing, low-status period of the freshman year while *literature* is real English. Freshman Composition is remedial high school English, just as high school English is remedial grade-school English. "Composition" is a second go at Operation Head Start where young adults can practice knotting simple verbs to nouns, getting used to the dictionary, and discovering life isn't all true-false or multiple-choice. For the better beginners, it may mean writing like Addison and Steele.

---

**Composition . . . is commonly thought of largely as a skill subject not much more, academically, than typing or home economics. The task of the composition teacher is simply to bring students to the point where they can convey thought on paper with a fair degree of clarity and conformity to the conventions. . . . Composition teachers look narrowly provincial to many of their colleagues.—"*What Is English?*" *by H. A. Gleason, Jr., Conference on College Composition and Communication, October 1962***

---

Many good English teachers believe that all students are best served in meeting the very finest users of the English language, the classic poets, novelists, and drama writers. Such meetings, they say, will gradually form ideals of language use that will direct the student in his own life whether he becomes a lawyer, an engineer, or a dentist.

Note that they are speaking of *reading*. The ideal they hope to establish is a *standard of reading*. A good reading standard, they are arguing, will serve the student's *writing*, too. If the student will only read enough Smollet and Fielding, Burke, Macaulay, Bacon and Addison and Steele and Emerson, his own writing eventually will begin to show signs of their grace and exactness.

This is the hope. But it is a futile, false hope and deserves to be toppled. By the time students come to the classical masters, they are so reading-drenched and their language habits so unexercised they can't distinguish *imitation* from copying.

At his best, the literature instructor is an artist in his own right, able to lead the reader to such penetrating insights that the after-image of special visions will shine in the mind for life. He is a professor in the oral tradition, talking out his thesis and his studies, a minstrel singing his insights, experiencing the direct joys of the singer-actor. Such teaching may indeed inspire a reader to want to become a writer. Unfortunately, he won't become one through mere wanting.

No doubt the talking teacher gets more satisfaction from in-laying students with his own theories than from reading theirs. It takes heroic human generosity to give a captive audience its time to talk and write.

The college English teacher is a tourist guide *pointing at* salient or subtle features of writing to make sure we *see* them. Some structural lines—argument, for example—can possibly be learned from *looking* at an essay, but such visual charting doesn't help the writer when he faces blank paper. What's he to do—draw, I, II, A, B, 1, 2, 3, a, b, c and then fill in? All the outline scheme does for him is remind him to string out his points and to make some points bigger than others.

Rarely if ever does an English teacher take you into a story to let you see it from the writer's viewpoint as the writer was trying to shape it. Never does he make your mouth and throat feel the writer's sounds. Never, never does he describe the writer's audience so that you can understand his gropings to reach them through metaphor. Yet, unless a student can get into the writer's mind and see the writer's attempts to bridge the gap between himself and his readers, he won't understand what writing is, and he won't even be reading right.

Many classic models don't deserve to be imitated because their patterns of communication aren't clear to modern readers. Many wouldn't even be in anthologies if they weren't in the public domain. They're used because they're free.

At their worst, classic models wrap the student with inhibitions. The student's mind becomes so impressed with them that he doubts the competence of his own expression. Like the plain girl who sees too many beauty contests, he compares himself with the writers he admires and concludes he'll never be able to match them.

The inhibitive effect does a double wrong when it affects the future grade teacher. First, the models block her own writing. Second, they influence the standards by which she will edit the writing of her children.

ALL WRITING is one of two kinds: either I write something only for myself, with no intention of showing it to anyone, or I write something for someone else to read.

1) The first kind of writing is not the object of writing instruction because there are no standards that have to be learned. The writer makes his own rules. If I write a note to myself or keep a secret diary, I can invent my own spelling or shorthand. I can write with lipstick or with my elbows dipped in ink, if I like. Of course, if I expect to read what I write later, I'd better write legibly and use a spelling code I can remember. If I want to save the writing, I won't write on beach sand.

There is a kind of writing not meant for others to read, a thinking-out on paper, a doodling with words. Paper lets us fix thoughts in a space and then move them about without having to remember what they are. It's a cheap test for error. Paper lets us band ideas so that we can study the patterns of their flight.

2) The other kind of writing, the writing that we want to be read, is an extension of talk. As such it is subject to many of the same rules that normally govern spoken face-to-face communication. It has to make sense. It has to be clear.

The closer writing is to my immediate personal needs and for my own eyes, the freer I am to use any kind of code, handwriting, and spelling that pleases me. But when I write to *others*, I need to use conventional meanings, standard spellings, and a standard handwriting. When I write to be understood, I should abide by rules that assure me of being understood. Learning to use these rules constitutes writing instruction. The school is not obliged to show me how to write my own personal diary. The school is obliged to teach me to communicate to society.

There is another difference between writing that is strictly for myself and writing that is intended for others. For myself, I can arrange my ideas and word my feelings as I like in any way that suits my needs. But writing to someone else means that I must arrange my statements to meet the reader. I must respect his willingness and capacity to understand me. I must try to beware of any special conditions that might affect his reading, just as they might affect his listening if we were talking.

What makes Sammy Reader run? Who is he? How smart is he? How old? What does he do for a living? What are his prejudices and how is he biased? Is he complacent, suspicious, judicious? Is he friendly or hostile or indifferent? What threats does he feel? What does he fear and what does he love? Does he like to eat? Has he ever been to war? Has he ever been divorced? Where is he now? Where is Sammy running?

IN 1958 a conference in New York attended by representatives of the National Council of Teachers of English, a college English association; the Modern Language Association; and other similar groups discussed this question as one of its "basic issues": "How can a student ever acquire a sensitiveness to language without studying literary works which illustrate such sensitiveness?"

There are three kinds of sensitivity possible in the use of language. First, there is the sensitivity of the writer's language for his subject. Next, there is that by which his language is faithful to his feelings and his private, individual self.

When an English instructor talks about "sensitiveness to language" he is usually talking about these two kinds of sensitivity. He seldom talks about the third kind of sensitivity: that by which the *writer accommodates his vision of the real and tempers his self-*

*statement to the feelings, intellectual capacity, and culture of the reader.*

A student will learn his language as a result of success or failure using it, not by looking at it in a book, nor purely through random self-expression. Language without people isn't even for the birds. It's for nobody. It's nothing.

He'll learn sensitivity when he sees that words can make people blush, or cry, or walk away in anger. He'll learn it when someone smashes him in the face for something he's said. He'll learn after a few job interviews, after losing a friend, through making up with an old enemy. Through making excuses, through talking with lawyers and women. Talking to a nun, a cop, a tax man. To an old, old, old lady with loose skin stuffed into her black collar and with quivering jaw, sprouts of white hair leaping over her face. When he sees her eyes assert life at something he says, then he'll understand sensitiveness in language.

The writer who uses "sensitive" language merely for unrelated self-expression is a showoff and in the long reading tiresome. Just as he's a bore to listen to, he's a bore to read.

We welcome the writer who tries to be clear, who tries to figure out where we might not understand him. We appreciate his attempt to understand us. It shows respect.

A writer with something new to tell us is like a foreigner. We like foreigners who try to speak our language.

We like language that comes out to meet us.

The best writing does not burn with a "hard, gemlike flame." The best writing *warms*.

## HER INSTRUCTOR

What is the future grade teacher's English instructor's attitude toward writing? What does he know about writing? Does *he* write?

---

**Graduate instructors who direct masters essays and doctoral dissertations are shocked at the extent to which they must become teachers of "hospital" English. Yet we are aware that many of the candidates for higher degrees are already engaged in part-time teaching of freshman English. If they**

cannot recognize and correct their own egregious errors, what is happening to the end-products of their teaching?—*National Council of Teachers of English, 1964*

In big schools, English Composition is taught by badly paid teaching assistants (T.A.s) working their way through graduate school. The T.A. gets no special training to teach writing. He looks at the course as a job, a tribal rite required before passing to manhood in the Department. The time he gives to students has to be taken from his own graduate work, so he can't afford to be lavishly helpful even if he knows how to help. If a T.A. likes teaching composition, older faculty members see him either as a loser or a campus nut.

Among the members of the higher circles are those who teach literature *per se*. Analogous to those souls in Dante's circles of heaven, all of these are not on the same plane. There are those who teach specialized courses concentrating on one or two genres. They sit at the fountain of wisdom. Then there are those who teach surveys of specific periods. They are a bit farther removed from the divine light. More remote than these are the people who teach surveys of national literature. And so the distance from the inner sanctum becomes greater and greater until we arrive at the dubious place of those who teach composition. Sometimes they are considered worthy of a foot in heaven; but most times they are relegated to do penance in purgatory, neither being accepted nor damned.... What if a person knows that for students to be able to express themselves in writing is much more important to themselves, to the university, and to society than to be able to recall characters, plots, or professional allusions? If a person has such low aims, he will be thought either deranged, incompetent, or intellectually lethargic....—*Everett W. Gibbs*, College Composition and Communication, *May 1963*

# The College Image of Writing:
## It Is Not Communication But
## Measurable Self-Expression

**In school, writing is talked about as communication, taught as an art, and tested as thinking. It is neither taught nor tested as communication.**

IN JANUARY 1958 twenty-eight teachers of English from all parts of the country and representing their most powerful organizations met in New York City for a series of conferences to discuss the frustrations of their profession.

Their conferences produced a remarkable document defining and clarifying basic issues, hanging them by 150 question marks on a line only six and a half pages long. It is a model report, delivering valuable information in clear, graceful English.

But if you finger the conference laundry carefully, you'll discover tiny rips and blued holes telling of a vicious ballpoint-pen battle.

The very first matter decided by the conference was that "English" consists of proportionate parts of *language*, *literature*, and *composition*. The second matter decided was that no one could agree on the relative proportions of the three parts.

In 1964 Roger J. Applebee reported to the National Council of Teachers of English: "From the composite estimate of departmental chairmen and from our own observation, the teaching of literature clearly receives the most attention—from half to two-thirds—in regard to classroom time and emphasis. . . . On the basis of some five hundred hours of classroom observation, it would appear that only about twenty per cent of class time is given to the teaching of writing."

One of the aims of the 1958 conference was to identify English. Just what were English teachers supposed to teach? The "Basic Issues" report reveals a doubt: "We are uncertain whether our boundaries should include . . . journalism" and "Should students be taught to 'express themselves' or to 'communicate'? . . . Is learning to write primarily a matter of learning to think? This issue bristles with difficulties."

You bet it bristles. It is a muted revelation of the power scuffle between those who believe English is *reading* and those who believe English is *writing*.

The communicators know what writing is, but the reading people own "English."

English departments don't really like journalism. They sneer at "popular" magazines and "writing for hire." "Madison Avenue" is a dirty name. So are *Time*, *Life*, and *Reader's Digest* dirty names. The Hollywood writer has "lost his soul." The television writer never had one.

The Department despises journalism for being overconcerned with readers, for pop pandering at the expense of language and truth. It scorns mass-media writers for their false, fast, skimpy research, their impatience to hear the truth through their hear-and-run writing, and calls "foul!" at their insensitive, careless use of language, rhinestone wit, and Freshman I sentiments.

Frequently, the Department is right.

But journalism preserves the concept that writing is a relationship between writer and reader, while in the English Department, writing is an *object*, a hard, spatial, measurable pattern, an expression of thought unaffected by readers; it is never an interpersonal relationship. It's not journalism's fault that research and report are estranged. In journalism they're not. Journalism *is* research-report combined. Journalists rely heavily on oral interviews, and their writing tends to lie close to sound. They are forced to consider the reader's interests, intelligence, and language capacity because their reports have to sell on their own merits and therefore have to communicate. Their feeling toward language is pragmatic;

if it doesn't work, chuck it out.

A professor of English who had recently received an award for research work told me he planned to examine "excellence of writing in such magazines as *Harper's* or *Atlantic Monthly* as compared with writing in the *Saturday Evening Post*, for example." This is a typical Department remark and it reveals the basic Department image of writing. The *Atlantic Monthly's* writer-reader relationship is different from *Playboy's* or *Redbook's* or the *Saturday Evening Post's*. Each magazine, by reason of the publisher's concept of his readers, carries a different content, uses a slightly different language, offers different services, different illustrations, images, and references to accommodate the different interests and intelligences of the different readers. If the entire contents of *Foreign Affairs* were traded with those of *Mad* for a single issue, would that issue of *Mad* thereby become a more excellent magazine?

---

**Mr. Matthews, who was the editor of *Time*, said that the most important thing in journalism is not reporting but communication. "What are you going to communicate?" I asked him. "The most important thing," he said, "is the man on one end of the circuit saying 'My God, I'm alive! You're alive!' and the fellow on the other end, receiving his message, saying 'My God, you're right! We're both alive!' "—*A. J. Liebling*, The Sweet Science**

---

Once writing is limited to being an isolated, static expression unrelated to its readers it can then be measured as a hard, spatial pattern. The anxiety to measure and grade writing has helped force it away from its communicative function.

In the spring of 1965 Ellis B. Page of the University of Connecticut announced that he would program computers to read student papers. Dr. Page is director of the Bureau of Educational Research. He received funds for his project from the College Entrance Examination Board. The machine, he said, would "simulate the ratings of superior judges."

What do "superior judges" rate in a piece of writing? Here is Dr. Page's list of thirty-one "variables" programmed into the computer for "Project Essay":

1. Title present
2. Average sentence length
3. Number of paragraphs
4. Subject-verb openings
5. Length of essay in words
6. Number of parentheses
7. Number of apostrophes
8. Number of commas
9. Number of periods
10. Number of percentage marks
11. Number of underlined words
12. Number of dashes
13. Number of colons
14. Number of semi-colons
15. Number of question marks
16. Number of exclamation marks
17. Number of quotation marks
18. Number of prepositions
19. Number of connective words
20. Number of spelling errors
21. Number of relative pronouns
22. Number of subordinating conjunctions
23. Number of words on Dale common word list
24. Number of sentences with end punctuation present
25. Number of declarative sentences. type "A"
26. Number of declarative sentences. type "B"
27. Number of hyphens
28. Number of slashes
29. Average word length
30. Standard deviation of word length
31. Standard deviation of sentence length

Is this all "superior judges" look for in grading a paper? Who grades the judges?

If computers can simulate the ratings of "superior judges," why couldn't a computer "read" the judgments of "superior" critics and pretest new Broadway plays? Newman, Watts, Probst, Tynan, Kerr, and other New York and London theater critics could read their last year's reviews into the machine. Superior producers, superior backers, and superior actors could add their special whims and favorite roles.

The variables could include the number of acts, scenes, actors and actresses, costume changes, and songs. Following Dr. Page's formula, dialogue could be analyzed by counting the total number of words in each play, the number of lines for the leading man and leading lady, and the number of question marks and exclamation points. Superior backstage workers could add union requests—for example, the number of seats in the theater; the number of tickets available; the number of lights, props, and pieces of scenery; the average prop weight and standard deviation of prop weight; the number of drinks sold at intermission; and audience heat as measured by air conditioning needed.

Some mistakes and some injustices are inevitable if Dr. Page's system were adopted, but the loss of good plays would be more than made up in backers' savings.

Page's computer can't measure writing because all it can do is count. It measures feelings by counting exclamation marks or such interjections as Oh! Alas! My, my!

It cannot detect sarcasm or irony. It doesn't understand humor. It doesn't understand anything at all.

It can't read meanings. It can't read feelings. It can only read writing as a silhouette, the scratch of meaning on paper.

Dr. Page's grading machine straddles the foul line. On the *fair* side, it may possibly help correct punctuation. But Dr. Page is deceived if he thinks he thereby measures writing.

Mel Elfin, *Newsweek*'s Washington Bureau editor, gave the computer a terse review (April 5, 1965):

" 'It's a fair guess,' says Page, 'that words and phrases like 'moreover,' 'however,' 'on the contrary,' and 'in summary' are indicative of the more mature writer.' In summary, however, or on the contrary, should such writing get an A?

"Eventually, Professor Page may tackle the more difficult problem of judging essay content. 'There's no reason,' he says, 'why superior human graders, who are in very short supply these days, couldn't grade enough papers [with their own brains] so that their standards could be imitated by the computer. I know teachers would rather do research and smoke their pipes than correct endless exam papers.' And since many students would no doubt rather smoke their pipes than study, the next step may be for them to program their own computers to take exams, more-over."

## The Ph.D. of English System
## Is an Elephant Machine

QQQQQQQQQQQQQQQQQQQQQQQQQQQQQQQQQQQQQQQQQQQQQQQQQQQ

WHAT STAMPS college English? What is the master-stamp responsible for its reading-oriented set? College English is reading-biased because of the Ph.D. of English System. The System marks the teachers of English. The System stamps the English curriculum.

The English doctoral program is stretched toward research. Research in English is not like research in, say, geology or physics, which seeks to report new discoveries in an ever-growing field with an ever-widening frontier. Ph.D. English research drills around inside a period of English expression only a few hundred years wide. Inside this narrow field it limits its studies further by specializing in only one kind of English-language expression—that which is imaginative, namely, poetry, novels, and drama.

Ph.D. English research is *reading*, pure and simple, and a skinny patch of reading at that.

---

**Fifty years ago our association had a membership of a little over a thousand; today we number 18,000. There are too many workers in a vineyard that has barely increased in size, and many of the newcomers do as much trampling as vine-dressing.... I have concluded that out field is over worked. Too many people are trying to do too much in too small an area. Intensive cultivation has its limits, as every agronomist knows.—*Dr. Morris Bishop, to members of the Modern Language Association while he was president of the Association in 1965***

---

*The Ph.D. Eng. System is a reader-making machine*, an "elephant machine," as it would be called in industry, since it makes other reader-making machines. It is a vocational-training school for shepherds who will watch over flocks of students feeding and feeding and feeding on books of the past.

The System is self-perpetuating. Once you board it, you have to help drive it or it'll throw you off. You have to support it or risk losing security, prestige, promotion, and a number of other professional benefits.

The System gets its power from the Literature Experts who run it. They sit in the best-paid chairs. They control appointments to the English Department and promotions in it. They control the executive, judicial, legislative, and social branches of Department politics. They "influence" the "fields" to be researched. They direct and supervise Ph.D. candidates and judge their examinations. I almost expect they have the right to levy taxes and issue warrants of search and seizure.

---

... many would agree that the Ph.D. system, especially the thesis system, is dismally unsatisfactory. Our young candidate, radiant with literary enthusiasm and high purpose, is given the task of writing on a subject that nobody is interested in, in a book that nobody will read, a book that is not a book, a book from which at best can be drawn two or three special articles. He approaches his task with repugnance and he fulfills it often with loathing. And he is quite right. No good man or woman wants to spend precious years doing something futile, merely to prove his constancy under affliction.
—Dr. Morris Bishop, 1965

---

The Ph.D. System is as baffling as a labyrinth in the Yellow Fairy Book. It demands monastic poverty, chastity, and obedience, heroic hope, patience in the pinch of wasting time. Yet each year scores of candidates seek the Ph.D. in English. They will use from two to five years of their life in classrooms watching older professors plaiting the hairs in Shakespeare's ears. They will sit with their thesis directors and solemnly tweezer out the cubic quarter-inch of the field of English they will investigate and report on. They will bale notes. They will read till their eyeballs look like dyed Easter eggs. Eventually, they will grunt out a thesis nobody cares about.

---

I chose for my doctoral dissertation an interesting subject—St. Evremond in England. . . . I spent a winter in the Bibliothèque Nationale and the British Museum, and did not discover very much, though I had a very good time. I returned to America and showed my thin pack of thesis slips to my chief,

James F. Mason of Cornell. "Splendid!" he said. "Splendid! In about fifteen years you will have a very fine thesis." "Yes, but—" I said. "Yes, but—. What would you suggest?" Wise Professor Mason said: "Take a small subject, with clear limits, with a beginning and an end. When you are through you will know you are through." "Give me an example," said I. "Why not the plays of Jules Lemaître? There are only thirteen of them; they aren't very good, but they are interesting in showing what happens when a good critic tries to apply his critical formulas to creative work." "Very well," said I; *va pour le thèâtre de Jules Lemaître.*" I worked for exactly a year, and wrote exactly 365 pages on the plays of Jules Lemaître, proving what everybody already knew, rediscovering a great many facts that had been forgotten, and properly forgotten. The experience was profitable to me in many ways; but I wrote a false book, a pseudo-book, a non-book for which I received the Ph.D. I have often thought of extracting it, but I renounce that purpose on realizing that, so far as I can learn, no one has looked at it in 38 years.—*Dr. Morris Bishop, 1965*

---

WHY DO THEY DO IT?
WHAT MAKES THE PH.D. CANDIDATE RUN?

In 1965 I asked twenty men and women who had recently earned Ph.D.s in English how much time and money their degrees had cost them and what they expected to gain from their investment. Fourteen persons answered from universities in Indiana, California, Michigan, Ohio, New York, Arizona, Colorado, Pennsylvania, Washington, and Illinois.

Here is one of the questions I asked followed by some of the answers: "What difference in treatment do you expect as a result of now having the Ph.D.?"

. . . they call you Doctor—and the rank starts as assistant professor . . .

. . . I couldn't get a job at my present school without the Ph.D. but *if* I could, it would be an instructorship at about 7M. I'm now an assistant professor at about 9M.

. . . since my status would be lower without it, it would affect friendships that I have formed since these friends are peers.

. . . ease of securing tenure; ease of changing jobs; faster promotion.

238

... greater self-satisfaction and more solid self-image; of course the self-image is totally irrelevant and based on false assumption in so far as it depends on an artificial thing like Ph.D.

I asked: "Do you expect your dissertation will be sought out and read in the library? Will it be published?" Eight persons answered "Yes" and six said "No." One of the eight said, "Yes, definitely." One said, "Yes, occasionally," and one said "Possibly." One of the "No's" said, "Ha Ha Ha. No," and another said, "Are you kidding? No."

When I asked "Do you expect your dissertation to benefit others?" nine persons answered "Yes" and five "No." Two of the answers follow:

Probably it will be of little benefit, but it is factually oriented and is carefully documented—so a number of facts have been gathered and organized.

Chose it to get the hell through. But it has scholarly value.

| How long did it take you to get your Ph.D.? (Years) | How long did you take to write your thesis? (Years) | How much money did getting your degree cost you totally? | What difference in salary do you expect to enjoy as a result of having a Ph.D.? |
|---|---|---|---|
| 15 | 4 | $15,000 | $2,000 |
| 9 | $2\frac{1}{2}$ | 15,000 | — |
| 6 | 2 | 20,600 | — |
| 6 | 3 | — | 2,200 |
| $5\frac{1}{2}$ | 9 mos. | 10–15,000 | — |
| 5 | $1\frac{1}{2}$ | — | 372 (Immed.) |
| 5 | 1 | — | 10,000 (Ult.) |
| 5 | 1 | 30,000 | — |
| $4\frac{1}{3}$ | 31 18-hr. days | 12,000 | 2,000 |
| 4 | 1 | 5,000 | — |
| 4 | 8 mos. | 13,200 | — |
| 4 | 4 mos. | 7,300 | — |
| 3 | $1\frac{1}{3}$ | 1,000 | — |
| 2 | 1 | — | — |

The significance of the figures above is that they affect writing instruction. In the present Ph.D. System it pays to be a reading teacher. It doesn't pay to teach writing. No young Ph.D. Eng. who has just spent five or six years and $18,000 getting his degree in eighteenth-century literature wants to become famous for his composition classes. There's no future to being King of English I.

But reading—now *there's* a *future*. Books are visible, collectible, measurable, catalogable, Government issuable, stock-pileable, cost-accountable, destructible and replaceable, status-symbolical. You can't beat books.

---

... graduate students are usually literate English majors. They face a major conflict in graduate school: the more time they spend with their freshman students the less time they have to spend on their own graduate work. This is self-defeating. Some of the best teaching in the universities is being done by vital, alive, interested TA's. Those who reject the students to face their own studies, go on and finish their degrees. The good teachers often flunk out on this level. The pedants and dullards often remain....

—*A letter from a new Ph.D.*

... the smart grad student knows that if he wants ever to get out of school he must neglect his students; he has divided loyalties. Even as his own profs ignore his needs in order to publish and maintain or augment their professional image so he must neglect freshmen in order to have sufficient time to finish his thesis, etc. The system above all cheats the tuition-paying freshmen.

—*A letter from a new Ph.D.*

---

# The Persecution and Assassination of Writing As Performed by Inmates of the Department of English Under the Direction of the Ph.D. System

MOST COLLEGE GRADUATES who want to write fiction fail because they don't know what a story is. In school they were *shown* stories as plot outlines—I. A.
                  B.
          II. A.
                  B. 1.
                      2. a.
                          b.
                          c.—etc., or dotted-line charts with abrupt peaks to indicate climax and a drop to indicate the end. Poetry was also taught to the eye. Rhythms, which should be *felt*, were stretched out on paper to be *scanned:*  —|-|—|-|—|-/-|—|-|

Some English Departments attempt to teach writing by teaching etymology, semantics, or linguistics. But a student may know the origin and life story of every word in a six-pound dictionary and still not be able to write a story or even an essay. At some stage he'll have to stop analyzing his words and piece them together in a story. He won't be able to because he won't know how. Analysis and synthesis are distinctly different operations and to learn the first does not mean automatic learning of the second.

Story writing is not an educational frill. Stories give us a chance to theorize about, guess at, and explore human conflicts. We imagine conflicts as they might have happened or conflicts that

241

*could* happen. They let us daydream life in advance of realizing it. They save us time, for if we could only progress by direct experience or if we had to creep along the measured findings of behaviorists we would scarcely move anywhere.

The failure to teach forms and patterns to students who want to write is one of the English Department's most shameful failures.

All college departments—not only the English Department—should require factual writing. The English Department should provide courses in developing fiction. It should not teach finished fiction but fiction at its raw, unworked beginnings. It should help students adapt proven story patterns of the past to modern language, to contemporary conditions and subjects, and it should help them experiment with new forms. Every college, every advertising agency, every publishing house has brilliant sentence writers able to produce pure little spills of feeling and self, but unable to tell or write a story. This is not because story writing is a mysterious gift. It's because the would-be writers were taught *to see*, not *to do*.

As things are now, there is no English Department in any university in the United States that can offer full instruction to a person whose goal is to become a professional writer. The person who wants to become a writer must make up his own course. He must hop from school to school looking for that unusual professor here or there who is able to help him. Meanwhile, he must dodge a great number of others who will distract him from his purpose, waste his time, misdirect him, discourage him, and in other ways do him actual harm.

Whose fault is this? By whose orders can the rights of students be so arrogantly frustrated? Here, clearly, is the stamp of the elephant machine. This is evident in the remarkable December 1964 issue of *College Composition and Communication*, published by the National Council of Teachers of English. Its editor, Dr. Ken Macrorie, opens the issue by saying: "Ever since I entered graduate school in English in 1964, I have been called to dark corners of corridors or asked to sit in faculty offices behind closed doors and listen to chapters from a book I would title: 'Tales of Neglect and Sadism.'"

Dr. Macrorie presents ten unsigned case histories describing "the Graduate Experience in English." The ten cases are an angering account of vicious egghead pettiness. They are titled by excerpts; for example, "One wins a Ph.D. by being a drudge," "Literature here is studied as if it were a dead cat," "An interruption rather than a preparation," "I could not recommend the total experience to anyone."

CASE #10, titled "A nagging sense of dislocation," describes a graduate-school student torn by the conflictive demands of the Ph.D. of English System and his own desire to be a creative, independent writer. The author states his case in such perfectly fit language that I gladly yield a piece of this book to him. He has asked to stay nameless.

Dear Ken,

. . . It may seem wilfull to begin this record in the wheatfields of eastern Colorado, but my relatives have a good deal to do with what I want to say, and they live in eastern Colorado. Each summer I go home to help harvest the family wheat. For one or two weeks I work under a heavy-hot sun, doing all the things that once were the daily stuff of my life. I deal with wheat, not with ideas: Wallace Stevens forgotten, I crack the fat red berries between my teeth to see if they are ready to thresh, and the setting of the straw-walker on the combine is more important than allegory in the *Faerie Queene*. I drive the combine through the delicate shafts of straw watching warily the thunderheads in the west that might hold hail, and I scoop grain in the galvanized heat of a bin. All of this gives me a pleasantly deceptive feeling of really being home, a sense that is strengthened by certain constant parts of the homecoming ritual. I can look for a sour-cream raisin pie at noon meal of the second day of my visit, I know that my father will recall the year the wheat made 58 bushels to the acre, and sometime during harvest one of my cousins will offer me a chew of tobacco and a faintly taunting remark about the habits of professors, both of which I will accept.

*243*

But this convivial chinking together of the homecoming ritual doesn't obscure the fact that, to most of the members of our large family, I am a failure. The more positive of my uncles and cousins think of me as an "educated fool," belonging roughly in the same class as the county agent who laboriously identified bindweed by looking it up in a book, while others take the softer view that I am a student merely because I am too lazy to be a wheat farmer. This judgement is an old fact of my life, and I don't think I'm overstating it. That I was a lazy, muddled, skewed child, one who would probably be walking down by the river if he were needed to take a broken combine part to the blacksmith for welding, was decided by the bright suns of my juvenile sky, the men who broke horses and drove combines. They knew what they were doing—that showed in every movement of their thick bodies—and so they had to be right about me. I knew I wasn't lazy, but I accepted their estimate; when I fell asleep while driving a tractor and dragged a one-way plow through a barbed wire fence, for example, I didn't tell my uncles that I had stayed awake all night reading *The Grapes of Wrath*. To account for my drowsiness that way would have been useless, even impertinent, so I simply said that I couldn't stay awake, thereby furnishing the whole community with a cherished joke.

I don't tell you this in order to exhibit myself as a sensitive young plant trapped in a wheatfield. It does have some bearing on my life as a graduate student, as I hope to show. But for now the point I want to make is that I had early practice in accepting two contradictory ideas about myself: I knew that what my relatives saw as slothfulness in me wasn't that at all, but I accepted their judgement of me.

This wouldn't have been so clear to me three weeks ago. On my last harvest trip this summer I garnered more than wheat; I saw how deeply the arrogant values of my relatives had penetrated. And even though what happened at home this summer seems to me improbable, something more fitting for a

Steig cartoon about Dreams of Glory than for an important event of my life, it is true that a silly, childish quarrel did allow me to glimpse something of myself, and this needs to be churned up with the rest.

The way it began was not unusual. Uncle John, the wit in our family, needles me every year about my effete student's life. Last year it was the shorts and sandals I was wearing when I arrived: "Is that what schoolmarms are wearing?" This year he mined the vein that I had gotten too soft to stay aboard anything more dangerous than a swivel chair. At the huge harvest table, before an appreciative audience, or out in the field, while we greased and gassed the machines, he talked of a two-year-old filly he owned. She was still unbroken, having thrown John twice, and he kept challenging me to break her. (Once this wouldn't have been a joke; it is part of the family mythology that anyone so muddle-headed as I was as a child had to be good with animals, so if this had happened while I was a teen-ager, I would have been asked seriously to do the job, even though John has always been a better rider than I.) Although it's been ten years since I tried to act like Jim Shoulders, John and the family left me no out, and when my young relatives began to snicker at the bare mention of the horse, I thought I had to say I'd ride her. My wife was angry. She said it was adolescent of me—"Maybe you should brawl with the football player who sneers in class: it would be the same thing"—and refused to go out to Uncle John's place with me.

So I found myself, late one Sunday afternoon after the wheat was cut, standing in a corral with my hand on the wet, quivering hide of a sorrel horse, waiting for John to chinch up the saddle. The horse was scared and so was I: once I had known more about horses than about Henry James, but that had been a long time ago. About twenty cousins, uncles and other relatives sat along the fences, waiting for what promised to be a very short rodeo. I wished insanely for the audience to be blindfolded, as the horse was. I was sure I'd be thrown.

But I wasn't. I rode her, rode her down until her legs were flaccid and her coat lathered and I don't think altogether in my life I have felt a sweeter moment than when I whipped the reins across her flank and she shambled into a tired trot. My jaw was numb from my leaning too far forward in the saddle when she tossed her head, and the insides of my legs were rubbed raw because I hadn't worn chaps, but a broken leg wouldn't have been too much to pay.

Later, sitting in the yellow, noisy kitchen that had been built by my great-grandfather in 1885, we drank and talked. The occasion was festive. I'm not sure why my relatives were pleased—and I suspect most of them had been John's victims too, and perhaps that was part of it—but for myself, I was happy to be completely comfortable for the first time in my life with my family. As I sucked whiskey through my teeth that barely opened it struck me that riding the horse should have brought me closer to the family—as it had, but in a strange way. I was comfortable not because I felt I was really one of them, not because I had proved myself according to their rules: rather, it was because I could accept the differences in myself.

Now, all of this sounds, even to me, suspiciously like one of those hokey *Reader's Digest* stories: I Rode a Bronc and Found Security. When I went home, a little drunk, and told my wife about it, she said as much. Banal or not, the thing happened, and my attitude toward myself changed.

And even though it is a long and circuitous route from a wheatfield to corral to seminar room, the incident helped me to understand my feelings about being a graduate student. Throughout the past year, I have felt a disquieting sense of having been here before; something in the atmosphere reminds me of a past visit, a visit that was blandly unpleasant. There is nothing really ominous or fearful, just a nagging sense of dislocation, of being a displaced person. It is, of course, the atmosphere of my childhood, in evidence again here at graduate school. For just as the values of my family

246

marked me off as an odd duck and made me at least apologetic for my strangeness, the values of my graduate school (not the stated values, the ones you feel and breathe) are also not mine. My uncles thought me hopelessly wrong-headed for preferring to collect wild flowers over installing new piston rings in a truck motor; my faculty, more refined and polite, merely suggests that the main business of my life is to be a critic. Another book about the allegory of the *Faerie Queene*, even another article for graduate students to mull over, would do more for me professionally than would a novel.

There. It's out. I've taken a long time to get around to repeating a cliché—namely, that graduate schools are less interested in creative effort than in critical ability. Everyone except me apparently knew this: I assumed that anyone who adopted literature as a profession would naturally be concerned with the production of a modern literature. But this is a naïve assumption for me to make, showing that I am heir to my uncle's mistake: they assumed that anyone who lived on a wheat farm in eastern Colorado could ask for nothing more. At any rate, it is too easy to call names and too hard to prove charges, so I must identify my point as an entirely personal conviction that is unsupported by any statistics or polls: I am regarded as less of a student at my university for being a writer.

Not that I came to this university to learn to write. I wouldn't have gone anywhere, except to my books and my typewriter, to learn to do that. But I expected a certain community of interest, a certain encouragement or at least tolerance, so that a published short story would be roughly equivalent in value to a speech given at MLA on "Whither the Subjunctive?"

So my sense of *déjà vu* during this first year of doctoral study stems from the resemblance of my situation as a graduate student to my childhood. In both I have been subject to an avuncular patronizing: in both I have pursued my own course more or less in secret. I realize that the production

*247*

of wheat is the main business of wheat farming, just as the production of scholars is the main business of graduate schools, and I am ready to go along with these propositions so far as it pleases me. I can do and have done a good job of overhauling a truck motor, and I can and will write a competent dissertation, but I will be damned to Huck Finn's Hell before I grant that I should feel furtively ashamed of myself for being less than a dedicated mechanic or scholar. One needs money and one does what is needed to get it—but one needn't believe with Coolidge that the main business of America is business.

Of course I would like to drop out of this doctoral program, but I want to teach. I can't make my living by writing, at least not yet, and I don't want to return to driving a tractor or working as a carpenter or selling vacuum cleaners, nor do I want to continue teaching four sections of freshman composition, with 120 themes a week, as I've been doing for the past three years. I hope my tone here isn't truculent—I certainly don't feel aggrieved at having to earn a living. Not all of my reasons for wanting to teach are negative or economic, of course, but the more respectable reasons do sound pretentious and empty when spoken. The most I can say with any degree of truthfulness is that I am engaged with and committed to literature and ideals. I should like to do better. I should like to say I hope to inspire my students by showing them the great liberal tradition of thought and feeling, but that has an uncomfortable ashy taste in the mouth. Inspire them to what? One of the best students I taught last year is now in jail, convicted of rape; another, a boy who barely passed, is in Mississippi this summer, risking his life and whatever faith in humanity he possessed by working in the voter registration drive. I spoke of Milton to both of them. It's another of those questions I can't answer; I have to leave it dangling here as it dangles in my mind. . . .

# Summary of Charges, Part II

THERE IS no businessman, no professional person, almost no college graduate whose ability to communicate has not been damaged by the reading bias that streaks down through our educational system from graduate school to kindergarten—Ph.D. to K.

The Department of English must be given its share of blame and, because of its prestige and authority, it is a big share. It is the Department that forces college English to be *reading* English.

The graduate school of English has contributed nothing to the design of a secure, reasonable introduction to the English language. It has failed to give elementary-school teachers even the most primitive understanding of writing. It has denied any responsibility for the elementary-school curriculum. It has done nothing to create an attractive, common-sense sequence of elementary-writing instruction.

The graduate school of English wants nothing to do with the teaching of grade-school teachers, but I should think love of the English language would interest some Doctors in how children are introduced to it. Shouldn't *"philosophy of English"* have something to do with English's ultimate causes? A philosopher examines beginnings, not just yesterday's but tomorrow's beginnings in the light of yesterday's.

The English Department continues to encourage and publish unneeded research in literature of the nineteenth, eighteenth, seventeenth, and sixteenth centuries, ignoring research needed to support and develop writers of the twenty-first century.

The Department of English keeps flagging young graduate students back down the hallways toward Chaucer and Beowulf,

249

meanwhile letting reading specialists choke the expression of this nation in a bottleneck system of controlled words and fill-in writing.

The Department believes students can learn to write if they expose themselves to (i.e., read) enough good writers of the past. But if writers are made merely by what they read, doesn't it bother the Department to realize that 98 per cent of our children are reading Dick & Jane?

If the Department would concern itself with laying down a proper bottom-grade curriculum of writing instruction, English in high school would not have to be remedial grade-school English and English I in college wouldn't have to be remedial high school English. The English Department could then devote itself to criticism if it wanted, to research for developing and improving sequential programs for grade school, to editing and aiding professional work in fiction and nonfiction.

# 5—THE NEW EDUCAND

## Two Reasons Why
## the Early Writer Is a New,
## Totally Different Educand

THE SIX-YEAR-OLD i.t.a. writer is a totally different educand. The first-grader who can put his mind and feelings on paper is a new kind of student, one we've never had before in our schools. He becomes a different educand for two reasons.

**1. The i.t.a. writer is a new educand in our schools because he can reveal more exactly and clearly what is educable in his personality; he reveals it verbally and independently, without having to ask for spelling help.**

The maturity of a child's expression as shown in writing may help show the depth and balance of both his mind and feelings. The qualities of interest and clarity in his writing can reveal how he understands others and how he feels toward them.

In May 1964 the *Bethlehem Globe-Times* described a "rising" against i.t.a. in the Buchanan School in Bethlehem. I telephoned a first-grade teacher in that school and asked her what her children thought of the controversy. Four days later I received a packet of letters, one from each member of her class.

The Buchanan School writers had heard that some people were rejecting their alphabet. Some answered emotionally, some tried to explain i.t.a., and some avoided the conflict entirely. I quote these letters not for any charm they may have but to illustrate how each child's writing shows his own peculiar way of coping with a problem. It is his problem-solving attitude and his methods for solving a problem that reveal how he may be instructed.

Nine children (seven boys) *numbered* their sentences, though they had not been instructed or shown how to do so.

1. wie dœnt yœ liek ar reediŋ
2. it is fun tœ lern
3. ie thiŋk yœ ʃhœd vœt yes.

4. yœ ʃhœd lern it tœ.
5. yœ can liek it tœ.   —*Karl, 6*

There were several invitations in the packet (the Invitation Letter is a second-grade *copy* project in the Dick & Jane system):

Wee liek ar reeding.  Wee luv ar reeding and wee never wont tœ stop ar reediŋ.  Ie wish yœ can beeleev ar reediŋ. yœ don't noe hou wee get eezee werk.  Wee get out at 3 av clock and at lunch tiem wee goe at 11 av clock.  we goe out for reeses.  Wee luv ar reeding væree much.  yœ ar inn nœ yorck sitee ie wish yœ can cum tœ ar rœm.  cuz wee hav a nuf chaerz.  yœ can sit bie mis danchoe if yœ wont.
—*Brenda, 6*

The packet also included several Letters of Regret, a form not expected from Dick & Jane writers till they are twelve years old and in sixth grade.  And there were letters not even mentioned in the T.O. curriculum—angry letters, a letter of disgust, some complaints, and even a sales or promotion letter.

whie dœn't sum peepl liek ar reedin.  every wun in mie rœm lieks it . . . if yœ dœn't liek ar reediŋ.  if yœ hav reediŋ then wee dœn't liek yœr dummy reediŋ.

. . . sum peepls sæ ita is for ᚦe birds.  mie muᚦer and faᚦer liek ᚦe reediŋ.

ᚦis is about ita evry boddee shœd liek our reediŋ becus it's fun and mor instreteiŋ and our teeᚦer lieks it tœ but if yœ ever hav sum ᚦhilldren ask ᚦem mæbee ᚦhæ'll liek it and ie ges ᚦat's aull but don't forget it's fun.  mie muᚦer and faᚦer liek it tœ if yœ dœnt liek it yœ shœd eeven mie cusent lieks it tœ and hee is œnly a bæby eeven mie grand muᚦer and faᚦer liek it and a boi in ar class hee miet gœ tœ anoᚦer scœl and a girl in our class ʃhee mœvd.—*Susan, 6*

**2. The i.t.a. writer is a new educand in our schools because he relates verbally to his teacher in a way never before possible.**

Reading, since it is inward-aimed, tends to isolate the child from his teacher.  Some children deliberately use reading to escape from their teacher or parents. But writing is a social act and is outward-aimed. Writing gives the lonely child the chance to reach out from his loneliness and touch someone. Reading cannot establish a warm, strong relationship between teacher and reader any more than it can between librarian and library-card holder or between a newsstand vendor and his customers. An interpersonal relationship is best established through interpersonal talk. But if the child isn't free to talk and the teacher doesn't have time to listen, the relationship's only chance to be formed will be through writing.

The early, freed written expression of i.t.a. children offers teachers a new, direct, intimate look into the six-year-old. As a writer, the six-year-old is honest, frank, open. He says what comes to his mind without deception, without much trying to protect himself. Later he may learn to be more guarded, but right now he runs freely. He is not ashamed of his feelings.

---

Dear Mrs. E. yœr sweet jenɑrositee is cristl cleer. Mrs. E. this shows that I love you very very very much. and you ɑre ɑ darling and ɑ sweetheart you ɑre and you ɑre ɑdoribul. Thank you for teaching our class many old and new things for the hole year on all ov the things that you tot our class was very fun it was so fun that today wen you look at my paper I am going to kiss you and I am going to rite letters on your back I love you so much that I will give you seven kisses you ɑre so ɑdoribul and sweet and cient that I will eat you up becus you ɑre so sweet and yumy cud I cume over to your hous on Feriday niet and stay until Monday after school yes! or no! Love Barbarɑ—*Barbara, 6, first grade, Long Island*

Dear Mrs. E

I wonted yœ for a teecher bee coʒ yœ lœk nies and yœ ɑr. I dœnt nœ if yœ liek mee. I thingk evree boi wd liek yœ for a teecher.—*B. J., 6, first grade, Long Island*

In the morning as soon as I awoke I went into the breakfast room and opened the Easter egg and I found a pearl necklace and in the other small egg I found Topo Gigio [a cartoon mouse].

My mother said the necklace was very beautiful. And Topo Gigio is beautiful too, but I wanted two more presents.

Then my mother told me that I was never content with what I had and I began to cry.—*Adelia, 7, second grade, Milan*

---

One boy, Charles, six, of Bethlehem, sent his first-grade teacher a series of love notes:

miss——I luv yco. yco ɑr mie drɛɛm gɹl. we ɑr ɑulwæz plæiŋ jœks on yco. luv  Charles

dɛɛr miss——I luv you gæɹɛɛ and charlz and jæmz and mie we fallœd yco ɑull œver ɹhe plægroun we ɑull luv yco luv  leslɛɛ and gæɹɛɛ and charlz and jæmz.

miss——I will kiss yco after scœl. I am your love boy. Here is ɑ report to you. When we sit by you and you go we be quiet. This is how you write my names Charles I love you.

dɛɛr Miss——, when I am apsint I do not smile but when I'm here I have ɑ big smile. In the afternoon I will kiss you. Saturday Sept. 25 nineteen sixty four. love  Charles

i.t.a. allows children to vent feelings of protest, annoyance, jealousy, and resentment, feelings of love and affection, worried feelings, sad and unhappy feelings. But rather than merely vent them, they share them with the teacher:

evrɛɛ worm niet mie mother œpens the windœ and the kricits kɛɛp sæing it is gœwing tco bɛɛ ɑ gcod dæ tco morœ. and sum ɑthr tiems thæ sæ it is not gœwing tco bɛɛ ɑ gcod dæ tco morœ and thæ kɛɛp sæing it œvr and œvr and œvr and I kant slɛɛp with thœs kricits I jes wish I ccod get up and clœws the windœs but I wont ɑ kcol bed rcom and I haf tco lɛɛv the windœs up sœw I haf tco. the end—*B. J., 6, first grade, Long Island*

Children in one Bethlehem first-grade class were invited to rate their teacher:

my teecher sumtimes is mad and sum times is nice. I no
when she is mad and I no when she is nic to us. when all
the childrin ɑr heer then she's mad. when the children go
to church school than she is nic and kwiet.—*Sandra, 6*

deɛr miss w     I like your riting and I like your clothing.
I hope you don't get sick eny more  I like the way you count
the muny. I like your blue cɑr very very much.—*Mirna, 6*

deɛr miss w.
I liek yꙮ because yꙮ look liek ɑ beedul. I liek your beedul
haircut. I liek your blꙮ dress. I liek storɛɛ tiem. I liek
number werck.—*Debra, 6*

"Mister X" is the principal in one of the i.t.a. schools. The first-
graders were asked what a principal's job was:

ie wunt tꙮ seɛ yꙮ hit ɑ boi. dꙮ yꙮ hit hard? yes, ie dꙮ.
yꙮ nœ ʃhat mie faʃher hits meɛ hard. wun dæ heɛ brœk
ʃhe stick œver meɛ sœ luv, Ellen—*Ellen, 6*

mister X iʃ our prisipal. if sumwun iʃ bad heɛ will spaŋkc
him. mister X iʃ ɑ verry verry gꙮd wun. heɛ prints pappr
and heɛ helps ʃhe ɖhildren dꙮ ʃhiŋgs wen ʃhæ neɛd him.—
*Wendy, 6*

ʃhe prinsipal in our scꙮl iʃ mister X. heɛ's ɑ nies felœ.
when peɛpl run dꙮn ʃhe haull heɛ mæks ʃhem waulk back.
when peɛpl ɑr bad heɛ givʃ ʃhem ɑ patliŋ.—*James, 6*

deɛr misstr X. yꙮ hav ɑ patl yꙮ yꙮsit on bad boiz and girl.
yꙮ ɑr nies tꙮ ʃhe teɛɖherz. ie wunt yꙮ tꙮ beɛ mie frend—
*Charles, 6*

The mere *expression* of feeling doesn't by itself mean healthy
emotional development since a child may express feelings which are
not understood or which are contradicted, frustrated, or suppressed.
The child develops as a result of *engaged* expression. He yields his
*self* to the teacher on paper and the teacher accepts his statements,
not as unfelt, impersonal copyings, but as authentic, personal
revelations. These revelations can bring child and teacher together

257

for that most important of human meetings, which Reuel L. Howe in *The Miracle of Dialogue* defines as "the meeting of meanings."

Dialogue transforms both persons who are party to it. Both teacher and pupil become fuller, more authentic persons because of this exchange. Such meetings repeated during the various stresses of a normal school year are essential for a healthy communication habit.

The excitement many teachers feel in an i.t.a. classroom is not from its "novelty effect," as some critics insist. For the first time these teachers are "hearing" an *inner* side to the children they're with, a side they could only guess at before. In answering that inner side they often discover a new, unused part of themselves as teachers.

Before i.t.a., teachers knew their children from listening to them talk, watching their behavior, and studying the results of true-false, fill-in, or multiple-choice psychological tests. But it is impossible to give much careful listening and watching time to twenty-five or thirty children, many of whom are competing with each other for attention. Often only the bolder or more interesting children strike through. Often only the weakest get picked out for special help.

But a dialogue in writing can be established only when the teacher honestly engages with the child. The teacher's assignment must first be honest and her responses to the returned papers must also be honest. The teacher will be interested in a written answer only if she was first of all interested in her own question.

" 'Here is a little toy house. It is for you.' 'Oh, father,' said Sue. 'A little toy house for me!' " is dull talk but this is a venial wrong. The mortal sin of such talk is that it prevents the teacher and child from ever meeting. No teacher in the world is actress or actor enough to fake genuine joy while reading the "stories" of Dick & Jane writers. Bright kids they may be but as writers they're awful.

The habit of dialogic communication is not an easy one to acquire and keep. It has to be set young. It has to be kept clear and new during all the stages of growth and development. Writing can support such development and can help communication become an easy, natural act.

## Early Writing:
## The Cyrano Chance

ԵԵԵԵԵԵԵԵԵԵԵԵԵԵԵԵԵԵԵԵԵԵԵԵԵԵԵԵԵԵԵԵԵԵԵԵԵԵԵԵԵԵ

DURING 1964 stacks of children's writings were sent to me from i.t.a. classes in Bethlehem, Long Island, and Cleveland. I came to know certain children entirely through their writings. I grew to like them and looked forward to a day I could meet them and see what they looked like. Who wouldn't be curious about the six-year-old named Barbara, from Long Island, who wrote:

on sandy beaches the wind blœs. and pœshes the sand and the trees bend œver wæ to the geround. and the berds flie and the clouds skip cross the skie

At the end of the school ýear, I drove down to Bethlehem, where I made the surprising and provocative discovery that most of my favorite writers were *not* the children I wanted them to be. Here were children I had come to know and like for their thoughts, their way of looking at things, their individualistic expression, and now I was disappointed. Some looked dull or sleepy, others—well, they just didn't catch my interest. In class after class I had the same experience. The children who appealed to me face to face, whose looks I liked, whose manners or personality caught my eye were seldom the children whose writing had won my interest and admiration.

I couldn't help thinking of Cyrano de Bergerac, the poet-swordsman in Rostand's play who loved Roxane but didn't dare tell her directly because of his grotesque, ugly nose. Instead, he expressed himself by ghost-writing love letters to her for a handsome young officer who also loved her. Roxane fell in love with this oaf body-god only to discover later that he was hollow and that the person she really loved was Cyrano.

Writing, I saw, gave some young children the *Cyrano chance* to express themselves unburdened by any hangdog self-image of how they looked or dressed or talked.

I saw that over the years I had accumulated certain visual biases and prejudices toward children and adults too, and that my visual tastes were often opposed to my deeper true appreciations of their personalities. The people I liked for looks frequently were not the same as those I liked as persons.

I wondered next whether teachers might be affected the same way. Did visual prejudices affect a teacher's relationship with her class? Couldn't it be true that a teacher, not realizing what was happening and unable to help herself, almost automatically rejected certain children because of their outward appearance? Didn't she sometimes accept a child and invest her hopes in him because of the way he looked and then later lament the child's failure to live up to his "promise"? Didn't teachers make up their minds a child was dumb because he looked dumb? The sad thing about this is that a child may too readily adopt his teacher's image of him and conform to it instead of asserting his distinct, individual self. If his teacher thinks he's dumb or bad, he may help her prove she's right.

Here is one more serious fault with the basal-reader controlled-vocabulary system. Dick & Jane primary-grade teachers are forced to judge children by their appearance and by their spoken expression. But are all children at their best *speaking* and do all children *look* their best?

Among the letters I received as a result of the Buchanan School disturbance was this defense of i.t.a. written in a hard-pencil scrawl by a six-year-old girl I will identify as Bertie.

Why dœn't you like ɑr reeding. We take time to leern ɑr reeding and you doet rspet it. wee luv ɑr reeding. Why doet you Set doun and Let ye Chindren reed to you. And see if you like ita.

The more I thought about Bertie's letter the more interesting it grew. Her thinking was orderly, her direct appeal was reasonable and cogent, her attitude had a strangely mature dignity—she says,

"We take time to learn our reading and you don't respect it." What was Bertie like, I wondered.

I telephoned Bertie's teacher, who told me that Bertie was the slowest learner in her class! "At Christmas I had just about decided to keep Bertie back another year," her teacher said. "Then, in January, she began to catch on. I can't get her to answer in class and she's still in the slowest group but she'll pass with the others."

Later, from talks with Bertie in Bethlehem, I found out she was afraid to hear her voice out loud. She was also ashamed of her clothes so she didn't like to stand up. She had an excellent mind, but a poor image of herself kept her from expressing herself before others.

No true-false or fill-in or multiple-choice paper could have given me a better understanding of Bertie. She was able to write down her own talk as she heard it, and what she heard was not the diction of a professional radio announcer but the voice of a little girl with a stopped up nose. Her feelings about i.t.a. were similar to the feelings of other children but there were distinct and important differences, too, and Bertie was able to reveal them. i.t.a. spellings gave her the freedom to individuate herself. She didn't have to ask her teacher to act as her stenographer and neither was her voice lost in a homogenized class-dictated letter.

i.t.a. gave Bertie the Cryano chance. It was through her writing that her teacher learned how to reach her.

# Early Writing Is a Versatile Diagnostic Tool

ℓℓℓℓℓℓℓℓℓℓℓℓℓℓℓℓℓℓℓℓℓℓℓℓℓℓℓℓℓℓℓℓℓℓℓℓℓℓℓℓℓℓℓℓℓℓℓℓℓℓℓℓ

EARLY WRITINGS can be a valuable diagnostic tool for the educator, the social worker, and the educational psychologist. The i.t.a. first-grader's writings could be saved as a sourcebin for generalizations regarding his education.

Psychologists now study children's drawings for social attitudes or for signs of emotional disturbances. The reason they haven't studied early writings is that before i.t.a. such writings were not available for study. In the controlled-word system children still aren't able to write what's on their minds.

Unless they are extraordinarily secure, children flinch from making spelling mistakes. Dick & Jane children write words gingerly, tentatively stepping along on each new spelling as it comes up, unsure whether it will hold up or not. They avoid hard words and use easy words. They keep wondering if they're going to make some face-reddening boo boo. They choose words they hope will win approval.

The following defense of i.t.a. was written by a Buchanan School first-grader whom I shall call Jana. Jana's argument has several good points in it, but her statement yawns with ellipses, maybe from trying to write too fast. Her communication is faulty but it would be a mistake to say her mind was confused.

This rediŋ is yosd in Ita it helpt me to lern to red faster and helpt me lern the old afabet I lik mi rediŋ. You shɷd lik it bacaus it helps mi clas tɷ. its not ar rediŋ. its that sum pepl doent red bɷks. maby if thae wunt teech so meny souns at wuns and I Thic its a teeny bit hard the old afabet is I mean—the nue is pritty eezy I Think. I hope you don't feel unhapy becaus your children dont lern as much. Mi best story is The very best sumer and I luv it. I hope yɷ dɷ to. so chaer up. mi sister liks mi rediŋ. I no becaus evey time I cum home with a bꝏk she reds it befor I can.

Jana may go through life giving people the false impression that she is fluttery-minded. This would be unfortunate. Her writings reveal that her communication habits need correction through a proper writing and speech program.

Early writings can reveal the child's basic understandings and interests. They often tell how he gets along with his family. They describe his social attitudes in school. They prove his memory and attention. They reveal his personal ambitions. Are the child's wishes the father of his life goals?

The papers below were written by six-year-old children in Long Island, Bethlehem, and Cleveland.

Success:

wuns apon a tiem ʃhæ wos a kiig and a kwen ofter a wiell ʃhe kwen got a bæbe. it wos a bɔi. ʃhæ næmd it charlls. it wos verea cwꝏt. aftr a littl wiell ʃhæ had a partea for it. wen he wos æt he thrꝏ stons at the gess and ducs and he didit hit them wen he wos ætean he went tꝏ colog and wen he wos nientean he wrckt on a farm he got ten dollrs and æteen sens and he got vere rich and got maread. the end

Autobiography:

ie yꝏs tꝏ hav an appl treɛ in mie backyard when ie wos wun. ie yꝏstꝏ luv ʃhem when ie wos wun. mie muʃher yꝏstꝏ mæk appl piɛs wiʃh ʃhem.

Eating:

weɛ ɛɛt arownd 6ꝏo. ferst weɛ sæ peɛræers then weɛ ɛɛt. weɛ cannot tawk antil weɛ finish. if weɛ dowt ɛɛt weɛ dowt hav disert  ie liɛk hot dog ie downt liɛk aspæruges

Self-Image:

I liɛk ʃheɛ klɔun ʃhats ax funeɛ ax meɛ and I liɛk ʃheɛ elafuntx ʃhat ar ax fat az meɛ and I liɛk ʃheɛ horsix ʃhat ar dirteɛ just liɛk meɛ, ʃheɛ horsix ʃhat kan run az fast just liɛk meɛ.

## Mother:

ie gæv mie muʃher ʃhe muʃher'z dæ kard and ʃhe flouer.
mie muʃher liek't ʃhem. but wen ie askt wie ʃhee wos dꝏiŋ
aull ʃhe wrk ʃhee sed it iʒ just wun of thœs ʃhiŋʒ.

## Sisters and Brothers:

wun time wen I woz sleeping. My sister poot her feat on
bœth of the pilœs. But . . . My hed was off of the bed.
then I wœk up an I fel off of the bed and got a spancan for
messing up the bed but Donna did it. wun time wen wee
were cleeing our room but shee wod not cleen it with me
an I got a spancan.

mie bruʃhr œeeʒ wons too sleep wiʃh mee and I sey nœ. yꝏ
hav a bed and mie bruʃhr mæcs nois sumtiems beecausʒ he
cant go too sleep. and in ʃhe mauniŋ mie bruʃhr cumz in
ar rꝏm and hee wæcs us up and hee got scœlded and at
brecfist hee starts a fit and mie muʃhr yeld at him.

I went tꝏ the marry poppins moovy and it's tꝏ bad that my
bruther had tꝏ cum alaug and bræk up the car and my
father tœld my bruther tꝏ hoock the dog and my bruther
left the dœr œpend and my father started tꝏ back up and
the garaug dœr hit the car dœr.

## Friends:

The person I work Best wiʃh is B.J.E. I wons gæv a nikil
for his muʃherʒ dæ pres-int. ʃhen I gæv a nuʃher nikil for
his milk monee. so now yꝏ see wee ar frens

I like Alison beecaus she is smart and she nos all ʃhe ansers
tꝏ ʃhe ariʃhmutik and ʃhen I can get all ʃhe ansers rite and
she can tel mee ʃhe wurds that I don't no.

My best is Richard and Billy. Richard is my friend becaus
he reads too slow and he is bad in spelling. And you no
why I like Billy becaus he is bad in Arieʃhmic And today
in ariʃhmic he had 8 wrong 5 right.

# 6–THE WRITING-ORIENTED CURRICULUM

# The Six-Year-Old Writer
## Is a New Educand. He Deserves
## a Writing-Oriented Curriculum

SINCE THE six-year-old writer is a new educand, he deserves a new curriculum, one that will serve his intellectual and emotional development while teaching him to communicate. He deserves no less than a writing-oriented curriculum.

Before we can deal with this new educand properly, we will have to clear the curriculum and methodology of the Rube Goldberg devices created to cope with T.O. distortions. We will have to reset correction standards used by teachers in evaluating child writing. The standards currently imposed are based on limited T.O. achievement possibilities. We will also have to redefine the basic elements of communication instruction. The definitions currently used are related to T.O. conditions and are false and injurious when applied to i.t.a. writers.

The Initial Teaching Alphabet let us put reading and writing back together where they belong. An ideal i.t.a. course would begin with children learning to read each other's writings. They would get books after they'd learned that writing is an extension of talk and that they must be clear to be understood.

The i.t.a. educand can be given a writing-oriented curriculum and can be taken off of the passive, reading-oriented curriculum he now has. He can be given a curriculum which will meet his life's needs for writing. Those needs start in school since, obviously, life doesn't wait for graduation before it starts.

A curriculum is writing-oriented if it has the following characteristics:

1) It is designed to graduate a writer who reads. The basal-reader curriculum graduates a reader who can't write.

267

2) It sees writing as an extension of talk, and therefore uses some kind of temporary alphabet reform so that primary-grade children can write all the words of their speaking vocabulary.

3) The child's writing needs determine his transition from the instructional-alphabet spellings to our traditional-alphabet spellings. The transition is not arbitrarily decided by Reading Experts eager to have his achievements compete favorably with the arbitrary Dick & Jane reading "levels."

4) The child's writing instruction fits his life's needs for both exact and imaginative communication.

5) Writing instruction tries to match and pace the child's psychological development. The Dick & Jane controlled-vocabulary structures should be unscrewed, dismantled, and junked. Out with Dick & Jane visual and rhythmic patterns. Out with the progression of sentences from short to long, simple to complex. Out with punctuation-mark rationing.

6) History, science, social studies, and other elementary-school subjects are restructured in such a way that the child can learn through observation and report writing rather than through reading alone.

7) The teacher herself is able to write and has been trained to teach writing. The teacher's standards for correcting papers are directed toward encouraging and improving clear, original communication. Teachers are quick to recognize personality differences in children through their writings. Teachers don't exaggerate the value of spelling and handwriting but cast these skills in their proper communication roles.

8) In a writing-oriented school the teacher's superiors value and reward writing instruction.

THE temporary-reform alphabet I recommend as the foundation of a writing-oriented curriculum is the Initial Teaching Alphabet—i.t.a. I recommend it because its design is suited for the beginning writer better than any other new instructional alphabet.

The curriculum that already uses i.t.a. but fails to note and exploit a child's individual qualities as revealed in writing misses and wastes i.t.a.'s gains. The curriculum that uses i.t.a. but assumes i.t.a. reading is the key to educational success and ignores i.t.a. writing, or regards it merely as a "charming" side effect, wastes the child. Children do not grow merely by passive reading any more than they grow if they're fed in bed and never allowed to exercise.

## First Steps of a First-Grade Writer

SINCE THE first object of reading instruction is the independent, comprehending reader, the *first object of communication instruction ought to be the independent, clear writer.*

The first product of a beginning writer in first grade ought to be one *clear, original sentence written without help from any person or book.* One clear sentence written without help may sound like very little to ask, yet many, many sentences written by lawyers, clergymen, engineers, psychoanalysts, congressmen, and businessmen fail to reach this minimum mark.

### "INDEPENDENT"

i.t.a. delivers two kinds of independence: one *internal*, the other *external*.

The i.t.a. writer is externally independent in that he is free of the controlled vocabulary and its ramifications. He is freed from first having to memorize how a word looks because he can write his talk as he hears it.

The i.t.a. writer is free to communicate what he wants to communicate and is not tied down to what the word lists let him communicate. His reading program, therefore, doesn't dictate his writing program. He doesn't have to wait to learn his sentences and punctuation marks in a sequence determined by books, and he isn't helpless if he doesn't have a secretary to take down his dictated words.

The i.t.a. writer gains an interior independence in being able to state his meanings and feelings in his own personal rhythm and intonation, using the vocabulary most familiar to him. i.t.a. spellings thus allow him to individuate himself. He can then communicate himself in a way different from speech, a way with certain unique advantages of its own. He can communicate his personal differences, his individuality.

Independence is an essential condition for the writing habit, because the habit while being formed seeks its own secret foundation bed. A writing habit cannot be imposed. It can be directed, encouraged, and helped, but its footings must be sunk by the one who will possess it. Independence assures the writer of his unique and distinctive viewpoint stated in the authentic rhythm of his own voice.

## "ORIGINAL"

Every child has his own unique isolation, an isolation that grows with growth and with the development of expanding differences. It is from the center of this isolation, which is the *self*, that the child's original statement must come. An "original sentence" is one that is authored by the child, that comes from the *origins* of his *self*.

## "CLEAR"

No curriculum guide or primary-grade language book I have seen requires clarity as an element of early writing, yet it is communication's most essential characteristic; without it communication is frustrated. Clarity as a desirable quality of communication was demanded by masters of rhetoric back in classic Greek times. Its necessity predates the Greeks, of course, for without clarity there could have been no oral tradition, no verbal history.

The term "clear" as applied to writing is a metaphor originally comparing language with glass or air or water. It implies that language is a medium—that is, something between a mind and an object known by the mind, or between one person and another. The metaphor says that just as a pool is clear when we can see its bottom and air is clear if we can see long distances, language is clear when it lets us see long distances into the user's mind or see an object distinctly without distortion.

271

In learning to be clear, the child must practice selecting words to fit the state of his mind and feelings, to fit the object he is writing about, and to fit his reader or audience. The child must try to fit three pieces of "glass" together with a minimum of distortion. If there is distortion in a speech or piece of writing, it means either the writer doesn't understand his subject or hasn't organized his own thinking or simply doesn't care about his readers. It may mean all three.

Clarity in writing is a struggle between one's feelings for self-expression and one's responsibility toward society. Most of writing's educational benefits probably are wrung from this specific struggle, for the writer's strivings to define and explain his ideas and feelings lead him to intellectual discoveries and insights.

Self-expression is a personal achievement of maturity and dignity. It is man asserting the loneliness of his individuality, his privacy, exclusivity, and separateness from society. But clarity is the sign of willingness to share. It asserts the social direction of language and the writer's need for others. Clarity is an attempt to escape from loneliness. It is through clarity that a writer lifts writing from being a *thing* to being a social act. It is an achievement of social maturity.

*Writing Instruction Should*
*Fit Life's Communication Needs.*
*The Needs Are Two: Exact and*
*Imaginative. We Need Both.*

### EXACT COMMUNICATION

The research proposal, research itself, and the research report—these three activities function as the growing edge of American culture. Research isn't born unless it's first articulately defined and proposed. Research dies unless later it's articulately reported. Proposals and reports can be delivered by video tape, tape recorder, telephone, charts and graphs, and in person orally. But the forms most commonly used to communicate exact and factual information all through school and adult life are written forms.

The children in a writing-oriented school will start writing reports and proposals in first grade. They will develop habits of acute observation and clear communication. Their writing-instruction program will eventually prepare them to communicate in a natural, easy way.

Before scientists and artists and technologists can communicate with each other they must have shared a course in communication that was common to them all. It is inefficient and too late to establish such a course in the graduate school, college, or even high school. It is best established in the primary grades, where the disciplines themselves have their beginnings and where all arts and disciplines are usually taught by one person.

As things are now, when history and sociology teachers get badly written papers, they blame the English teacher. This is unfair. Communication instruction is every teacher's job. But unless writing and reading are taught as complementary skills, English teachers will continue to be blamed and students will continue to write bad papers in history, science, and social studies—yes, and in English too.

---

**The English Department often resents having to give a service course for the entire college or university, and composition teachers frequently protest that this kind of work carries little chance for development, promotion, and professional prestige. Besides, basic training in fundamentals belongs in high school, not in college. But if it is to be given in college, why isn't it the responsibility of everyone on the faculty—in history, sociology, chemistry, or whatever—to see that his students write well?**—*Introduction to Basic Issues, New York Conference of English Teachers, 1958–61*

---

Some educators say that children who are taught early math and early science are learning a form of exact communication. They are, indeed, but their model for exactness is a limited one stated in numbers. If they learn communication only from this model, and if they don't learn how to be exact with words, their education is distorted. It's important for them to value language for its ambiguities and to respect the differences between words and numbers, for these ambiguities and differences are associated with human variables and differences.

But will children respect words if they are given "Oh, Sue! I have a toy for you. I have a big, blue toy for you"?

The six-year-old child who can communicate what's on his mind, can state a difference of opinion, can make a distinction, can protest, observe, and reflect—all *in writing*—is new to our schools as a teachable subject. i.t.a. has made him possible, but before he can be graduated as a capable writer he must be delivered from Dick & Jane and Jimmy & Sue. They're bad company and we all know what happens to children who keep bad company.

IMAGINATIVE COMMUNICATION

The writing-oriented school will not strive to turn out fine poets and novelists, but rather to teach all children the skills and crafts of communication. Since these same skills and crafts serve the art of literature those children who have literary talent

*274*

can rise from surer grounds. They will be paced and stimulated by readers who can better appreciate the *art* of literature because they are familiar with its *craft*.

Stories have forms or patterns, as sports have certain forms and as music is written to certain patterns. We could hardly sit still during a baseball or football game if the game were not measured by innings or quarters, by chalk stripes on the field, by the clock and whistle, by a limit to the number of outs, strikes, or downs. But while the forms of a game affect the attention and appreciation of its watchers, they first of all affect the performance of the athlete on the field. The forms affect his decisions, guide him, help him pace himself, give him his sense of direction and purpose.

Similarly, forms help the spectator enjoy ballet, music, and drama. He likes them most when they don't threaten to be endless. Chapters, scenes, acts, and stanzas give them the illusion of progress. No matter how funny or engrossing a book or play may be, if we recognize its pattern we intensify its sweetness and focus its light.

Forms should not be confused with mechanistic formulas. Knowing the rondo, the sonata, and the Mass forms doesn't cramp the composer; the forms free him. Forms free the writer too. They let him run with his story, knowing where he is and where he's going.

Our basic patterns were created deep in our past history. They took shape in the process of being told to live, reacting audiences. Tellers discovered that certain patterns usually got instant attention and held it to the end. These were the patterns that survived.

The printing of books automated the storyteller out of business, just as the phonograph has almost done away with "live" musicians. There was no Petrillo to save the minstrel or town crier. Consequently, the *joke* is the only talking-story pattern that has survived.

In losing the storyteller, we also lost the story listener and valuable story-listening habits—patience, for example. We lost face-to-face criticisms that help us refine the art of storytelling— boos and refunds, yawns and glazed eyes, heads nodding and heads shaking. We lost the tension that made storytelling an art similar to singing and acting, an art that depended on an immediate artist-audience relationship, a relationship sustained by sound.

At the University of Nebraska, Paul Olson and Frank Rice have developed an English course that deserves a book of its own. Olsen's course draws children through the myths, fables, adventures, and fairy tales of our past. It relies on reading but is not reading-oriented. It is expression-oriented, designed to conduct a child along a channel interweaving language, literature, and composition. The channel bed is oral—spoken English. Briefly, children learn how to tell stories from hearing stories of classic literary excellence. They learn to shape them for the best effect on the listener. While learning to tell stories they also learn how to write them. They learn how to construct the story of Cinderella, the Sleeping Beauty, and David and Goliath and then to invent stories of their own along these classic patterns. Pitting protagonist against antagonist helps children learn logic and persuasive rhetoric.

Nebraska's English channel winds in a spiral direction from kindergarten through high school. The primary-grade story forms have bold, simple patterns. More sophisticated versions of the patterns are repeated in the middle and upper grades. "Little Red Riding Hood," for example, evolves to become *Ulysses*. "Peter Rabbit" one day becomes *To Kill a Mockingbird*. Thus, Nebraska's English curriculum is related to any child's changing needs as he grows and develops.

Nebraska's curriculum serves two functions: while educating the child it offers elementary teachers a sense of place and a sense of direction in the teaching of English.

Unfortunately, Professor Olson didn't equip his curriculum with i.t.a. Nebraska teachers, consequently, have to work as "secretaries" to their pupils and are run ragged through clouds of chalk dust as they spell out stories their children can't write themselves.

Earl H. Greeson, principal of the Delmar-Harvard School in University City, Missouri, was the first to bring i.t.a. to a St. Louis-area school. Then, in 1966–67, his school become the first in the country to integrate i.t.a. and the Nebraska Curriculum. The samples below were written by i.t.a. graduates early in the second-grade stage of the Nebraska Curriculum.

### When my d.x. Getaway Chase
### game came to life

One day my whole family went shopping so naturally, I was left alone at home. All of a sudden, I heard this sirene noise! At first, I thought it was a regular fire engine. But then I found out that it was coming from my third floor. So, I went up to the third floor and did I have a shock! My D. X. Getaway chase game had come to life!!! to anybody else it would look natural but the cars weren't running on battery power and the police cars light was really flashing and you could hear a sirene comming from it. The porch-lights on the houses were really lighted up. The guy in the crook car, the one that had the machine gun, well, the gun was shooting real machine gun bullets! Then, the police shot a hole in the tire of the croock car and it slowed down but, the police car kept going and knocked it off the board and they both broke in two. Then the porch-lights went off. So, I put them back to gether and everything went back on for a strange reason. Then, I had an idea. [Electric bulb drawn here.] I picked up the cars and turned them on. Everything blacked out like it did when the cars fell and broke in two. Now I found out how to operate them the peculiar way: off turns them on and on turns 'em off. So, I kept it a secret and every chance I got, I played with them that way. Then I woke up found I was taking a nap & had had a bad dream. The End—*Dwight, 7*

### Journey in a balloon!
### Chapter 1 finding a balloon!

My name is alder I am 10 years old I went for a trip in a balloon! with to friends ther names were anlogen and

ildorrel. the people in the town call us ac bc and cc and wen they wer talking about all of us tegther they called us "ranegers". this is a story about wen me and my frends went for a trip in a Balloon!!! well it all happened on a sunny day wen we were resting on a hillside looking at the sun. it's a nice day sied ildorrel. Just the day sombody wood fly a balloon. after saying those wourds a uncanny silens fell on the company. I brocke it by saying "well" wot are we waiting for"! "animal cracers"! so the company got up in search for a balloon we came to a preastorik forest and we fond a balloon that was full and had sand bags in and a sign saying For sale FREE so we got the balloon and a instruck shons and we got to sale all over the world we hade supper in the balloon and we desided it was time to go down so we poped the balloon and we watched the ground come to meet us it hade been a lovely day in a balloon and fun. we landed and looked arond there was a wonderful smell we had landed in the elven vally "riverdell" there we staded and lived. the end
p.s. is this anoffe—*Ann, 7*

What do Dick & Jane offer? Below is the Tyler, Texas, program for second-graders. It is typical of the basal-reader "creative writing" course.

Creative writing is fun and is stimulating

1. The first word in each paragraph is indented.
2. All sentences in a paragraph are about one topic.
3. Sentences of a paragraph must be placed in proper sequence.
4. Proof reading is always necessary.

Enjoy creative writing

1. Look at pictures, read stories and poems, and tell about experiences in order to get ideas for creative writing.

(See "More To Do Activities," Book II.)

2. Engage in creative writing and read written story to class; evaluate.
3. Paint a picture and write a story to fit the illustration.
4. Discuss and evaluate creative writing of others.
5. Use words *first*, *next*, and *last*, as aids in keeping ideas in order.
6. Proofread creative writing to see if first word is indented and all sentences are about one general idea.

Below are some anonymous Dick & Jane writers, age seven, second grade:

There once lived a cat who was very wise.
A wise cat he was.
Once a very little boy,
who was not in school,
asked "What is one and one?"
The cat said, "What is your name little boy?"
"My name is Jeffrey Hill.
But what is one and one?"
"One and one is two."
"Thank you."
And the boy went off happily.   The end.

Billy siad, "I can count, Mother.
   Listen—1, 2, 3, 4, 5, 6, 7, 8, 9, 10."
"Good," said Mother.
"Tell Father."
"Oh, boy," he said.
"Listen, Father, 1, 2, 3, 4, 5, 6, 7, 8, 9, 10."   The end.

In 1964 certain i.t.a. teachers in Bethlehem gave their first-graders an assortment of spices contributed by French & Company. The children were asked to taste or smell them and then write what their spice made them think of.  Among the papers handed in was the story below written by six-year-old Cora.  Cora comes from a storytelling and story-reading family. She was able to read T.O. books given to her as presents at Christmas time. Maybe we shouldn't be surprised to find her story imitates classic fairy-tale structure.

### the peper that mæd me sneeze

Wun dæ I sau a littl box. And when I got 10 feet away sumthing very strænj happend. The littl box blew sumthing at me, and it mæd me sneeze. Everybody in toun wer sneezing. And even the peepl in Easton wer sneezing! Because the littl boxtop is open Then the hole wurld woɤ sneezing. Because thær woɤ a hole famaly ov majic peper boxes. And thær wer five little bæby boxes. do you know why the hole wurld woz sneezing? because the tops ov the majic pepper boxes wer off. Then wun dæ I noetest it. I wuz bræv enough, that I went over to the little pepper boxes, but I cot a bad cold. For a fue weeks I wuz resting. Then wundæ I woz better. This time I wor an oxygen mask and cot a little cold but I pœoton the tops ov the little pepper boxes. The End

What will happen to Cora's story-writing ability as she moves upward from grade to grade? Will she be guided and taught how to perfect her talent? Will she learn how to develop stories after other classic patterns? Will she be shown how to create characters and dialogue?

No, no, no. There are no books to teach her. There are no teachers to help her. There is no curriculum guide to help her teachers.

# Writing Instruction Can Pace and Serve the Early Writer's Intellectual Growth and Development

THE POLICIES COMMISSION of the National Education Association says that seven "values" underlie the spirit of science, and it urges teachers to promote these values. The seven values are:

1. Longing to know and understand
2. Questioning of all things
3. Search for data and their meaning
4. Demand for verification
5. Respect for logic
6. Consideration of premises
7. Consideration of consequences

But William C. Warren, Dean of Columbia University Law School, believes that the study of law is just as good as the study of science for training the intellect and wonders why teachers haven't borrowed some law-school methods for teaching their own subjects. Dr. Warren explains why law-school instruction methods provide good mental training: "A lawyer always deals ... with facts—the tale of a client, the selection and ordering of facts in litigation, the fact basis of a judicial decision. As a means of enlightening students on the business of wrestling with facts, analyzing, discriminating, criticizing, and selecting what will sustain generalizations, our [law-school] methods have much to commend them."

The intellectual habits required for law and science can be started in the early writer at the age of six and can be exercised and developed by proper writing instruction.

Italian second-graders are regularly assigned papers to train them in observation. Since the Italian child acquires his power to spell all at once, he can freely express his observations on Italian history, geography, science, social studies, or anything else his intellectual and emotional powers permit. He is not restricted to a controlled-word list, as the papers below demonstrate. (Bracketed numbers next to certain words indicate the word's grade level for writing according to *A Core Vocabulary*, 1960. That is, "antenna [6]" is a fifth-grade word for reading, *sixth* grade for *spelling*.)

Today I observed an ant.

With his small antenna [6] he picked up a crumb [5]. I tried to watch in order to see what he'd do with it, then I touched [5] him, I thought he'd run away with the crumb but instead he ran away without the crumb. But later he came back for it. Then he returned to the hole with the crumb and put it in some other place. I saw many ants trying to move a nut. I wanted to play a joke on them. I got a pebble [7] that was on the ground on which the ants were crawling and when I lifted it all the ants began to fall. The nut had been saved [5]. All the ants ran away and the nut sat there all alone—*Fulvia, 7, Caionvico.*

## Observations [8]

Today, in a ray of light I saw two swallows [5].

The swallows were ready to fly.

On their back they had black feathers and underneath [7] on their bellies they had white ones.

I didn't see their legs because they were hidden. After a while they flew. I thought "How beautiful they are!"

If I had a beautiful cage I would be able to look at the swallows. But I thought:

"If I put them in a cage they would die [4] of unhappiness [4]."—*No name, 7, Caionvico*

## A visit to the zoo [9]

One day I went to see the animals in the zoo.

I saw the giraffe. He had a long neck and continued

[4] to eat grass which I gave him and stuck out his tongue [4].

There were parrots [4] of many colors. The one I liked the best was blue.

There were also lions and lionesses. One lion kept roaring [4] like he had pneumonia [9].

The jaguars slept on the stones attached [7] to the wall but there was one young one quarreling [6] with his brother.

In a cage nearby there was a black panther who was sad perhaps [4] because he didn't have any company [5].

Those which I liked the best were the brown bears who were drinking. There were two of them and maybe they were husband [4] and wife [3].

In a field there were three or four fawns and I wanted to go into that meadow [4] to pat them.

I saw a real eagle [4] who was small but if he opened his wings he would have become very big.

In a small pool there were strange seals a little black and a little brown. There weren't any small fish to feed them.

I also liked the monkeys because they were climbing here and there on a hanging [4] vine [4].

There was a turkey [4] together with some ducks which spread their wings which were many different [4] colors. One duck had no feathers on his neck and you could see his skin [4] but the rest of him was covered with feathers.—*Camilla, 7, Brescia*

## The giraffe [4]

The giraffe has some strange points, he is the tallest of all the animals but is also weak [5] in all of his body except [4] for his front legs which are strong enough to kill a snake [4] with one blow.

The beaver is an animal similar [7] to the Boxer puppy, but it has a large tail, and with one bite he can split [5] a finger [4] or with his breast [5] break a stick in two, but he is a good swimmer and I bet that if there was a race between the beaver and a seal [5] the beaver would win. His teeth [5] are all incisors, and he makes his house in the middle of the river with the lynx but he doesn't eat him.—*Roberto, 7, Brescia*

The six-year-old first-graders who wrote the i.t.a. papers below were never given specific training in observation, interpretation, and report writing, yet their papers show sprouts of all but one of the seven values listed on p. 283. These intellectual skills can be cultivated and strengthened by writing, but never in the Dick & Jane curriculum.

Six-year-olds ask questions endlessly but don't normally *demand verification*. Skepticism is a later development. At six, children believe what they're told by adults. They are keenly concerned with consistency, however, and through this concern can be led to a rudimentary understanding of logic, which is really a respect for law and order in thought.

"Longing to know and to understand" and "Questioning of all things"

Mie trip to the librery we wauks to the librery. and ie liekt the Libreryin. she is nies. but wun thing ie wꝏd Liek to nœ is wie duz she tauk sœ Lœ. pꝏrhaps ʃhæ œlny pik peepll hꝏ know hou to bee kwieit. our clas woz not sœ kwieit and ie did not hellp it very much but nœ boty reelly did nether.
—*Gary, Long Island*

"Search for data and their meaning"

I hœp I gœ to the beech and wen I cen find the rest uv ɑr shell cleshen and wen I get it dun I wil ʃho yoo it. doo yoo think I ʃhood rit the nam uv the ʃhells down or doo yoo think I shood get ene kind.—*Denise, Long Island*

On mundæ we went too ʃhe Bech with ɑr cllas wen we got ʃhær we cllecdid chells and we fownd ɑ gelle fich and

*284*

bornuclls and jigll [jingle] chells and shiprs chells and sum ciend of thigs that PoP and ʃhæ feel funɛɛ. Thæ tigll Thæ scwrt wotɾ owt at yoo it is funɛɛ vere funɛɛ and we fownd crabs and we went owt sied at scooll we had ræset and we pllæd on the swings Then we cæm in and we ficst ɑɾ chell cllecchon and Then we pllæd in sie and Bobi mæct pichrs and ie tooc off mie choos and socs ʃhe sand wos cœlld it tiglls it dus tigll verɛɛ much Then we æt ʃhen it storted too drisll [drizzle] sœ we saing and ʃhe Busis cæm and we went bac too scooll—*No name, Long Island*

"Respect for logic"

mie mommy iꙅ in ʃhe hospital. ʃhɛɛ haꙅ ɑ bæby. ʃhɛɛ iꙅ gœiŋ tɷ briŋ it hœm. it iꙅ ɑ boi. ie wonted it tɷ bɛɛ ɑ girl. sœ it iꙅ ɑ boi and it will reck mie toiꙅ.—*Becky, Bethlehem, Pa.*

"Consideration of premises"

I hav trubliz becuz mie muʃhɾ telz mɛɛ tɷ clen ʃhe selɾ and it iz clen.—*B. J., Long Island*

"Consideration of consequences"

her muʃher tœld her tɷ get sum bred ʃhɛɛ got ɑ 100 cɷkeɛz but when ʃhɛɛ got hœm her muʃheɾ had ɑ fit and nou yɷ nœ ʃhat yɷ can't trust kidz.—*Gregg, Cleveland*

ʃhe wagon has nien pakejes ov cɷkeɛs. ges hɷ woz pɷliŋ ʃhe wagon. yes ɑ girl hɷ lieks cɷkeɛz but when ʃhɛɛ got hœm her mommy woz mad. ʃhen ʃhɛɛ hated tɷ briŋ ʃhem back—*Susan, Cleveland*

The writing habit of mind is founded on a cluster of simpler habits. The writer develops a certain way of seeing reality, a certain way of thinking, and a certain way of explaining himself. He develops an acute sense of awareness. He acquires a habit of noting details, of making accurate identifications, of discerning differences and making accurate distinctions. He must be able to collect details and then generalize from what he has collected. He must respect sequence and consequence in time and space. He must be able to discern patterns and be able to associate concepts and experiences.

Admittedly, many able writers don't have all these qualities. My purpose in listing them is to describe some of the educational values of the writing process itself.

It can be argued that these same intellectual processes are exercised by reading, and that in addition reading is the greatest bank for saved experiences of our past. Why, then, does the reader need to write? How can writing develop the intellect better than reading?

We have said it before: the reader must wait for his book to speak before he can react by agreeing or disagreeing. The writer must take the initiative and advance his own judgments, make his own distinctions and qualifications.

In this book I have never denied that reading is important. What I deny is its singular, dominating importance. Reading cannot achieve its proper values unless it is matched by a vigorous and demanding exercise of expression, and by that I mean writing. True, reading opens the doors to new worlds, but after the reader has entered those worlds and had his fill of wandering and looking he will eventually come back out and want to tell others what he has seen—and if he cannot tell them, who will know he's ever been away?

# 7 – THE ANTI-WRITING COALITION

# Lock-Out in Lehigh Valley

ALLENTOWN AND Bethlehem stand as close to each other in Pennsylvania's Lehigh Valley as A to B in the alphabet—Allentown's alphabet, not Bethlehem's.

Teachers, principals, superintendents, and reading experts from every state in the Union, from England, Canada, New Zealand, and Australia have traveled to Bethlehem to watch i.t.a. at work. Many have gone back home and installed the alphabet in their own primary grades.

Yet here is next-door-neighbor city Allentown, so close to Bethlehem it can share city-limit sign posts, and not one Allentown classroom has even tried i.t.a. Why not?

For that matter, why isn't i.t.a. in *your* school? Between 150,000 and 300,000 first-graders will be starting i.t.a. this year. If you have a child starting school, why isn't he one of them? As of 1967, every state in the Union except South Dakota had some i.t.a. program, so that certainly your school has at least heard of this new alphabet. Why isn't it being used? You may find your answers in Allentown.

Allentown, like Bethlehem, has about fifty first-grade classes. Most of these use the Betts Basic Readers.

A year after Bethlehem started using i.t.a. in 1964, Allentown tested a new program of sound-and-pattern drills with several slow-learner classes. This "linguistics approach" was considered so successful that it was extended and used with regular classes as well. As noted earlier, the linguistics program does not replace the regular Jimmy and Sue basal-reader books, but merely dubs sound into them.

So, while Allentown's first-, second-, and third-graders are

*289*

yawning through dull stories about dull Jimmy and Sue and their boring dog, Pepper, in basal readers with skim-milk titles like *On Our Way*, *Time to Play*, and *All in a Day*, Bethlehem's i.t.a. kids are reading about Flanagan and Finnegan, Christopher Robin, Mrs. Doodlepunk and the Five Chinese Brothers, Magellan and Vespucius, John Glenn and Dinosaur Ben, and the Beatrix Potter books and *Winnie-the-Pooh* and *When We Were Very Young*.

---

Jimmy and Sue look and look.
It is fun to look for a toy.
"Here is a blue toy," said Jimmy.
"Here is a big blue toy for you."
Sue said, "A big toy!
I do not want a big toy.
I want a little toy.
I do not see the toy I want."
                            —*Betts Basic Readers*

---

While Allentown children are copying "See the ball. The ball is red," Bethlehem's i.t.a. first-graders are writing book reports. Some are writing their own absence excuses or passing love notes.

There is no ceiling on the Bethlehem writer's words. He was never bundled in baby-word swaddles and stuck in a controlled-language playpen with Sue and Jim. Neither was he fed a day-after-day diet of "bat the rat, Nat" jingles. He writes freely and confidently the vigorous language that wise, imaginative six-year-olds are apt to talk.

Clearly, the Bethlehem first-grader is a different educand than the Allentown first-grader. Why doesn't Allentown seek to have this new educand too? Allentown is next door to a sizzling educational revolution and refuses to join it.

Allentown schools understandably don't like being compared with Bethlehem's, but like it or not the fact that Bethlehem has converted 100 per cent to i.t.a. while Allentown is 100 per cent non-i.t.a. raises a few fair questions. Maybe Allentown knows something about i.t.a. that Bethlehem doesn't know. Allentown is neither backward nor too conservative to try an innovation like i.t.a. Its "opportunity program" for mentally superior children is a national model. It has one of the most imaginative and yet practical vocational-school systems in the country.

Is jealousy, perhaps, keeping Allentown from imitating Bethlehem? One might get that impression from talking with some people in Allentown. A school-board member commenting on the number of visitors to Bethlehem wasped: "They've all come just for the novelty." A school official told me flatly: "Bethlehem wouldn't have taken i.t.a. if it hadn't received a grant." (Not true. Dr. Stewart had already taken steps to try i.t.a. on a small experimental scale before Dr. Mazurkiewicz received his Ford grant.)

But while robust competitive feelings may stir the attitudes of some school officials, neither jealousy nor pique nor the spirit of rivalry is keeping i.t.a. out of Allentown.

Is it *cost* that's keeping i.t.a. out of Allentown? Probably not. An Allentown school-board member told me that i.t.a. had never been described or presented to the board for consideration. There was nothing unusual about this, he explained, as the board was not responsible for curriculum decisions. "But we would have heard about it if it had been a question of money."

Allentown's Assistant Superintendent, John T. Shuman, grumped, "If it's so good, why doesn't *everybody* use it?" He admitted he had no specific professional reason for rejecting the alphabet and denied it had been rejected because of cost. He further observed that the decision to reject or accept i.t.a. had never been his to make. "I can't stand the way it's being promoted," he added, but declined to amplify or explain what he meant.

The decision to refuse i.t.a. had been made by the city's former Director of Elementary Education and Reading Expert. i.t.a. had been defined solely as a "reading method" and on that definition rejected.

The city's new Director of Elementary Education is Otis J. Rothenberger, a thoughtful, old-family Pennsylvanian with courtly manners. "I do not view i.t.a. as an unsound program," he told me. "The Bethlehem teachers who have spoken to me about it

*291*

have such dedication and enthusiasm that one cannot help but admire them. Nevertheless, the basic feature of the program is rather cumbersome and I think this can be justified only if the results are significantly better than in a program using traditional orthography. In the development of reading skills, I see no significant improvement and am not particularly impressed."

It becomes clear when you have asked enough questions around Allentown that i.t.a. was the victim of reading bias. Not one teacher or school official had seriously examined i.t.a. writing or considered the alphabet in any other way than as a method for teaching children to read.

# The Reading Expert

THE BIGGEST MOUTH in grade school belongs to the Reading Expert. He or she is a School of Education graduate who has specialized in reading and reading measurement. He is a professor teaching teachers or he works in a school district or state department of education.

An extremely small number of Reading Experts manage to become publishing consultants or textbook editors and authors. In these positions their power can claw out in all directions, for not only do they collect and edit the stuffing for basal readers but they write the manuals that show teachers how to teach reading. Their influence through these manuals can be great or little, depending on the teacher's ability and sense of professional security, but the influence is usually great, according to a 1964 Columbia Teachers College report on reading instruction.

The authors of the report, Allen H. Barton and David E. Wilder, say that 66 to 70 per cent of the first-, second- and third-grade teachers they queried believed either "strongly" or "mostly" that the suggestions to teachers in their reading manuals were based on definite scientific proof; only 7 per cent disagreed. Elementary-school principals went the way of their teachers: 58 per cent either "strongly" or "mostly" believed the manuals used by their teachers were scientifically based, while only 9 per cent disagreed. Barton and Wilder conclude: "But the experts ... are much less impressed by the scientific status of reading manuals; almost half disagree with the statement that they are based on 'definite scientific proof,' and only a third agree 'mostly.' The experts thus think much less highly of their own product.... Perhaps the teachers have been oversold—and the principals are almost as sold as the teachers."

The ultimate source of the Reading Expert's power is his controlled-vocabulary system. By strictly controlling which words and how many words a child will learn year by year, the Reading Expert determines the child's grade level. By determining grade levels, the Reading Expert also controls the readers and the social studies, history, science, and other textbooks the child will use. He influences the selection of concepts these books will teach because the concepts must be expressed in words that fit the grade levels he has rigged up.

It's easy to see why i.t.a. bothers the Reading Establishment since i.t.a. saws clean through the rungs of the controlled-vocabulary ladder. By collapsing the ladder, it threatens to pull down the school's system of grades and levels which are knotted into the controlled words. It frightens teachers who feel secure and at home in the apparatus of the controlled-vocabulary lists. It threatens publishers with expensive revisions of their materials. Publishers have caught the knack of feeding concepts into books by grade levels and by following controlled-vocabulary guidelines. It's convenient and profitable to sell books in graded series. Now they are faced with an educand who breaks up the numerical progression of their series, who wants grade-four or -five books instead of the grade-two or -three book he was expected to use.

I can sympathize with teachers who have become addicted to the controlled vocabulary. Their dependency reminds me of a middle-aged woman I read about a few years ago who had been living in a body cast for twenty years although she had completely outgrown her original need for it. As a young girl she had broken her back and doctors had enveloped her in a plaster-of-Paris coat. After a year or so she was released from the cast, but she found room temperature too harsh for her sensitive skin and preferred to sleep inside her cast. Gradually, as other problems and tensions disturbed her she slept more often in the cast and eventually moved back into it to live.

More than anyone else in school, i.t.a. confounds the Reading Expert who has set up shop within the controlled-vocabulary economy. He has figured out his Blue Cross, the mortgage on his swimming pool, his retirement pension, and his next Mustang, convinced that controlled words are as solid as U.S. dollars.

It doesn't take ESP to guess that you won't get i.t.a. or a writing-oriented curriculum in your school if it threatens the job ego or income structure of the one person who can keep it out, your Reading Expert.

Since the same word list that regulates the child's reading eventually regulates his spelling, the Reading Expert is automatically in charge of written expression. Through his readers he gives children short words before long words, simple sentences before complex ones. Their schedule of sentence structures for writing must follow his reading-instruction timetable. Children spend weeks learning dozens of uses for capitals months, even years, in advance of any practical writing use for them. This sequence too is drawn to suit the Reading Expert.

But the need to communicate is dynamically present in every child as, month by month, he pushes up through his stages and phases of growth, as he develops psychologically, emotionally, intellectually, and socially. The need can't be satisfied orally in a class of twenty-five to thirty children. The need doesn't wait for second-grade words or fifth-grade words.

What about the child who has compound thoughts and complex feelings and would like to express them? He must wait. He must manage with the baby patterns till he's big enough to get bigger patterns.

Thus we see that *the Reading Expert controls a child's social and emotional expression as well as his intellectual growth.* He decides the child's word-spending allowance. He is Customs supervising the child's communication export. Who hired him for all this? Has anyone challenged his qualifications?

Reading Experts are fond of saying that reading is "the heart of education," mindless that the heart has several chambers serving different functions, some receiving, some sending. Reading Experts know next to nothing about "sending," about the reader's expressive needs.

A miraculous golden flow of new writing has been coming from i.t.a. first-graders, but no one is doing anything to learn from it or to direct its course. Some Reading Experts comment on its charm, others step warily around it and let it wash by without comment; still others remark at the "atrocious spellings" floating in the stream

*295*

or worry about the ungraded words they see. All seem to be too preoccupied with reading to realize they're dealing with a new educand.

> sum peepl can see
> sum peepl cannot see
> peepl that cannot see cannot see prity things
> —*Jane, 6, first grade, Bethlehem, Pa.*

## THE READING LOBBY

The Reading Expert amplifies his voice by joining other Reading Experts. In 1956 two organizations, the International Council for the Improvement of Reading Instruction and the National Association for Remedial Teaching, merged and became the International Reading Association (IRA). According to its by-laws, the IRA has three goals: the first is "to improve the quality of reading instruction at all levels"; the second is "to develop an awareness of the impact of reading upon our citizenry"; the third is "to sponsor conferences and meetings planned to implement" these purposes. The IRA has more than 55,000 active members including 40,000 teachers in over 500 separate councils zealously pursuing these objectives in the United States.

**4 out of 10 fifth-graders will become high school dropouts—mainly because of *reading* problems. . . . A million kids a year leave high school before they graduate. Experts say that the key is *reading*.—*International Paper ad***

Reading Experts have persuaded the government to believe that for every reader there is one less dropout, one less juvenile delinquent or criminal, one less unemployed person, and that reading is the way out of poverty. Their argument is that since reading is *the* key to success, when someone doesn't succeed it must be because he can't read.

The IRA is a healthy, active organization doing the job it was intended to do. Its success, exactly, is my single criticism of the IRA, for what is good for the IRA is not necessarily good for education. Since there is no comparable lobby promoting speech or writing, the primary grades are sent on a sinister, biased course.

No one agitates for the improvement of writing instruction or seeks to impress our citizens with writing's importance or calls conferences and meetings to advance these two objectives. There is no international writing association, no national writing association, and no regional, state, county, or school-district writing association.

By creating the general impression that reading is the *king* subject, Reading Experts have persuaded teachers to feel that reading instruction is the one all-important study of their professional careers, and that they can never ever get enough information about it. The National Council of Teachers of English asked elementary-school teachers what school subjects they wanted to learn more about and which they considered most professionally valuable. "The overwhelming national choice was reading," the Council reported in "The Continuing Education of Teachers of English" (1964). In spite of the swamp of seminars, institutes, and workshops all promoting reading, 79.1 per cent of the teachers said they wanted still more.

There are magazines called *The Arithmetic Teacher* and *The Mathematics Teacher*. There is *The Reading Teacher*, of course. But no one has published a Writing or Composition Teacher.

The Council for Basic Education has only one message to grind out month after month in its bulletin and other publications: "Go back to basics." In the CBE, "basics" means reading and arithmetic. The Council has never sponsored or reported on any writing research. For that matter, Ford and Carnegie both have spent thousands and thousands of dollars for reading research but neither has put down a cent for a report on early writing instruction.

Elementary-school administrators have become so bookcentric that they *hear* "reading" when you say "writing" to them. I invite anyone to make this test: talk with a grade-school authority about your child's writing. Before you have spoken three sentences, see if he will not have switched the talk from writing to reading. "Illiteracy" ought to refer to both reading and writing but you will hear it used only to mean reading. The Encyclopedia of Educational Research index reference to "literacy" sends you through its pages to an article about adult reading ability. The article doesn't even mention writing illiteracy.

---

MAKE A QUACKING NOISE . . . and you're speaking a duck's language. In fact, a duck call may be the hunter's best way to communicate with his feathered audience. Communicating with people, in language they can comprehend, is more difficult.

To help them master the skills of communication, your students require, first and foremost, a sound reading program. . . . —*Inside-front-cover advertisment in* The Reading Teacher, *October 1966*

---

The Reading Expert has convinced parents, too, that reading is boss in school. Many parents are only too happy to agree if for no other reason than that books are good pacifiers. Books are kid mufflers. Reading is a sound-soaking mat to be flopped over talking too much, yelling, and wrecking the house—but especially asking questions. After television, there's no better way to keep a kid quiet than by putting him in a big, warm, mothering library and feeding him a book.

In 1966 a thousand parading New York City parents drummed and blared along by a forty-piece band demonstrated against poor reading instruction in the schools and demanded a summer remedial-reading program. You couldn't find *three* New York mothers willing to carry a sign against bad writing instruction. You couldn't even get anybody to hum through a comb.

In 1964 the *Ladies' Home Journal* titled one of my articles "A Bizarre Alphabet Teaches Johnny to Read" in spite of the fact that the article was about writing. I quoted over twenty other magazine articles with both "Johnny" and "Reading" together in their titles, but I couldn't dissuade the editors. They were convinced that a title with "writing" in it would attract fewer readers. They were probably right. *Journal* readers, no less than readers of *Atlantic Monthly* or *Saturday Review*, have been sensitized to the formula R = E—reading equals education.

The Office of Education catalogue lists a single pamphlet on writing instruction called "How Children Learn to Write." It is out of print. The bad consequences of bad writing instruction show up all over Washington. The *Congressional Record*, for example, is a massive record of bad communication, as is distressingly clear when you compare it with its British counterpart, *Hansard*. The neglect of writing instruction is reflected in the needs of other government agencies and departments. The Department of Labor, the Treasury Department, the Air Force, and the Department of the Interior each has published more instruction material for writing than has the U.S. Office of Education.

*Has anyone in the Office of Education ever thought of reducing the number of reading illiterates by reducing the volume of bad writing?*

## THE READING MEASURERS

Educationists explain the vacuum in writing research by saying they have no valid tests for measuring writing. Now this seems odd because there are stacks of tests for evaluating reading. Dr. Albert Harris' book *How to Increase Reading Ability* cites at least fifty different reading-measurement tests. There are easily as many reading-measurement experts as the total number of Fuller Brush men and Avon ladies combined. Wouldn't you think at least one among them could turn up some simple test to measure writing?

The fact that they haven't makes me doubt the testers—not their sincerity or honesty, but their ability. If they can't measure the child's written statement, which they can feel with their fingers, which they can hold up to the light and pass around among psychologists, speech experts, parents, administrators, taxpayers, and teachers, how am I to believe they are able to measure an event such as reading, an event that happens in the mind, hidden, entwined with cognition itself?

Writing is as complex and subtle an event as reading, but while reading ends in the mind, writing ends out in the open where we can all look at it and have some opinion about it. Writing is not some-

---

judy and I have a seecret labrtory and wee do difrent things everyday and wee arn't going too tell enywon wot wee do in the labrtory—*No name, first grade, Long Island*

---

thing in a black felt bag whose nature we have to guess at by feeling it with thick leather mittens.

What happens to the written word that drops into a reader's mind is a mystery only dimly lighted by objective tests, because reading measures are feeble soundings of an extremely complex and subtle event—the act of *becoming* itself. But the written word that drops *out* of the mind is no mystery. There it is, captured by paper, dyed into its fibers, a voice print, a mind print. It exists to be known. It can be run through baths of criticism. It can be tossed from expert to expert.

In a certain few tests, Reading Experts have given sidelong glances at i.t.a. writing. Their reactions to what they've seen testify to their ignorance of the nature of writing, the need for writing, and the importance of writing. For example, William B. Gillooly, an assistant professor of education at Johns Hopkins University, concludes that "the promise of i.t.a. is a delusion." Yet he reports, in the June 1966 *Phi Delta Kappan:* "In Chasnoff's study, 616 writing samples were collected after 120 days of instruction. The samples were transformed so that the four judges could not tell in which group they originated. They were then rated for 'communication of meaning.' A significant difference favored the i.t.a. group."

The failure to design an adequate measure for writing, besides dramatizing the favoritism shown to reading and passivity in our educational attitude, suggests that there is no adequate measure of reading, either.

---

wun dæ ſhe kiŋ ov ſhe ɛɛmuez woz runniŋ ſhrω the bruſh land. hɛɛ sau mister kaŋgrω. aʂ ſhe ɛɛmue ran bie hɛɛ nœtest sumſhiŋ in mister kaŋgrω'ʂ pouᴄh. ſhe ɛɛmue slœd doun until hɛɛ woʂ ɛɛven wiſh mister kaŋgrω. and askt "whot iʂ in yωr pouᴄh." wiſh a nies ekspreſhon mister kaŋgrω replied happily wiſh a sie "a picnic baskit. ie hav enuf fωd for 2 austrælɛɛan animalʂ. and sœ mister kaŋgrω tœld ſhe ɛɛmue ſhat hɛɛ woʂ hopiŋ tω a buetifωl plæs just across ſhe hill. œ kæ ſhær wer nœ snæks. œ ſhæ bœth had a fun tiem. ſhat niet ſhæ bœſh had nies drɛɛmʂ about aull ſhe fun ſhæ had ſhat afternωn—*Gordon, 6, first grade, Long Beach, Calif.*

---

# There's More Money in Reading

BETWEEN 1960 and 1966 International Paper illustrated the message "Send me a man who *reads!*" in thirty-two different ways and ran it in *The New Yorker, Look, Reader's Digest,* and *The Saturday Review.* Six million reprints of the ads were sent to school teachers and librarians, who hung them on classroom and library walls where children were sure to get their message. The message was always the same: success in getting a job or career, success on the job and success in life depended on reading—"International Paper believes the future lies with men who read . . ."

The "Send me a man who *reads!*" ads were often false and always misleading. What makes them *seem* true is our reading bias. We're willing to believe almost anything good about reading. For example, a typical International Paper ad reads: "The average U.S. Senator reads 27 newspapers a week—more than any other occupational group ever interviewed by International Paper. He reads three books per month and four magazines every week. I-P believes the most important thing that's ever done with paper is putting words on it."

What International Paper says about the average U.S. Senator's reading may be true, but most Senators' *speeches* are ghost-written. Perhaps they're too busy reading, but I rather suspect it's because they can't do the "most important thing that's ever done with paper" —they can't put words on it.

A good letter may land a job interview at International Paper, but a list of books the applicant has read won't. The only people hired solely for their ability to read at I-P are messenger boys. The ability to communicate clearly on paper and in speech is as necessary and important there as in any other business. I pointed this out to an I-P executive, who agreed readily but defended the ads by saying: "Look, we're paper salesmen, not educators. We'll sell more paper by promoting reading. How much paper can a writer use?"

The only products ultimately needed for writing instruction are blank paper and something to write with. In today's market, a good salesman expects to earn from $10,000 to $18,000 a year selling textbooks. He won't make it selling tablets and pencils.

Elementary schools buy almost 40 per cent of the textbooks published—more than $2 billion worth each year. Very little school money goes for books teaching communication, as is quickly apparent when you examine textbook catalogues.

I have before me Ginn & Company's 1965–66 price list. Ginn, a leading textbook publisher, presents 156 *reading* items for sale to all elementary-school grades. The sale of this total package would earn the company $433.44. The *spelling* package consists of eighteen items costing a total of $22.98. On the other hand, under the subject "English" Ginn offers only fourteen items. Of the fourteen, four relate to literature (which is reading, of course) and four relate to the classroom library (also reading). Of the remaining six items, one is *My Picture Dictionary* and one is a set of alphabet wall cards. Two books teach correct language usage and *two*, finally, *concern writing*. The two writing books are for seventh- and eighth-grade use only. They sell for $1.70 and $1.95.

The 1967 Ginn catalogue shows little change. It contains fourteen page-length columns devoted to reading materials, two columns covering "English," a half column describing a vocabulary-building program, and one and a half columns listing spelling books.

Scott, Foresman is the publishing house that Dick & Jane built. Scott, Foresman's total reading package in 1966 sold for $368.82. The Basic Reading Program lists sixty-one items for $82.78. There is a "Reading for Pleasure" series, an "Enrichment for the Accelerated" series, an "Invitations to Personal Reading" series, a "Reading for Independence" series, an "Easy Reading" series, and an "Easy Reading and Simplified Classics" series.

Scott, Foresman's list shows books for writing under "Additional Materials." The first six items in this category are:

Big Book for We Read Pictures $6.60
Big Book for Before We Read 5.10
Big Book for Pre-Primers 4.68
Big Book Holder 9.00
Comprehensive Card Set 16.50
Speech Improvement Cards 4.95

There is also *My Little Pictionary*, *My Second Pictionary*, *Beginning Dictionary*, *Junior Dictionary*, and *Advanced Junior Dictionary*.

Finally, there is *Learn to Listen, Speak and Write*, for sixty cents, and *My Practice Pad* for thirty-six cents. It comes in six parts. Total cost, including teachers' editions: $13.92.

Scott, Foresman also sells plastic cubes imprinted with words. There is a First Rolling Reader, a Second Rolling Reader, and a Third Rolling Reader, all three for $9.90. You can buy Rolling Consonants for $3.30, too. Rolling Vowels cost more: $7.50.

---

**Step Up Power In . . . Writing. . . . Strengthen . . . awareness of sentence patterns, of the function of words in sentences and the significance of word order. . . . There are noun blocks, verb blocks, adjective blocks, adverb blocks, and alternates to provide variety and extend children's vocabulary of instantly perceived words. Fifty words in all are used. Each time children toss the blocks they can build a grammatically correct sentence, following sentence patterns they are used to hearing. . . . With 10 additional blocks children now can make thousands of sentences ranging in length from 3 to 7 words.—*A Scott, Foresman advertisement for its "Rolling Readers"***

---

# The Alphabet Is a Two-Way Street

**The decision to reject or accept i.t.a. merely as a device for reading or to review it merely as a bundle of books is an arrogant misuse of power and trust. It is a presumptuous decision because it pretends that reading is all that counts in education. It is false and misleading for a Reading Expert to pretend to be promoting all the language arts when all he or she knows is reading. Since there are no grade-school writing consultants to speak up on behalf of writing instruction, it is irresponsible for Reading Experts to assume that early writing is an interesting, charming, delightful phenomenon but a trivial one for all that.**

RESEARCH into reading isolated from writing may profitably absorb the piecemeal, bricklaying behaviorist research, but it shouldn't satisfy the master educator concerned with a child's total development and education. Unfortunately it often does.

Nancy Larrick, a past president of the International Reading Association, wrote an article for *Parents' Magazine* (October 1965) in which she compared two new learning alphabets and what they mean to education. The alphabets were i.t.a. and Unifon. She starts her article with the typical Reading Expert bias: "The purpose of the new alphabets? To make it easier for beginners to read."

Dr. Larrick does not ignore i.t.a. writing but the bias of her point of view creates the general impression that an alphabet is made for reading only. Yet there wouldn't be any readers if there hadn't first been some writers. (I made this latter observation to a Long Island Reading Expert recently. She answered: "Oh, that's just like which came first, the chicken or the egg.")

Dr. Larrick skims along describing first i.t.a., then the Unifon, then i.t.a., then Unifon again, and in the end she blithely concludes: "An impartial and dispassionate appraisal of I.T.A. and Unifon is hard to make, because the new alphabets are still young." Now it is obvious she was thinking only of reading because in the article itself she reports she saw no Unifon writing, and that in fact the children she observed had been told *not* to attempt to write with it. But somewhere she reports that she saw writing, writing, writing in the i.t.a. classes, that to capture the flow of words children were using the backs of used sales-record sheets from an ice cream distributor.

i.t.a. was begun in England as a reading aid and introduced into the United States by Reading Experts as the medium for a new approach to reading. Consequently, and no wonder, it has so far been cheered or cursed only by Reading Experts.

It is typical of the reading favoritism that pervades our culture and stubbornly obsesses our educators that i.t.a.'s value in writing instruction is repeatedly overlooked and grossly undervalued.

Since i.t.a. was first demonstrated in Bethlehem, about fifty research studies have compared i.t.a. and T.O. reading at a cost of at least a million dollars in state and federal aid alone. On the other hand, I know of only one study that has compared i.t.a. and T.O. writing. Lenore Sandel of Hofstra University wrote "The Comparison of Oral and Written Responses of First Grade Children of i.t.a. and T.O. Classes." She received $6,800 to conduct this study. Workshops instructing teachers in the use of i.t.a. may devote an hour or two to writing, but many ignore writing completely. At the annual international i.t.a. conferences, it is typical for three or four days full of talks to go by with perhaps only one speaker concentrating on i.t.a. writing.

The i.t.a. Foundation names almost a hundred publishers who publish i.t.a. materials for various reading programs. There are storybooks and social studies, science, geography, geology, zoology, and biography books. But no i.t.a. writing-instruction program has yet been developed nor are any publishers jostling each other to be the first to develop one.

One big scare for the publishers is that very few teachers would be interested in picking up and handling a writing-instruction program. No one has been trained to teach writing. Before a publisher can sell a proper writing course he'll have to fight his way through the various bands of reading favoritism wrapped around our school system. The strength of these bands is well known to salesmen who serve education. When Smith-Corona put its first i.t.a. typewriter on the market it prudently announced "Breaking through the reading barrier with Smith-Corona."

It is possible to use i.t.a. without buying any books at all. For example, it can be used in Dr. R. V. Allen's "Language Experience" system, which has children learn to read through reading their own writings. It can be used with the Nebraska Curriculum, as demonstrated in University City, Missouri, and described earlier.

When I interviewed Dr. Allen in Arizona in 1965 he had not used i.t.a. nor did he seem willing to introduce it. Children in his "Language Experience approach" dictate to their teachers and then read what their teachers have written down for them. Gradually, as the children learn to copy and write, they need only spelling help.

The LE papers I read showed the same adult organizations and intonations one gets used to seeing on experience charts. They are unmistakable signs of teacher presence, just as a child's direct look into the camera betrays the "candid" cameraman. I told Dr. Allen I thought his LE children would succeed more quickly and more fully if begun with i.t.a. because they wouldn't need to get writing and spelling help from their teachers. Dr. Allen doubted this and offered to pit a class of i.t.a. children against one of his LE classes in order to show me his LE class would produce more and better writing. Dr. Allen is right in putting so much confidence in his teachers, but his challenge reveals a common misconception of i.t.a. one meets everywhere, namely, that it is a *method* of reading instruction. A fair test of i.t.a. would be to match an LE-trained teacher using i.t.a. against an LE-trained teacher using the traditional alphabet.

i.t.a. is merely the alphabet temporarily extended to fit English speech more exactly and consistently. It is a medium, not a method, and therefore it fits both reading and writing and is adaptable to any teacher's methods provided the methods do not depend on the controlled-vocabulary system. Educators who are afraid i.t.a. may disrupt their own carefully engineered programs betray their view of i.t.a. as a competing arrangement of books.

Some people regard all innovations in school as "drastic." To them the mere sight of i.t.a. makes them shiver and get cramps. Mark Twain claimed that such people once delayed the adoption of the alphabet itself. In the excerpt below, Twain, who was an active Simplified Spelling advocate at the turn of the century, describes how Cadmus tried to persuade the Egyptians to abandon their hieroglyphics and adopt the alphabet:

Uncle Cadmus began with an object lesson, with chalk, on a couple of blackboards. On one of them he drew in outline a slender Egyptian in a short skirt, with slim legs and an eagle's head in place of a proper head, and he was carrying a couple of dinner pails, one in each hand. In front of this figure he drew a toothed line like an excerpt from a saw; in front of this he drew three skeleton birds of doubtful ornithological origin; in front of these he drew a partly constructed house, with lean Egyptians fetching materials in wheelbarrows to finish it with; next he put in some more unclassified birds; then a large king, with carpenter's shavings for whiskers and hair; next he put in another king jabbing a mongrel lion with a javelin; he followed this with a picture of a tower, with armed Egyptians projecting out of the top of it and as crowded for room as the cork in a bottle; he drew the opposing army below, fierce of aspect but much out of drawing as regards perspective. They were shooting arrows at the men in the tower, which was poor military judgment because they could have reached up and pulled them out by the scruff of the neck. He followed these pictures with line after line of birds and beasts and scraps of saw-teeth and bunches of men in the customary short frock, some of them doing things, the others waiting for the umpire to call game; and finally his great blackboard was full from top to bottom. Everybody recognized the invocation set forth by the symbols:

it was the Lord's Prayer.

It had taken him forty-five minutes to set it down. Then he stepped to the other blackboard and dashed off "Our Father which art in heaven," and the rest of it, in graceful Italian script, spelling the words the best he knew how in those days, and finished it up in four minutes and a half.

It was rather impressive. Then he said:

"My argument is before you. One of the objections to the hieroglyphics is that it takes the brightest pupil nine years to get the forms and their meanings by heart; it takes the average pupil sixteen years; it takes the rest of the nation all their days to accomplish it—it is a life sentence. This cost of time is much too expensive. It could be employed more usefully in other industries, and with better results.

"If you will renounce the hieroglyphics and adopt written words instead, an advantage will be gained. By you? No, not by you. You have spent your lives in mastering the hiero-glyphics, and to you they are simple, and the effect pleasant to the eye, and even beautiful. . . . But I appeal to you in behalf of the generations which are to follow you, century after century, age after age, cycle after cycle. I pray you consider them and be generous. Lift this heavy burden from their backs. Do not send them toiling and moiling down to the twentieth century still bearing it, still oppressed by it. Let your sons and daughters adopt the words and the alphabet, and go free. . . .

The Opposition rose and combated his reasonings in the usual way. Those people said that they had always been used to the hieroglyphics; that the hieroglyphics had dear and sacred associations for them; that they loved to sit on a barrel under an umbrella in the brilliant sun of Egypt and spell out the owls and eagles and alligators and saw-teeth, and take an hour and a half to the Lord's Prayer, and weep with romantic emotion at the thought that they had, at most, but eight or ten years between themselves and the grave for the enjoyment of this ecstasy; and that then possibly these Revolters would shove the ancient signs and symbols from the main track and equip the people with a lightning-express reformed alphabet that would leave the hieroglyphic wheelbarrow a hundred thousand miles behind and have not a damned association which could compel a tear, even if tears and diamonds stood at the same price in the market.—*From* Mark Twain: *Letters from the Earth, edited by Bernard De Voto.*

## THE "GREAT DEBATE" IS ONLY A FAMILY FIGHT

Jeanne Chall's book, *Learning to Read—the Great Debate,* is the result of a three-year study of grade-school readers and reading instruction. The study, sponsored by the Carnegie Foundation for the Advancement of Teaching, is a model report: it interests, it informs, it communicates. Even the usually sour and gloomy Council for Basic Education says that it "is not only a fascinating and informative book but an important one, possibly a revolutionary one."

Dr. Chall's report defines and describes the various approaches to reading instruction that have been devised in recent years to meet the inadequacies of the incumbent basal-reader system. It is based on Dr. Chall's examination of sixty-seven research studies, visits to 300 classrooms, and interviews with 500 teachers and school administrators. Her style is clinical but warm, her language professional but surprisingly free of jargon. Many educational events, research projects, market surveys, and books in years to come will refer back to Dr. Chall's report. Some will agree with it, some will disagree. Unfortunately, the ferment it will stimulate will be an Establishment ferment.

The "great debate" alluded to in the report title turns out to be only a family fight as told by a member of the family, a wrangle among Reading Experts described by another Reading Expert.

In a curious departure from the bittersweet objectivity of her report, Dr. Chall says: "I make a special plea for caution concerning the use of ITA because I see it as the most expensive and drastic change that could be made in beginning reading. It is expensive because it means developing and buying new books for grades 1 and 2—not only readers, but arithmetic, science, and social studies, as well as library books. It also means constantly retraining teachers and administrators. It is drastic, because a child moving from an ITA to a non-ITA school, or vice versa, during his first or second year will have to learn a new alphabet in midstream; this would be troublesome in the United States, where people move around a great deal. Of course, if all schools adopted ITA simultaneously there would be no problem, but educational change in this country is usually slow and sporadic."

A discussion of i.t.a.'s expense is out of place in my book because I am pledged to discuss writing, and expense is a reading problem. The expense of writing consists in pen and paper costs. But I want to comment on Jeanne Chall's "special plea for caution concerning the use of ITA" because her plea will be grabbed up and hugged by many educationists only too happy to use her and the prestige of the Carnegie Foundation as an excuse for their own immobility. I object to the following three statements:

1) *The use of i.t.a. means "constantly retraining teachers and administrators."* It takes only two or three days to show teachers how to read and write with i.t.a. Though administrators sometimes attend workshops to see whether they want to introduce i.t.a. to their schools or not, there is no training of administrators needed. Teachers need only one exposure to i.t.a. There is no constant retraining.

2) *The use of i.t.a. is "the most expensive change that could be made in beginning reading."* By this time, i.t.a. publishers must have showered Dr. Chall with price lists showing that their books compete in cost with any other grade-school books on the market. *Winnie-the-Pooh*, for example, costs $2.95 in the i.t.a. edition as compared with $3.50 in the T.O. version.

It's hard to believe that Dr. Chall is sincerely worried about i.t.a.'s "expense." She doesn't volunteer the caution that Omar K. Moore's "talking-typewriter" costs $30,000 to $40,000 for each machine. Even if a manufacturer could eventually jack the price down to $400 or $500, the per pupil cost would still be beyond most school budgets. This is not meant to be a criticism of Dr. Moore's machine or of teaching machines in general. I just wonder why Dr. Chall enters some thirty or so references to the "talking-typewriter" without pointing out that you can stuff the old *Queen*

*Elizabeth* deck to bottoms and stem to stern with books for $40,000.

If it's educational bargains Dr. Chall wants, why didn't she make a special plea for Dr. Allen's "Language Experience" system? Its materials are free, since they are written by the children themselves. Or why doesn't she refer readers to the Nebraska Curriculum, which was developed with government funds and is therefore mimeo-paper cheap? Dr. Chall doesn't warn the reader about the expense of basal readers, and yet elsewhere in *Learning to Read* she says: ". . . a basal-reading series is one of the most expensive and extensive ventures a publisher can undertake. . . . I was reminded of how bulky a basal series and related materials can be when the generous editor . . . wanted to know how much space I had in my office before sending his complete reading program for grades 1, 2 and 3. . . . I would have needed a storage room!"

i.t.a. is expensive if a school already has a deep stock of Dick & Jane books that the publisher will not take back. The expense will come from having to cast out a collection of books. The decision to take a loss on Dick & Jane books is a test of values: *which is more important—to waste the books, or keep them and waste the children who must use them?*

3) *The use of i.t.a. is "the most drastic change that could be made in beginning reading."* Dr. Chall's fear is really nothing more than a combination of the old "two-alphabet" fear and the "unlearning" fear that bothers most people who look at i.t.a. for the first time— she alludes to learning "a new alphabet in midstream." But Dr. Chall formulates a new argument against i.t.a., namely, that it is unsuitable because United States citizens are a nomadic people.

I don't think that educational philosophy should be determined by the possibility that some first- and second-graders may change schools in midyear. What happens if a child starts a new math program in one school and then switches to another? What if he goes from a nongraded to a graded school? What if he abandons Dick & Jane to embrace Jimmy & Sue or if he flees to a phonics-method system? If the mobility of our citizens is an argument against i.t.a., then it is also an argument against any innovation in any school. If our nomadic patterns are as serious and bold as Dr. Chall draws them, the ultimate solution would be that all schools

*311*

adopt exactly the same books in all grades—Uni-Ed, one united, nationwide set of books and methods.

Dr. Chall is right in saying that i.t.a. can cause drastic changes, but it is superficial to say the changes are drastic because they may affect families who move. They are drastic for far deeper and more serious reasons. The changes that follow the adoption of i.t.a. are pushed by the i.t.a. child himself. He changes his teacher and the two of them change the curriculum.

Bethlehem is an excellent showcase for drastic change. The first book to be thrown out by Bethlehem's first graduating i.t.a. classes was the old T.O. second-grade speller. Next to go were three thousand unused Dick & Jane language books. New spelling lists had to be devised to meet the i.t.a. child's different spelling attack.

The social-service material usually given to Bethlehem second-graders was rejected by the i.t.a. classes as "dumb and silly." They preferred a geography-social studies-economics book described as "hard" for third-graders. When Dr. Stewart decided to use a book on colonial America with her second-graders the worried publisher reminded her that the book had been developed for fourth-grade classes. He said: "I fear it will be too hard and your disappointment will turn you against the series." The publisher's worry was wasted.

Dictionary work used to be started in third grade in Bethlehem and limited to picture dictionaries. World Books and other simple encyclopedias were usually introduced to fourth-grade or high third-grade children. But Bethlehem second-graders began to use the World Books and work with honest T.O. dictionaries and encyclopedias.

In Bethlehem before i.t.a., it was believed children could not understand time and space concepts until they'd reached the fourth-grade level. The i.t.a. wave has proven this false. Some map and globe work is given in first grade and is regular subject matter for second grade.

Yes, i.t.a. is expensive and i.t.a. does mean drastic change, but not for Dr. Chall's reasons. i.t.a. is a rebel who threatens to kick down the house that Jack (and Dick & Jane and Jimmy & Sue and Mr. Gray) built.

# The Reading Hawks

THERE IS evidence that the basal-reader system means the basal rot of communication development, yet when school starts this September three and a half million first-graders will once again be greeted at the door by Dick & Jane and Jimmy & Sue and all their dogs. Year after year these tint-faced baby-word frauds continue to cheat the United States out of several million writers—your own children among them.

If i.t.a. can give us our first clean chance to teach communication properly, why don't the schools dump Dick & Jane and adopt i.t.a. as the start of a writing-oriented curriculum? Or, forgetting i.t.a., why don't schools make an honest move to teach the basal habits of clear, articulate communication?

It's not easy and may well be impossible. Dick & Jane are backed by a rich, squat, and slothful Reading Establishment that's had half a century to settle down tight. The Reading Establishment consists of reading experts, curriculum developers, school principals and superintendents, teachers, school psychologists, librarians, school-board members, education-research organizations, education writers, publishers, and education foundations who collectively believe that the three R's of education are reading, reading, and reading: $E = R$.

The Reading Establishment has treated *reading* to lush expense-account lunches but let *writing* eat out of brown paper bags. It has piddled away the meaning of writing instruction until it now means little more than "correct spelling" or "handwriting."

Jeanne Chall's bleat about i.t.a. "expense" unintentionally echoes a slur heard when i.t.a. was first introduced to the United States. An Associated Press education writer, G. K. Hodenfield,

*313*

told *Phi Delta Kappan* readers in January 1966 that i.t.a. was "a bonanza for the Pitman publishing interests."

John H. Fisher of the Modern Language Society in discussing i.t.a. during an interview told me that i.t.a. was "commercial" and insisted that James Pitman was exacting a royalty from everyone who used his alphabet.

Both Hodenfield and Fisher are mistaken. Pitman and his publishing firm do not profit from other publishers using the augmented alphabet. Pitman has copyrighted the alphabet to insure that its design will be kept intact, but he has formally given the use of the alphabet *free* to the world.

About a hundred publishers and printers are involved in producing, selling, or distributing i.t.a. materials. The nature of their involvement and its degree vary: Harcourt Brace & World publishes achievement tests in i.t.a.; Scholastic Magazines, Inc., has published at least fifty i.t.a. paperbacks; F. Warne & Co. has published all the Beatrix Potter books in i.t.a.; E. P. Dutton has published Milne's *When We Were Very Young* and many of the Pooh stories in i.t.a.; Remington Rand, Imperial, Royal, and Smith-Corona sell i.t.a. typewriters and I.B.M. offers an i.t.a. ball for its Selectric typewriter.

I have called a number of these manufacturers and publishers and they have assured me that they pay Pitman no royalty. I have checked with The Composing Room in New York City to verify the fact that typographers and printers pay no royalties either.

One of the easiest ways to dismiss an innovation in education is to accuse the innovator (not to his face, of course) of seeking profits. In Pitman's case this accusation is both cruel and false. Rather than allow the interests of his publishing firm to conflict with the growth of i.t.a. and its interests, Pitman initially subsidized another publisher in England to produce the first i.t.a. materials. These materials are now the most widely used i.t.a. textbooks in England.

Pitman offered his alphabet to a dozen American publishers, but they decided its potential market was too small and turned him down. It was only after all other publishers here refused i.t.a. that Theodore Dolmatch, president of Pitman Publishing Inc., formed a new company and put Margaret Bushnell at its head. i/t/a Publications, Inc., the new company, is located in New York City. While i.t.a. is far from being a "bonanza" for anyone as yet, it does appear to be paying its own way.

i.t.a.'s most agitated critics are the reading hawks, namely Reading and Handwriting Experts who are fatly invested in the baby-word business. Jimmy & Jane are the child stars of an annual two-billion-dollar elementary-school textbook market. Even failure is big in this market: four million disabled readers are dragging through our elementary schools toward dropout. And don't overlook that dropout market.

Professor George D. Spache told eight hundred teachers attending a conference at Marquette University in Milwaukee that i.t.a. was failing in Britain and that therefore its promoters were pushing it hard in the United States.

Dr. Spache is director of the reading clinic at the University of Florida, and is the author of a series of basal readers.

According to the *Great Neck News* (November 24, 1967), Dr. William Sheldon told a conference of Long Island teachers: "The i.t.a. is something the British will drop directly and we in America will do the same, simply because it breaks most of the laws of learning."

Dr. Sheldon is author of the Sheldon Basic Reading Series.

Arther S. Trace, Jr., sums up an anti-i.t.a. chapter in *Reading Without Dick & Jane* by saying that i.t.a. was England's "jolly good way of getting back at us for having won the Revolutionary War."

Dr. Trace is author of the Open Court Basic Readers.

Dr. Emmet A. Betts told a convention of five thousand reading specialists in Pennsylvania that i.t.a. made "reading more hazardous" and criticized it for teaching only nursery rhymes.

Dr. Betts is professor of education at the University of Miami and is also author of the Jimmy & Sue basal readers.

*Science News*, in its February 11, 1967, issue, quotes a criticism of i.t.a. by Dr. Arthur Gates: "The expanded alphabet is artificial, cumbersome, expensive (because of the cost of additional printed material) and often perplexing. . . . It is unsuitable to the many

*315*

children who can learn to read easily without it." Dr. Gates' statement was taken from a booklet published by the National Education Association: "Teaching Reading," 1967.

A letter defending i.t.a. came to *Science News* from W. H. Pahrman, Supervisor of Elementary Education at Oregon State Penitentiary. It was published in *Science New's* Letters to the Editor on April 1, 1967:

Dr. Arthur Gates has published materials for the use of teaching reading. His criticism is of a personal nature because Dr. Albert J. Mazurkiewicz [an author of i.t.a. materials] has dared to invade this sacred field.... We have enjoyed outstanding success using i/t/a and feel it definitely has a place in the teaching of reading, particularly to the non-English-speaking, the illiterates, and semi-literates. We advocate its use to all who inquire as to its success at our institution.

Dr. Edward Fry, director of the Rutgers Reading Center, obtained $30,000 from the U.S. Office of Education to compare i.t.a. children with children using the Diacritical Marking System, an alphabet that has slashed and dotted symbols. He reported that i.t.a. children were "significantly inferior" to children using DMS in making periods, commas, and indentations, but he conceded that i.t.a. children wrote "significantly longer stories."

Dr. Fry invented the Diacritical Marking System.

Romalda Spalding has criticized i.t.a. for being "unduly complicated." During a talk sponsored by the Reading Reform Foundation in 1963 she said: "We ... believe it to be wrong to teach a new and complex alphabet, which *must* confuse and delay the child's basic education in conventional English."

Miss Spalding has designed the Unified Phonics Method of introducing children to reading, and she is author of "The Writing Road to Reading." The "writing" in the title means handwriting.

Dr. E. A. Enstrom asked sixty-six flinty questions about i.t.a. in the January 1967 issue of *Elementary English*, a professional magazine produced by the National Council of Teachers of English. He asked, for example:

"What about successful beginnings in handwriting? With the

more difficult i/t/a symbols (designed from adult concepts rather than child capability) will there be many handwriting failures? From my observation, pupils using i/t/a generally produce very poor script. It is tight, pinched, and written with undesirable tension and strain. Poor habits of holding the pencil are being established which will plague and handicap many of these writers for life. Lefties (over ten per cent of the school population) under observed instruction are doomed to the less efficient and awkward appearing, ever-smearing, crab-like "hooking" approach. These things are so because everything seems to be disregarded except the hoped for reading gain. Does not the total picture deserve consideration, or shall we continue to ignore all other related problems?"

*Elementary English* identifies Dr. Enstrom in this article merely as "a Research Specialist," although six articles that appeared during 1963 and 1964 in the same magazine describe and acclaim him as a *handwriting expert*. Dr. Enstrom is in fact Director of Research for Peterson Directed Handwriting, an educational-materials producer.

Another of Dr. Enstrom's questions is: "Are there other less confusing ways of achieving similar goals? What about color coding for the various sounds of the letters and combinations?"

By "other ways" could Dr. Enstrom be referring to *Adventures in Handwriting for Grades 1–8*, prepared by his company? According to an ad, these textbooks feature "the Colorgraph: step-by-step letter forms in color that guide the pupil in writing every letter."

The title of Dr. Enstrom's *Elementary English* article is "Wanted: Unbiased Answers."

---

"ie hæt yω!" sed wun ov ʃhe dogꭗ. "ie reeally hæt yω! ie'm gœiŋ in ʃhe hous." well, ie thiŋk hee duꭗ not liek mee. well, ie will teeʧh him a lesson. ruf! ruf! ruf! ouʧh! ʃhat's whot yω get!—*Eric, 6, first grade, Bethlehem, Pa.*

---

# Can We Beat the Reading Establishment?

ՉՉՉՉՉՉՉՉՉՉՉՉՉՉՉՉՉՉՉՉՉՉՉՉՉՉՉՉՉՉՉՉՉՉՉՉՉՉՉՉՉՉ

ALMOST ALL technical failures and many psychological difficulties in communication can be blamed on the first four years of grade school. These four years are owned by the Reading Establishment. They are the years of the basal readers, of the controlled vocabulary, and of the Reading Expert.

If we intend to set up a writing-oriented curriculum, we will have to lay its foundation in kindergarten and the primary grades. This means busting into the Reading Establishment's "iron quadrangle."

Can we do it?

We can, and I propose a three-part offensive to do so. English teachers interested in writing will lead the attack. They will be joined by school-board members who will apply pressure at city, county, and state levels of school administration. Superintendents, principals, and teachers will cooperate with them from inside the school system and classroom.

As long as Reading Experts "own" the alphabet, the Reading Establishment will not be dislodged. Control of the alphabet guarantees that reading must be taught before spelling and writing. Once this priority is fixed, the Reading Expert can dictate the course of reading and writing instruction.

The task of the English teacher will first be to pry the Reading Expert off the alphabet, and then make the alphabet work coordinately for both reading and writing. Her course will instruct children how to communicate as well as how to be communicated to.

School-board members normally leave curricular matters to the professionals, but in the matter of communication *they* are the professionals. Who better than the lawyer, businessman, engineer, and clergyman knows the cost of communication failure in life? The average layman may easily be put off by the Reading Experts' defense of reading instruction. But reading measurers are the alchemists of education, and are not to be trusted. The board member will not have to take anybody's word that a school is teaching communication. He can ask for samples from the children and see for himself.

All of this will take time. School-board pressure will do no good if the English teachers aren't ready to put in their curriculum reform, and the English teachers aren't going to get rid of the Reading Expert overnight. Are we to do nothing in the meantime?

No. Right now superintendents should reward school principals who get their schools to write, and school principals should reward teachers who teach writing. In the end the teacher herself, all alone, will be the one who teaches anyone to write. But isn't that exactly how it happened with us? If we learned anything at all about writing wasn't it because of one teacher back somewhere in our school life, one teacher who cared about what we had to say and made us keep trying to say it better?

# Epilogue

ᦉᦉᦉᦉᦉᦉᦉᦉᦉᦉᦉᦉᦉᦉᦉᦉᦉᦉᦉᦉᦉᦉᦉᦉᦉᦉᦉᦉᦉᦉᦉᦉᦉᦉᦉᦉᦉᦉᦉᦉᦉᦉᦉᦉᦉ

EVERY EASTER SUNDAY over ten thousand citizens of Denver gather at dawn above their city in the Park of the Red Rocks amphitheater. They pray, they sing, and they marvel at the vast natural metaphor that has the sun-awakened world describe the Resurrection. Then they go home and about their business in peace.

It wasn't always in peace. For many years, until 1948, the crowds who came to pray were forced to stay, cursing the traffic jam that was their inevitable and immediate earthly reward.

In 1947 twenty thousand cars drove up to Red Rocks, although its parking lots could accommodate no more than four thousand cars. Half a day after the Easter service was over, eight thousand of these cars were still stuck in the park, unable to leave because of blocked exits. More than a dozen cars had been forced off the road and were hanging over the steep banks; three hundred cars had burned-out clutches.

Then Denver hired Henry A. Barnes as its new traffic commissioner and ordered him to correct what was being called "the biggest traffic jam west of New York City and east of Los Angeles." Barnes discovered that drivers who came up to Red Rocks parked *head in* at the lots. This meant they had to make a complete U-turn to get out. He changed the traffic flow so that drivers entered the lots from the rear and drove at once toward the front exits. They parked ready to go.

The new pattern was a success. That year for the first time no one got stuck on the grades. No car went over the bank. There were no burned-out clutches or bent fenders.

The United States suffers from the same one-way thinking. In all its parts, in foreign and internal policy expression, in its professions and sciences, in business, from its President to its last illiterate citizen, we are all congealed by the same communication jam caused by the fact that only a few of us can write.

Thousands of Reading Experts, parents and publishers, Congress and the Office of Education, teachers and librarians are flagging books into children willynilly, helterskelter, pell mell, while no responsible provision is made for orderly, efficient exits. The idea-flow is all one way. There are no *out* arrows.

The Reading Road is a multicolored, day-glo-lighted twenty-four-lane superhighway. The Writing Road is a miserable, dark back way, unsigned and unattended—true-false, fill in, and multiple choice, copying, controlled-word lists, and "creative writing."

The *literacy* on which democracy depends does not mean the mere ability to read directions, to read the laws, to be able to identify the names of candidates for office and read their promises.

Democratic literacy must also mean the ability to question, to make distinctions, to disagree—not by the stark minimum check mark after a candidate's name but by an exact statement of each individual's dissent through speech in primary debate, through the press, and through letters to one's government and one's representatives in government.

The ability to write is especially important to modern democracy because the written statement is subject to less prejudice than the spoken statement. Paper can screen off age and sex, whether the writer is male or female or homosexual, whether Negro or Sioux or Bostonian, whether Unitarian or Jew. Freedom of the press is not guaranteed only to owners of press machinery, but to every last citizen with something to say or ask. The United States was not meant to belong to a *worded* aristocracy.

The greatest natural resource of any nation is the thought of its people. In the United States, this resource lies passive, inert, unexpressed, and unengaged. How many grand plans, great ideas, and inventions live in exile out among us, locked within persons we see each day at work or on the street, pacing the floors of their minds, destined never to be released because their possessors don't also possess the keys of expression?

*321*

Our educational system thus neglects one of its primary constitutional obligations, for the right to freedom of speech does not come automatically coupled with the ability to speak freely. The ability to speak and write with ease and clarity must be taught. The idea-flow *out* of the student must be respected—researched, measured, and tested if need be, but encouraged, developed, rewarded, and engaged with. *The student's organized expression must be the goal of his education, for truly his expression is his knowledge.*

Of course, reading must be taught, too, for the ability to express with neither the patience to listen nor the humility to read produces the baseless guerrilla rebel. It is by listening and reading that the values and gains of the past are preserved. But reading should not be the end of education. Reading is not *the* key to educational success, merely one of the keys.

The school product, then, should be a spoken, drawn, performed, and written product.

The minimum graduate is the writer who reads for both information and pleasure. An eloquent writer with acutely refined listening and observational powers—this is the maximum graduate.

To produce such a graduate I propose the writing-oriented curriculum. It is not the curriculum itself, but a relationship with the student that I suggest we change. A writing-oriented curriculum would require the student step by step to communicate clearly on paper what he has learned. This new student-teacher relationship will itself force the curriculum content to change.

The United States will make its mark in history by what it writes and does. Nobody remembers a nation for its readers.